Rethinking Reading in College

Rethinking Reading in College

An Across-the-Curriculum Approach

Arlene Fish Wilner
Rider University

National Council of Teachers of English
340 N. Neil St., Suite #104, Champaign, IL 61820
www.ncte.org

Staff Editor: Bonny Graham
Manuscript Editor: Leigh Scarcliff
Interior Design: Jenny Jensen Greenleaf
Cover Design: Pat Mayer
Cover Image: iStock.com/enjoynz
NCTE Stock Number: 41229; eStock Number: 41236
ISBN 978-0-8141-4122-9; eISBN 978-0-8141-4123-6

Library of Congress Cataloging-in-Publication Data

Names: Wilner, Arlene Fish, 1950– author.
Title: Rethinking reading in college : an across-the-curriculum approach / Arlene Fish Wilner.
Description: Champaign, Illinois : National Council of Teachers of English, 2020. | Includes bibliographical references and index. | Summary: "Argues for more—and more systematic—attention to the role of reading comprehension in college as a necessary step to address inequities in student achievement that otherwise increase over time"—Provided by publisher.
Identifiers: LCCN 2020014195 (print) | LCCN 2020014196 (ebook) | ISBN 9780814141229 (trade paperback) | ISBN 9780814141236 (adobe pdf)
Subjects: LCSH: Reading (Higher education)—United States. | Reading comprehension—United States. | Academic achievement—United States. | Interdisciplinary approach in education—United States.
Classification: LCC LB2395.3 .W565 2020 (print) | LCC LB2395.3 (ebook) | DDC 428.4—dc23
LC record available at https://lccn.loc.gov/2020014195
LC ebook record available at https://lccn.loc.gov/2020014196

For Polly and Sam, and for Jeffrey and Maizie

Non scholae sed vitae

Contents

ACKNOWLEDGMENTS

Writing, as everyone knows, is both solitary and collaborative. While any weaknesses in this book are entirely my own, whatever may be valuable has emerged from decades of shared pursuits focused on higher-education pedagogy. Over the course of my career, I've had extraordinary opportunities to learn from peers and experts in venues such as the Center for the Study of Writing in New Jersey, the Writing Across the Curriculum workshops on my campus directed by Katharine Hoff and Anne Salvatore, and the Carnegie Academy for the Scholarship of Teaching and Learning (CASTL), which supported my early forays into holistic classroom-research.

Kathy and Anne provided unflagging encouragement and mentorship as I developed and led campus faculty learning communities that borrowed from their exemplary model and from the multidisciplinary CASTL structure. The most extensive of these programs, BRIDGE, was inspired and initially codirected by Kathy. As a BRIDGE mentor for many years, Anne Law, professor of psychology, contributed key pedagogic insights and advice on research design. Elaine Scorpio, chair of psychology and consummate scholar of teaching and learning, was a sage and generous colleague and advisor.

The resulting classroom research and publications testify to the dedication and resourcefulness of faculty across the curriculum and our ability to mentor one another. I owe special thanks to my colleagues whose projects, representing a wide range of disciplines but convergent in their emphasis on reading, are summarized in this volume: Danielle Jacobs Duda, Steph Golski, Brooke Hunter, Terra Joseph, Phil Lowrey, Susanna Monseau, Reed Schwimmer, and Bryan Spiegelberg. I am also indebted to Mort Rozanski and Phyllis Frakt, who, in their respective roles at the time as university president and provost, encouraged my application for the CASTL grant and generously supported BRIDGE in the ensuing years.

Discussions with Kendall Friedman, Amy Atkinson, and Isabel Baker deepened my perspective on the challenges that confront learning center professionals. My department colleague Kelly Ross kindly allowed me to use my observation of her composition class to illustrate notable strategies for teaching a writing course that is also an education in rhetorical reading. The talents and dedication of Anne Osborne are reflected in the sample assignments for supporting the reading of history students (Appendix 2 of this volume); Pamela Brown, an astute teacher and valued colleague with whom I have copresented at conferences many of the ideas developed here, sharpened my thinking and stretched my imagination during countless conversations about teaching and learning. Along with Anne Salvatore, whose expertise in writing pedagogy has proven a boon to faculty across the campus, Pam influenced in vital ways the shape and content of the sample first-year curriculum that appears as Appendix 4.

Essential to the completion of this project was the assistance of the NCTE Books Program staff. Kurt Austin was a genial and gracious mentor; I am deeply grateful for his optimism and persistence. The anonymous readers who assessed early drafts offered thoughtful and expert feedback. The copy editor's efficiency and attunement to authorial intention surpassed my expectations for editorial review. Bonny Graham's indulgence of my requests during the production stage was a welcome source of reassurance.

Finally, I want to thank my sons, Peter and Richard, whose rigorous expectations I have tried not to disappoint, and my husband, David, for the priceless gifts of time, space, and abiding confidence.

INTRODUCTION

[I]t would be the cruelest of ironies for a school, of all places, to assume the mastery of its curriculum at the outset rather than to teach toward its gradual accomplishment over time.

—ROBERT KEGAN, *In Over Our Heads: The Mental Demands of Modern Life*

More—and more systematic—attention to the role of reading comprehension in college is needed now. This book explains why and suggests practical ways forward. These include (1) a reconception of "freshman composition" in the direction of rhetorical-reading instruction and (2) reading-across-the-curriculum programs that support faculty in teaching not just the "what" but also the "how" and "why" of their respective disciplines. Expertise in developing and implementing such measures would increase the potential of faculty to improve learning, increase retention, and better prepare students for complex challenges beyond graduation.

To argue for reading across the curriculum is to confront the stigma attached to "teaching reading" in college and to reimagine undergraduate campuses as sites where instruction in rhetorical reading is given emphasis equal to that on instruction in writing. On the college level, "reading" implies not merely basic decoding but also critical analysis (including mature understanding of generic constraints, audience, and purpose), synthesis and, often, problem solving. Increasingly, college graduates are perceived as insufficiently prepared to demonstrate such sophisticated competency.

For example, surveys conducted in 2013 and 2018 by Hart Research Associates for the Association of American Colleges and Universities revealed that the majority of employers are dissatisfied with the ability of college graduates to think critically and communicate effectively. The findings in 2011 by Richard Arum and Josipa Roksa indicating "limited learning on college campuses" (*Academically Adrift*) are supported by reports from information-literacy researchers and classroom instructors across the curriculum. Studies of conventional remediation offer mixed results or suggest few positive long-term effects. Yet the responsibility for cultivating the needed skills is rarely assumed consciously by college instructors, even those with the highest dedication to teaching and learning. The revelation experienced by a team of researchers investigating how students write in response to reading in first-year classes epitomizes the issue: "Although we were all interested in critical reading before this inquiry, none of us realized how absolutely central it is to our ideals of postsecondary education but how marginal it is in our actual practice" (Manarin et al. 87).

Adding to the difficulty are unconscious assumptions that can tacitly inform campus practices. I am thinking of common misconceptions such as these:

- Plagiarism is best dealt with as a form of dishonesty that will invoke swift and rigorous penalties.
- "College-level texts" is a catchall category with meanings common to faculty across the curriculum.
- Textbooks are a natural basis for teaching a course in most subject areas and at all levels.
- "Critical reading" is practiced the same way across the curriculum.
- Remedial or developmental courses should break down holistic skills into "building blocks" taught sequentially.
- Learning complex concepts is a linear process.
- Self-focus and "relatability" are good criteria for assignment design.
- The emphasis in research-writing instruction should be on accessing academic sources.

To complicate matters further, research forces us to confront a growing inequality, whereby those who arrive at college highly skilled consistently acquire even greater skill while weaker students fall further behind. In this context, the need to align equity with excellence has motivated strategic planning and policy statements by both governmental and private agencies and is apparent in the newly rigorous assessment criteria imposed by regional higher education accreditation boards.

Meanwhile, the Common Core State Standards, in an attempt to better prepare high school students for college work, have generated robust critiques (some based on faulty premises) and are not well understood by the college instructors tasked with acculturating recent high school graduates to new academic demands. Addressing the challenges posed by the gap between expectations and reality is both an urgent ethical issue, with implications for the strength of a democratic civic society, and a practical matter because of its impact on retention and on the value—real and perceived—of a college education.

General questions that inform this book include the following:

- What habits and practices are associated with expertise in reading?
- How can research findings be translated into curricular strategies in both first-year seminars and throughout the curriculum?
- Why does addressing inequities in student achievement require a shift in campus culture, and what approaches are most helpful in this regard?

To make the issues concrete, I begin with four provocative "scenes of reading" from my classroom experiences—moments that disconcerted me at the time—and posit reasons for the failure of college campuses to effectively address weak reading. Included in the framing discussion are distinctions among related terms often used interchangeably in the relevant literature but with somewhat different implications—*meta-reading, disciplinary reading, critical reading, rhetorical reading.* Since most students do not arrive in college habituated, as most of their professors were, to making connections as well as distinctions within and among texts, perspectives, and disciplines, we must design curricula that foster such habits. In the subsequent two chapters, I examine the challenges of the high-school-to-college transition, a topic that has gained increasing attention among practitioners in higher education composition and rhetoric.

Because the Common Core State Standards have generated some contention and because in many states they remain central to the preparation of students for higher education, I address in Chapter 2 the strengths and weaknesses of high school reading instruction based on the standards, with reference to published model lessons. In this context, I revisit the practice and predicates espoused by the iconic New Critics—whose close-reading approaches have been assailed as elitist and autocratic by some opponents of the standards—while also affirming the dangers of treating any text as "autonomous." Thus I aim to offer a balanced and informed perspective on the debate about the standards in hopes that the recommended changes to the college curriculum will be seen as helpful in bridging the divide between secondary and higher education.

Chapter 3 analyzes the reading-comprehension challenges for undergraduates that usually remain unarticulated and therefore do not inform curricular design. Research has shown how expert readers vary their comprehension strategies, using alertness to genre, discipline, audience, purpose, and conversational context to determine whether their reading (or rereading) will be fast or slow, close or selective, with or against the grain. By comparing these findings with studies of how students read (and how they write texts based on their reading), instructors can begin to conceive of ways to help students build expertise in rhetorical reading.

In the next two chapters, I focus on theory-to-practice, modeling what such a curriculum could look like and how it can be implemented—initially in first-year composition classes (Chapter 4) and then "vertically" throughout the undergraduate program and across disciplines (Chapter 5). In both instances, examples of assignments are analyzed and critiqued in light of theories previously discussed. Examples from the disciplines are derived from classroom research conducted in campus faculty-development programs I directed: BRIDGE (Bridging Research, Instruction, and Discipline-Grounded Epistemologies) and FFTF (Faculty Who Frequently Teach Freshmen).

In Chapter 6, I circle back to the "scenes of reading" that introduce the book, imagining alternative responses to the students based on the ideas developed throughout. I further broaden the implications of the thesis with reference to both ethical imperatives and the increased external accountability now required of higher education.

There are four appendixes. Appendix 1 considers how the practice of rhetorical reading can be applied to prose fiction. This question is invited by the standards' requirement that high school English language arts curricula shift their emphasis from literature to informative texts and literary nonfiction, mainly readings from which knowledge can be extracted. Analyzing strategies for teaching Harper Lee's *To Kill a Mockingbird*, a novel frequently read in both high school and college, I try to demonstrate why it makes sense both to favor a continuum over a divide between fiction and nonfiction and to consider how prose fictions are nonetheless distinctive in their capacity to affect our habits of mind. Appendixes 2 and 3 are samples of faculty work that supplement descriptions of development projects in Chapter 5. Appendix 4 outlines a sample first-year course sequence, with assignment groups that illustrate the principles of rhetorical reading endorsed in this book.

Chapter One

What's the Problem?

Scenes of Reading

Scene 1: A First-Year Composition Class

We are studying the Declaration of Independence. We have discussed the occasion for its creation, looked at earlier drafts with "peer review" notations by Thomas Jefferson's colleagues, and carefully read the document together once (in preparation for rereading). We are now discussing difficult words. I have asked students to define selected words not just by reporting their online dictionary meaning but by speculating on the connotations of each in the context of the passage in which it occurs and the document as a whole. At one point I ask what Jefferson meant to accomplish by submitting facts to a "candid world." I am expecting students to suggest "honest" or "not rehearsed" as conventional synonyms for candid, even though the latter would not make much sense in context. I am stumped when one of the suggested answers is "fake." Apart from my surprise at this understanding of "candid," I wonder why the student imagines that Jefferson would appeal to his audience by calling them fake. I assume I am missing some sequence of ideas and ask for a bit of elaboration. The room is silent, and I feel bad that I have apparently caused some embarrassment. Still, I wonder about the thinking behind this response. The explanation comes from a colleague, a professor of communication and journalism, well habituated to the varieties of students' attempts at acontextual meaning making. "Oh," she says, "the student was confusing 'candid' with 'canned.'" I am struck by this insight; it is one I would never have arrived at on my own.

Scene 2: A First-Year Honors Seminar

As part of a unit on secular and religious ways of viewing material and spiritual nature, we are reading Robert Frost's poem "Design." The poem's artfulness—including its close adherence to the discipline of the sonnet form and its oxymoronic imagery, ending with a couplet positing a possible "design of darkness to appall," or, alternatively, a random purposelessness—is satisfying to tease out. We discuss the philosophical traditions that might have informed the poem's vision and together ponder the ironic contrast between the esthetically pleasing tableau described by the speaker and the way the unfolding image in the octave is fulfilled and darkened in the rhetorically interrogative sestet, especially in the disturbing final couplet. In groups and then as a class, students consider the poet's choices of diction, structure, rhyme, and rhythm. We compare the poem with a much earlier version and use history and biography to reflect on possible reasons for the poet's revision. We discuss how the title inflects the text of the poem. We consider both the experience of reading and the overall effect once we see the entire "design." Students are interested and offer good insights. "Design" is an option for a writing assignment that requires analysis and synthesis of two or three texts. My co-teacher and I find that most students who choose to write on "Design" interpret it as an expression of faith in a benevolent deity, a conclusion at odds with the sonnet's language and structure. One such student, when asked to show evidence from the poem, offers none. Reporting that the source of the interpretation is prior discussion in a high school class, she has apparently chosen to affirm what she already thinks without reexamining either the poem or her thinking.

Scene 3: Another First-Year Honors Seminar

We are reading *Hamlet,* in this lesson focusing on Hamlet's treatment of Ophelia and her response. A student accounts for Ophelia's behavior by making up what she calls a "backstory," describing how Ophelia had been "dumped" by a previous boyfriend and how that experience affected her. The student is a theater major and has been encouraged by a drama teacher to use the backstory approach. Others in the class are happy to go along with this line of thinking, but I am concerned that we are moving too far from the text. When I ask the student and the rest of the class to paraphrase selected lines relevant to our discussion, no one volunteers. I offer time and hints, but still no takers—attention to Shakespeare's syntax and diction and to how selected lines mesh with larger contexts and themes is easily deflected in favor of imagined circumstances for a failed romantic relationship. While such imaginative constructs suggest engagement with the play's human complexities and are therefore encouraging, I worry that students are evading the hard yet rewarding work of actual reading. We parse the lines together, but the theater major, miffed by my insistence that we grapple closely with the text, lets me know my limitations: "My interpretation is just as good as yours." Taken aback by this display of arrogance, I wonder out loud what this student hopes to gain from my expertise.

Scene 4: A Class in the Literature of Adolescence

I have assigned a few essays outlining basic concepts for thinking about literature as compared with expository or argumentative writing. These include an article by Wayne Booth on the unique opportunities for emotional and ethical stretching that literature presents to readers who are willing to inhabit various personas ("Ethics"), Laurence Perrine's essay from *Story and Structure* on narrative point of view (Arp and Johnson, ch. 4), and Vladimir Nabokov's lecture to undergraduates on what makes good readers and good writers (from *Lectures on Literature*). Based on this reading, students are asked to select and respond to one of several posted study questions. A double major in psychology and education chooses the following: "Paraphrase the argument behind Nabokov's claim that 'one cannot read a book; one can only reread it.' Does this argument coincide with your experience as a reader?" Nabokov's point is that good literature demands from readers a complex response: a combination of "impersonal imagination and artistic delight" that is best experienced upon *re*reading, when we have a sense of how temporal responses fuse into a coherent sense of the whole. However, the prospective teacher in my class resists my prompt to consider Nabokov's insight that readers must have both an "artistic" and a "scientific" temperament—the ability to be simultaneously engaged and "aloof." Nabokov's essay focuses on literary texts, and one of the *misconceptions* he addresses is the idea that one should read literature primarily to be informed. The student, however, stays in her comfort zone: What stands out in her experience is the need to reread texts in order to "understand the information." She misrepresents Nabokov's point accordingly.

"A Huge Elephantine Problem"

Despite decades of teaching, I am regularly flummoxed by the habits and assumptions of students trying to make sense of texts. And I am far from alone. Evidence abounds that students at all levels and in all disciplines need better instruction and more practice in reading. In recent years, special issues of three influential higher education pedagogy journals—*Across the Disciplines, Reader,* and *Pedagogy,* in 2013, 2104, and 2016 respectively—have been dedicated to questions about how our students read and how we must reshape our practices to help them improve. Data gathered by standardized surveys and tests such as the NSSE and the ACT and by classroom instructors who struggle to help their students read effectively converge on an urgent point: As Writing Across the Curriculum has become increasingly institutionalized, it is now time to direct more attention to the support of reading, the reciprocal activity required in every high school and college classroom. However, while a clear consensus has emerged that more instruction in reading would benefit students across the curriculum, the arguments and research seem not to have had much influence on classroom pedagogies or campus faculty-development programs.

Over the past three decades, increasingly urgent calls for attention, deploying a rhetoric of increasing alarm, have marked the contributions of influential scholars representing various strands of English studies. A few examples of the shifting emphasis will make the point: Robert Scholes's lucid and engaging *Textual Power: Literary Theory and the Teaching of English,* published in 1985, offered exemplary lessons in pedagogic approaches grounded in a thoughtfully explicated philosophical perspective and an optimistic spirit. Writing in 2002, perhaps frustrated by the (mis)application of theories that seemed to make students *worse* readers of texts, he declared: "[W]e have a reading problem of massive dimensions—a problem that goes beyond any purely literary concerns" ("Transition" 165). In 1992, Peter Rabinowitz, while deploring the constraints imposed by prevalent strands of New Criticism, thought it likely that "many students engage dutifully in close reading" as preparation for discussion of literature ("Against" 239); subsequently (see, e.g., Rabinowitz and Smith; Smith and Rabinowitz), he seemed less confident of this assumption, mapping out strategies to help students "develop the literary knowledge they need to construct readings of coherence" while also honoring their experience as readers (Rabinowitz and Smith 115). In 2007, literacy specialist Alice Horning summarized the evidence of poor reading among students in the United States, noting the effects of this deficiency on degree completion and calling for intentional reading instruction across the curriculum from elementary school through college. In 2013, introducing a special issue on reading and writing across the curriculum in *Across the Disciplines,* Horning called the quality of students' reading "a huge, elephantine problem" ("Elephants"). In a 2008 study of students' reading habits on their campus, rhetorician David Jolliffe and composition specialist Allison Harl found that students generally dismissed assigned reading as boring, self-evident, or difficult (and therefore tried to dispense with it as quickly as possible), and, whether reading assigned or chosen texts, did not read "studiously," rarely making text-to-text connections (611–12). The authors proposed strategies for addressing these challenges and suggested that other campuses study the reading habits of their students as a critical step toward more effective curriculum development. By 2014, such steps no longer seemed adequate. Co-writing with Christian Goering an introduction to a special issue of *Reader,* Jolliffe lamented the trends evident in both systematic data and reports of classroom experience, asking whether, in response to students' lack of engagement with reading, both high school and college instructors had given up on designing curriculum that relies on students' careful critical reading of assigned texts. The only solution, it appeared, was a call for a "revolution in the study and teaching of reading, pre-K through adult" (3). What has been inhibiting such a revolution and what, if enabled, might it look like?

A major challenge has been institutional structures based on the assumption, despite evidence to the contrary, that college students arrive—or should arrive—on campus largely prepared to read college-level texts. While first-year composition classes or other comparable first-year writing courses are the norm, they do not typically entail formal instruction in reading. Reading classes in college are, by definition, deemed to be remedial, so that only the neediest students are placed into them, and often what is taught looks more like study skills than like critical reading. Moreover, such skills do not necessarily transfer well across disciplines and various types of assignments (Maxwell; Leamnson 40, 121; Jolliffe, "Learning to Read as Continuing Education" 474; Manarin et al. 11; Anson, "Pop Warner Chronicles"). Overall, despite the need for students in high school and college to consistently practice reading and interpreting texts of various kinds, the idea of "teaching reading" is regarded as unworthy of college-level instruction and therefore mostly avoided.

Addressing this problem will require, as Justin Young and Charlie Potter argue, an integrative approach that begins long before students are admitted to college and that continues an increasingly sophisticated skill-building through cross-campus attention in colleges to reading across the curriculum. In a 2014 conversation among secondary and postsecondary English instructors, literacy specialist Douglas Hartman observed that as high school lessons move from a focus on reading as a subject to the interpretation of texts, instruction in how to read those texts is not as systematic and purposeful as it needs to be (Mallette et al. 17). Horning points out that many high school teachers are not prepared to teach reading per se and that, typically, little instruction in reading nonfiction prose is offered after the sixth grade ("Reading Across"). Misconceptions about reading further compound the problem. For example, the unhelpful idea that reading is a finite skill once learned and then automatically applied (similar to a commonly held faulty view of writing) is shared by both students and instructors; this may be one reason that the focus in high school often turns to unpacking the text as an artifact rather than helping students consider ways of reading different texts. The notion that once it is taught in elementary school, reading as a skill need not be systematically revisited then stigmatizes reading instruction in higher education: "if you [say you're teaching reading] among the professoriate, that's a sort of diminishing or a dumbing down[;] . . . to say you're teaching reading is to say we've got a bunch of people who haven't progressed beyond fourth grade" (Roskelly in Mallette et al. 17–18). This stigma suggests that "reading" is understood mostly as decoding, a task students are expected to have mastered long before they enter high school.

And indeed there is ample evidence that students who, early on, achieve basic reading competency (i.e., phonemic awareness and the "spelling-to-sound code") reap lifelong advantages in comprehension, not least because, in struggling less to read, they tend to read more, increasing their knowledge and vocabulary as part of overall fluency, thus creating a beneficial loop that continues to deepen their expertise (Stanovich; Stanovich and Cunningham, "Studying the Consequences of Literacy within a Literate Society"; Cunningham and Stanovich, "Early Reading Acquisition and Its Relation to Reading Experience and Ability 10 Years Later"). The inequalities that over time are thereby magnified produce the "Matthew effect" (Stanovich), whereby, as in the Biblical passage Matthew 25:29, the rich get richer and the poor poorer. Certainly, some students entering postsecondary study, having gotten off to a slower start at the beginning, will not have had the benefits of this reciprocal process, and college professors will not have been trained to deal with the neediest of such students. However, even for students without such basic needs, the challenges of reading across the curriculum in college—considering the range of discourse conventions, genres, purposes for reading, and expected outcomes from reading assignments—will be substantial.

This is why, according to Ken Bain, the best college teachers understand that their students have typically received little prior instruction in how to read specialized texts and therefore incorporate such support into their classes, asking themselves, "What is unique and distinctive about reading material for this course, and how can I break that reading into identifiable strategies?" (56).

Such instructors realize, based on their experience, that support for reading on this level is, in effect, support for the deepest kind of learning in the relevant discipline. It is not surprising, then, that directors of campus tutoring have called for more systematic attention to reading, citing the need for the research in reading pedagogy that is "boiling up" to be recognized by writing centers (Adams 87) and for tutors to be familiar with the body of research that addresses college reading, and "not necessarily as a remedial enterprise" (Griswold 68). Understanding of this need appears to be gaining currency in theory, if not practice. "Writing centers are also reading centers," asserts Muriel Harris, founder of the Purdue University Writing Lab. "How could they not be?" (227). Harris deftly unpacks the ways that problems with writing derive from problems with reading, showing how tutors who understand this relationship can help students improve in both areas. But the call to train tutors accordingly has so far largely been resisted, with "no evidence of a widespread solution or response" in the literature or in institutional practices (Harris 241).

The prevalent notion that reading instruction in college by definition entails "dumbing down" is likely one reason that theories of reading, including many connected to pedagogy, while important in scholarly conversations, have not exerted much power in the design and delivery of curriculum. Compositionist Ellen Carillo has noted that work on reading pedagogies in the 1980s and 1990s "unfortunately remains terribly underrepresented in our field's anthologies, histories, and grad courses" ("Creating" 20). Participants in the 2014 conversation mentioned above concurred that helpful research on reading remains "widely unused, and unacknowledged by the field" (Mallette et al. 28). Chris Anson laments that "over the past three decades, research on the relationship of writing and reading in higher education has ebbed" ("Writing to Read, Revisited" 22). Similarly, Jolliffe, who observed in 2007 that "no clear, salient theory of what reading is or does prevails in college composition" ("Learning to Read as Continuing Education" 474), a decade later applauded the increasing interest in and contributions to the field but noted that the ongoing nature of "the reading problem" demands a much more focused and more comprehensive effort than we have seen ("'Learning to Read as Continuing Education' Revisited").

Ironically, even as reader-response theory gained currency in the academy, its natural connection to composition pedagogy remained suppressed. Skipping from literary studies to cultural criticism without meaningfully informing composition theory, it was paid lip service in argument textbooks where, as Patricia Harkin and James Sosnoski have argued, it was not entirely at home (111–21). Such books wanted to respect the idea of textual indeterminacy and instability as well as constructivist epistemologies but found these to be at odds with the idea that logic and reason, once understood, command assent and thereby promote consensus. As a result, students are guided in conversing with the reading but mainly with the purpose of discovering its essential meaning: "What has happened to reader-response criticism, at least in argument textbooks, is that it has become a set of instructions for 'finding' authorial intention as the stable meaning of texts" (104). For Harkin and Sosnoski, such textbooks betray the "critical, counter-hegemonic promise . . . of the early days of reception aesthetics" (102). They attribute this loss to the reduction of rich and complex schemas to oversimplified, more easily usable and less threatening versions of their antecedents, in effect, a transformation of theories to ineffectual "theoroids," virtual clichés (103). Thus, while skepticism of the writer's argument might be encouraged, consciousness of the cultural circumstances, motives, and ideologies that produced it (factors that might render it fundamentally unreasonable) was sacrificed for what might be called basic comprehension that repressed motives for dissent and alertness to the unstable meanings inherent in every text. As I see it, to call this translation of theory to practice a "betrayal" points to an ongoing tension between, on the one hand, the need to construct meaning for purposes of clear communication (thus enabling the achievement of common ground) and, on the other, the obligation to assess the tacit assumptions of an argument (thus enabling resistance).

A central reason for the disconnect between theories of reading and theories of writing may lie in the process by which composition and rhetoric defined itself as a field independent of literary studies and its offshoots. In their introduction to a January 2016 issue of *Pedagogy*, Mariolina Salvatori and Patricia Donahue not only remind us that the burst of interest in theories of reading and their relation to teaching evident in the 1980s waned considerably in the ensuing three decades but also observe that the professionalization of composition contributed to a divergence between reading theory and other research areas such as rhetorical or cultural studies ("Guest" 2). Given the prerequisites for respectability in the academy, including the definition of rigorous disciplinary methods as independent of teaching strategies, it may be that the seminal work by Louise Rosenblatt, beginning in 1938 and extending through the 1990s, in charting how adolescent readers make meaning of texts (particularly literary ones) via evolving "transactions" was long marginalized by composition and rhetoric precisely because of its focus on pedagogy and perhaps because, as Salvatori and Donahue suggest, "capturing meandering reading processes was difficult, or risky, or suspect" (2). Indications of the profession's declining interest, since 1991, in systematically exploring the reading-writing connection are vividly portrayed by Salvatori and Donahue in their historical examination of the calls for papers and program categories published by the Conference on College Composition and Communication. Why, the authors wonder, was the term *reading* "completely invisible for seventeen years?" ("What Is College English?" 210). After the promise of the 1980s, this trend suggests a sadly missed opportunity to which we may only now be summoning a sufficiently vigorous response.

Yet some positive signs have emerged over the past decade or so. These include the appearance of the category "Theories of Reading and Writing" in the 2008 CCCC call for proposals ("What Is College English?" 210), a slightly increased (but still insufficient) emphasis on reading in the 2014 revision of the Writing Programs Associates Outcomes Statement for First-Year Composition (Jolliffe, "'Learning to Read as Continuing Education' Revisited" 12), and an uptick in research and theorizing on the nature and pedagogies of college reading and its relation to writing by notable scholars such as Jolliffe, Horning, Carillo, Jamieson, and Anson. In the introduction to their recent collection of essays, Patrick Sullivan, Howard Tinberg, and Sheridan Blau posit the inseparability of theories of reading from the pedagogies of undergraduate writing (xix) and offer a range of convergent data, insights, and arguments on how to connect the increasingly compelling theory in the field with classroom practices. The task before us is to move in more purposeful and collaborative ways on these encouraging indicia of a shift in thinking.

The longed-for revolution in reading instruction can best be effected as a continuous process beginning long before college, and instructors in postsecondary settings who are alert to common high school pedagogies will have a keener sense of their students' thinking and habits. As is well known, attempts at curricular reform (or at least rigorous assessment that might ensure reform) have been salient in K–12 public education for some time, from George W. Bush's "No Child Left Behind" to Barack Obama's "Race to the Top" to the Common Core State Standards (CCSS), an effort to improve math and reading proficiency first discussed by state leaders in 2007, with details drafted in 2009 and a subsequent process of review and consideration for adoption by individual states. While the passage of the Every Student Succeeds Act (ESSA) in 2015 effectively reversed the CCSS federal mandate, it is important to note that the ESSA is not a curriculum but a policy that allows states flexibility in specifying standards keyed to college- and career-readiness. A major impact of this policy is that it does not make funding contingent on adoption of specified federal standards in ways that the CCSS did. However, many states are continuing to rely on the CCSS to meet the state (and federal) curricular guidelines. While the words *common core* are often omitted from revised state standards, the basic benchmarks remain identical or similar to those defined in the CCSS (Brown; Klein).

Moreover, the philosophy behind the CCSS will remain relevant because it addresses fundamental questions of pedagogy that continue to inform K–16 debates, including those concerning how best to teach reading comprehension in secondary and postsecondary settings (Coleman and Pimentel, 1, 3, 14). Thus it behooves college instructors to understand that some problematic elements evident in first-year reading and writing instruction—thinned-out theories, along with tensions in the uneasy accommodation of constructivism with an assumption of definite and stable meaning—also underlie the pedagogies recommended as paths to achieving the Common Core State Standards, which continue to shape precollege curricula. In Chapter 2, I propose to offer a fresh take on the theory and assumptions that generated the standards and on the intense backlash provoked by this latest attempt to prepare every child for success in college and careers (the standards' stated goals). I will argue that in attempting to correct ineffective reading pedagogies—summaries and "preinterpretations" on one hand and "springboard" reactions on the other—the Common Core directives are liable to go to a different extreme and thus diminish the importance of rhetorical reading. First, however, it will be helpful to consider some terminology.

Ways of Reading: Rhetorical, Meta, Disciplinary, Critical

Rhetorical reading, as defined by Christina Haas and Linda Flower, is a strategy whereby readers approach the text "not only as content and information but also as the result of someone's intentions, as part of a larger discourse world, and as having real effects on real readers" (170). Such readers notice particular textual features—not just what the text is saying but how it is constructed (e.g., the rhetorical function of the various pieces, such as an introduction, a statement of an argument, an example, a qualification of the main idea). Rhetorical readers also go "beyond the text itself" (176); they use prior knowledge to construct a sense of authorial persona, intended audience and purpose, and the larger debates, questions, or theories in the background.

Practices associated with rhetorical reading also define *meta-reading*. An explanation of meta-reading, and a persuasive rationale for teaching it purposefully across the curriculum, has been articulated by Alice Horning, who identifies three kinds of awareness inherent in reading by experts: (1) metatextual: the rhetorical organization of the text, the relation of parts to one another and to the whole, (2) metacontextual: the place of the text in an ongoing conversation or inquiry focused on a defined problem or question and directed to an audience with assumed background knowledge in the field, and (3) metalinguistic: specialized uses of vocabulary, syntax, and verbal patterns characteristic of practitioners in the field ("Where to Put the Manicules" 6; *Reading, Writing, and Digitizing* 7, ch. 5). Meta-reading thus entails awareness of both intratextual features (including part-to-whole connections and discipline-based uses of language) and extratextual frames (including motives for writing, historical contexts, and generic constraints), and the inseparability of all of these in the construction of meaning. While not usually named as such, meta-reading is desired by professors across the curriculum.

I am conflating rhetorical reading with meta-reading because the two accounts share an emphasis on the reader's role in constructing meaning as shaped by consciousness of both formal conventions and assumed or implied contextual frames. The "feature/function" aspect of rhetorical reading as described by Haas and Flower includes attention to particular choices of words and sentences as well as to the roles of larger units of meaning and therefore seems to underlie the metalinguistic and metatextual kinds of awareness described by Horning. Another congruence between the two conceptual frameworks lies in the similarity of Haas and Flower's description of expert readers' text "construction" (which depends on extratextual inferences) and Horning's "metacontextual" awareness. A third parallel has its roots in the broader notion of "critical reading." Haas and Flower speak of rhetorical reading strategies as central to such a skill, i.e., the ability of students, when confronted with a challenging text, to "build an equally sophisticated, complex representation of meaning" (170). Implied in such a representation is the ability to achieve an informed perspective that allows evaluation according to accepted disciplinary methods. Horning's description of "application skills"—students' ability to evaluate and synthesize texts with each other and with their own work—would no doubt depend on critical reading so defined. Thus the similarities between the two accounts of reading are quite salient.

If pressed, however, to distinguish *rhetorical* from *meta* reading, one might suggest that *rhetorical reading* as defined by Haas and Flower puts slightly more emphasis on the relationship between text and context than does Horning's *meta-reading*, which seems to emphasize intratextual understanding a bit more, perhaps because her primary aim is to help students "read informational prose texts quickly and efficiently" ("Where to Put the Manicules" 13). However, because the terms describe approximately the same expert habits, I will use them here interchangeably (and with the assumption that such habits are associated with what is commonly called critical reading). It is worth noting here that experimental research in discourse processing is consonant with these paradigms: a dominant model in cognitive psychology for representing reading comprehension comprises three levels of sense making—surface structure (decoding words and syntax), textbase (representation of gist), and situation model (connections with a larger conversation or context)—that correlate with the dynamics of meta-reading (Zwaan; see also Kintsch and van Dijk; Kintsch, "The Role of Knowledge"; Kintsch, "An Overview").

A fourth term, *disciplinary literacy*, is used to distinguish modes of rhetorical reading (and writing) specific to individual academic fields. Research on the reading and writing habits of academics in various disciplines—e.g., Bazerman (physics), Wineburg (history), C. Shanahan et al. (history, mathematics, and chemistry)—have revealed differences fundamental to the values, epistemological assumptions, and discourse conventions of each field. These findings have led literacy scholars to infer that beyond the primary grades, where emphasis is on decoding, reading is best taught not as a generic skill but rather as an aspect of mastering disciplinary content. Moreover, as I hope to show in the ensuing chapters, the effects of aiming for an enrichment of students' knowledge base from the earliest grades has not only cognitive implications but also ethical and social ones.

Broadening the Responsibility

My argument draws on the recommendations of literacy experts, who see instruction in rhetorical reading as "a gateway to disciplinary literacy" for high school students (Warren, "Rhetorical Reading as a Gateway"; see also Shanahan and Shanahan, "Teaching"; Moje). Concurring with the composition researchers noted above that interest in rhetorical reading, which seemed to surge a couple of decades ago among college instructors, never sufficiently influenced high school reading instruction, James Warren cautions against pedagogies that continue to reinforce the unhelpful idea that each text is sui generis ("autonomous") and that therefore its meaning can be gleaned strictly from attention to the words on the page. "Expert academic reading," he says, "*is* rhetorical reading" ("Rhetorical Reading and the Development of Disciplinary Literacy" 4). However, since "reading" as a skill is largely ignored outside of high school English classes, "the myth of the autonomous text" (4) persists in classes across the curriculum. In light of the similar limitations that affect college instruction, the remedy entails a dual approach: both a reconceptualization of composition as a course, or sequence of courses, that could better prepare students for the challenges they will face as they are asked to read sophisticated texts from many fields, and systematic faculty development to foster effective instruction in disciplinary reading across the curriculum.

We already have good evidence that the necessary changes, both in high schools and in colleges, will be hard-fought. The changes Warren proposes, if integrated across subject areas in high schools, would require two shifts: (1) a reconception of English language arts (ELA) classes, which have mainly focused on teaching literature and/or the arhetorical reading strategies common in basic literacy instruction, and (2) more intentional integration of discipline-specific instruction in reading in each of the other content areas. Proponents of such curricula are naturally alert to the difficulties of changing deeply embedded pedagogic practices so that ELA classes can help support critical reading in all subject areas and so that disciplines other than English can, in turn, foster skills in disciplinary reading. As Warren observes, each of the recommended moves invites resistance. For ELA teachers, the risk is that the field's traditional focus on general comprehension strategies that treat each text as autonomous will be viewed as inadequate and that therefore their role as the campus literacy experts will be diminished; on the other hand, restricting their classes to the content and methods of literary analysis (in which ELA teachers are typically trained) fails to advance the broad meta-awareness that secondary- and college-level students need to read proficiently. For teachers across the curriculum, there are reciprocal challenges: Teaching reading is perceived as outside the boundaries of their training and/or a threat to content coverage (Warren, "Rhetorical Reading as a Gateway" 393). Elizabeth Moje, in arguing forcefully for integrating instruction in disciplinary reading across the high school curriculum, notes that such a project is "complicated": The idea that epistemologies must be made explicit as a crucial aspect of disciplinary content "requires a radical rethinking of what constitutes a discipline and, in turn, a secondary school subject area" (100).

Resistance based on such aspects of entrenched culture is not, of course, restricted to high school faculty and administrators; it has also hobbled attempts to improve reading among college students. In their compelling study of discipline-specific reading habits by experts and the ways that high school teachers could help students understand and practice such habits, Timothy Shanahan and Cynthia Shanahan ("Teaching") document the disciplinary understanding and finesse required to encourage professors, teacher educators, and high school teachers to try strategies designed to enhance students' critical reading. Not surprisingly, the ideas that proved most acceptable were those most closely related to disciplinary epistemologies—i.e., those that helped students see how concrete data in the field related to "big ideas" or concepts and that offered scaffolding for enactment of expert practices (54–56). My own work with faculty on assignment design supports this finding. As I will demonstrate in Chapter 5, the needed pedagogic shifts that typically meet with skepticism or outright rejection can begin to permeate the curriculum if respect for the uniqueness of each discipline drives the approach to reconceiving one's mission. In this way, the proposed changes are revealed as integral to the essential meaning of the field and thus to the initiation of students into the specific values and practices of the discipline at hand.

Shanahan and Shanahan end by recommending major revisions in the teacher-education curriculum—including "explicit literacy certification standards for teachers who teach in the disciplines" (57). Acknowledging the challenges of such a requirement, Warren emphasizes the benefits of training ELA teachers to introduce students to the rhetorical nature of texts and the reading practices of experts, a change he perceives as potentially consequential even in the absence of cross-campus collaboration ("Rhetorical Reading and the Development of Disciplinary Literacy" 7). However, without a concerted and integrative move toward helping students read rhetorically and in discipline-specific ways in high school, the challenges for college instructors will continue to grow. And even if high schools across the country miraculously implemented all of the practices urged by disciplinary-literacy researchers, we would still no longer be able to pretend that sufficient instruction in reading and writing can be accomplished even in the most skillfully taught first-year skills classes and then somehow applied to various disciplinary contexts.

How, then, might college instructors address the needs of students throughout the four years by cultivating, in their design of assignments, the habits of mind that foster rhetorical reading not just in English classes but in all disciplines? Like Carillo, I imagine a foundational experience in which "first-year composition becomes about preparing students to productively engage with texts in a range of disciplines" ("Creating" 15). However, the possibilities for application and adaptation of skills based on metacognitive awareness of one's reading practices would be subject to the same limitations Anson outlined in his case study of writing transfer: The uniqueness and complexity of each reading situation (demands of discipline, genre, class level, instructor preferences, or even "idiosyncrasies and fetishes") require that students confront each reading assignment prepared to "create new, situationally determined knowledge." Anson observes that we cannot rely too heavily on a generic transfer of writing skills from first-year courses alone; rather, we need faculty willing to link concepts and strategies taught in first-year skills classes with pedagogies in courses across the curriculum ("Pop Warner" 542). The same, I would argue, is true for the reciprocal skill of reading. (In Chapter 5, I offer examples of the benefits such integration, if widely practiced, might confer.)

In addition, a first-year reading-writing curriculum should, I contend, include content elements that might help to redress inequities. In thinking through the design of such a curriculum, I would attend carefully to the selection of texts, choosing more than a few classic expositions and arguments commonly familiar to college graduates. (In Chapter 4, I illustrate assignments based on such a curriculum.) Not only would such a selection help enrich the cultural and intellectual capital of all students, but it is likely to play a role in reading comprehension, since the effective construction of a rhetorical frame is enabled by background knowledge (on this last point, see, e.g., Brent; Haas and Flower; Horning, "Reading Across"; Moje). Rhetorical reading will also require an awareness of genres and comparisons of the constraints and affordances offered by each of several, representing a range of disciplines. Assignments would be designed to support understanding of the meta aspects of texts, and to help students use such understanding in compiling a literature review, effecting a synthesis, or advancing an argument. Complementing and building on this course, classes across the curriculum would be revised to incorporate purposeful instruction in discipline-based rhetorical reading "as an integral aspect of subject area learning, rather than as a set of strategies for engaging with texts" (Moje). If a few classic or otherwise significant texts are taught across all sections of a first-year course, some instructors across the curriculum could revisit these texts in more specialized disciplinary contexts, thus increasing the potential for a more coherent curriculum that affords iterative practice in rhetorical reading and writing. In Appendix 4, I offer a sample of a two-semester first-year course sequence designed to meet these objectives.

In planning revisions to their courses, college instructors should be alert to the sorts of preparation first-year students are likely to bring with them. The literacy-instruction guidelines specified by the CCSS, intended to remedy the failed pedagogies of the past, promise to offer certain benefits but have been criticized for reinforcing instruction that is, in light of recent research, surprisingly arhetorical in its focus on the text in isolation. While regarded by some as mostly a move in the right direction (see, e.g., T. Shanahan, "The Common Core Ate My Baby"), this approach holds for others a dangerous affinity with the perceived elitism and rigidity of New Critical methods. I turn now to an examination of the Common Core pedagogies in hopes that by exploring their assumptions we can better understand some aspects of the controversy they have generated, appreciate their potential as well as their limitations in helping prepare students for college-level reading assignments, and imagine what an effective university-level reading-across-the-curriculum program might look like.

"Close Reading" and the Common Core

Expertise Does Not Equal Elitism

In a 2011 speech promoting the Common Core State Standards to New York State education officials, David Coleman (a co-developer of the standards who currently heads the College Board) explained that the new literacy pedagogies had been designed to address reading scores that tended to flatten out in the eighth grade ("Bringing" 8). Widespread failure to prepare high school students to read college-level texts was largely attributed to both content, i.e., a disproportionate focus in the early grades on literature (mostly narratives) as opposed to informative texts, and pedagogic strategies commonly used in English classes. Among the latter, two widespread approaches were deemed particularly detrimental because they deflect attention from the text: (1) the emphasis on "opinion" or "springboard" writing rather than argument based on analysis of evidence and (2) the priority given to "prereading" exercises or supplements supposed to serve as tools to introduce themes and topics and to encourage engagement. With regard to the use of texts primarily as prompts for personal reaction, Coleman cited with obvious frustration a study of literacy instruction in the culturally different states of Vermont and Texas, the main finding of which was that in both systems 80 percent of the questions posed to students—e.g., "what it reminds you of, or what you criticize, or perhaps how you feel or react to it"—were peripheral to the meaning of the assigned text. Presumably, he suggested, this practice is well received by students who want "to avoid confronting the difficult words before them" ("Bringing" 10).

As for the "prereading" material, it might include summaries, extensive background information, prompts to imagine or report on experiences with situations like those portrayed in the text, and the "reading" of illustrations. Coleman argued that such strategies constituted an "escape from the text" (17) rather than a means to foster careful reading. In introducing a lesson on Martin Luther King Jr.'s "Letter from Birmingham Jail," he reinforced the point with a parodic interpretation of how such teaching is commonly enacted:

> If I were to go to a film with you, imagine before it started, I want you to do a bunch of pre-film watching strategies. Then I ruthlessly interrupted you as it unfolded and said, "There's a train. Have you ever been on a train ride? What does this remind you of?" You would kill me before we were five minutes through. Why then is this appropriate with reading, which is also a task of deep observation and attention, where the author's story is the most interesting one to start with, whether it's informative or narrative? (18)

Tim Shanahan accounts for the preponderance of ineffective pedagogies by observing that practices based on questionable or overgeneralized interpretations of research (e.g., the importance of activating background knowledge) tend to become reified as pedagogic "rituals." He notes that an overemphasis on preliminary activities intended to motivate or inform can create "a veritable flood of extra information" that does not aid comprehension, and that the common alternative is equally unhelpful and even potentially harmful: "If students are to read about tide pools, for example, teachers are counseled to start out by asking questions such as, 'Have you ever visited a beach? What plants and animals did you see near the shore?' Or if students are to read *Charlotte's Web,* they might first learn the biographical details of E. B. White's life" ("Letting the Text" 7). On the other hand, privileging students' experiences and reactions as distinct from the text has had the deleterious effect of equating the value of all opinions, inhibiting critical thinking, and generally fostering "ignorance and helplessness" (11).

In this context we can understand why, in order to avoid the pitfalls of distracting intervention and the use of the text as a prompt for personal sharing, the CCSS advised teachers of classic documents such as the Gettysburg Address "to plunge students into an independent encounter with this short text [and] [r]efrain from giving background context or substantial instructional guidance at the outset." The exclusion of background knowledge, along with the intense focus on the document's meaning as revealed by the words on the page, supposedly sets all students on an equal footing as they undertake a "close reading" of the artifact before them and thus "levels the playing field" ("Common Core Unit" 3). To achieve this goal, the questions posed to students must be "text-dependent"; they must require strict attention to the words, sentences, and paragraphs on the page and avoid fostering discussion of merely tangential ideas and personal associations: "Text-dependent questions do not require information or evidence from outside the text or texts; they establish what follows and what does not follow from the text itself" (Coleman and Pimentel 6).

In a close reading of the Gettysburg Address, therefore, questions that call upon experience or opinions, such as "Have you ever been to a funeral?" and "Why is equality an important value to promote?" are rejected as prompts for expression of views independent of Lincoln's ideas; and historical questions that might normally seem relevant, such as "Why did the North fight the Civil War?" and "Did Lincoln think that the North was going to 'pass the test' that the Civil War posed?" are also rejected because they take students "outside the text." Indeed, such queries can even "undermine" comprehension, in this case, by making North-South distinctions not present in the speech ("Common Core Unit" 20). (Why such obvious distinctions seem to be deliberately avoided in this speech is a question that, while pertinent to comprehension of Lincoln's purposes, presumably would distract from the text.) Coleman and other developers of the standards apparently fear that the practices they need to correct are so deeply ingrained that teachers must be strictly prohibited from even being tempted by the lure of "non-text-dependent" questions. Certainly any instructor of English would embrace the value of "deep observation and attention" to texts (Coleman, "Bringing" 18). Yet it appears that the creators of the mandated CCSS pedagogies, in attempting to address the identified problems, overreacted.

Given the two types of questions that are forbidden, it is not surprising that the recommended literacy approaches embedded in the standards have invited backlash as an avatar of out-of-favor practices associated with New Critical close reading. Jason Endacott et al. deplore the standards as creating "robots teaching other little robots" and as "closed reading" that stifles creativity and represses competing interpretations. Ellen Carillo ("Reimagining") similarly posits that the Common Core shares New Criticism's insistence on separating the reader from the text and thus improperly "dismiss[es] [students], their experiences, and their backgrounds" (29, 33). Close reading as promoted by the standards, it is said, framed the text as a puzzle with a "predetermined meaning" to which students must be led and thus deprived students of agency in meaning-making (Connors and Rish); excluded as irrelevant any contexts, whether biographical, historical, or cultural (Shanahan, "Letting" 7); and denied that the reader's affective response might be essential to any determination of meaning or value, substituting "mechanistic inspection" of texts for thoughtful interactions (Gilbert 28). This pedagogic critique, it should be noted, also entails a political one. According to Sean Connors and Ryan Rish, "the CCSS's myopic emphasis on close reading in ways that are circumscribed by New Criticism constitutes a social justice issue" by privileging "certain texts, types of readers, and sets of literacy practices" over others (96). Endacott and Christian Goering attribute the emphasis in the standards on uniformity and accountability to the role of corporate interests in producing them. And Chris Gilbert observes how the top-down approach can affect teacher evaluation, tenure rights, and curricular options, thereby producing "submissive teachers" and compliant but "listless" students (29). To be sure, the standards' cramped textual focus has invited such critiques from dedicated teachers who rightfully resist efforts to commodify education in general and the humanities in particular. However, this reaction to so much prescription, while understandable, runs the risk of advancing a "theoroid" that is also rather reductive—that the New Critical discipline of close reading must be shunned as inherently elitist, conformist, and disrespectful of students. Indeed, the New Critics themselves would likely not recognize this portrait of their approach. Rather than reject them and what they allegedly represent out of hand, we can use the ideas they actually promoted as a frame for interrogating our own assumptions about reading.

It is worth recalling that the New Critics, in their desire to help students read literature with understanding and appreciation, wanted to avoid both the positivism they saw in other disciplinary epistemologies and the unconditioned relativism of personal reader response. If the CCSS were in fact faithful to the spirit of New Critical exposition, the resulting pedagogy, while still insufficient to address the current challenges, would be far more nuanced in its approach and less likely to provoke claims that it was trying to turn students into automatons or obliging corporate interests. When literature, especially poetry, was studied systematically prior to the emergence of the New Critics, the emphasis was generally not on the meaning generated by the text (because this could be simply a matter of taste or personal associations) but rather on authorial biography, psychology, or history of ideas. It was in this context that critics such as I. A. Richards and, a bit later, Cleanth Brooks and W. K. Wimsatt were attempting to regularize principles of literary criticism in the interests of both intellectual respectability and productive pedagogical approaches. However, in attempting to set down and apply methods for understanding poems, plays, and narrative fiction, these critics did not see themselves as priests unlocking the mysteries of sacred texts to worthy acolytes, a caricature often imposed on them, but rather as teacher-scholars of the profoundest sort, motivated to share their methods and insights with others while insisting that texts worth studying cannot be reduced to a single meaning or experience.

Far from seeing literature as a puzzle with a single solution or final meaning to be ferreted out in a cultural vacuum, these practitioners understood the importance of both background knowledge and ongoing transactions of the reader with the text. Brooks was careful to avoid reducing to an algorithm the reader's unfolding relationship with a work of art: "A formula can be learned and applied, but the full, concrete, appropriate response to a situation can only be experienced. Literature is thus incurably concrete, not abstract" (*Shaping Joy* 6). Wimsatt, while committed like Brooks to enduring and universal aesthetic principles, understood the role of the reader's unique perspective in discerning textual meaning, as indicated by this passage from *The Verbal Icon* (1954): "Our judgments of the past cannot be discontinuous with our own experience or insulated from it. To evaluate the past we have to penetrate it with our own intelligence" (258). Chicago School critic R. F. Crane, while skeptical of the New Critics' first principle of literary evaluation—the accommodation of paradoxes, tensions, and ironies into a finely balanced whole—nonetheless agreed with Brooks and Wimsatt on the urgency of charting a respectable disciplinary method and on its basic outlines in literary education. Such a method, he wrote in *The Languages of Criticism* (1953), would avoid both "mere impressionism and the evocation of irresponsible opinion" and also "the imposition on students of ready-made literary doctrines or canons of taste." It would depend on concepts and criteria and would keep students focused not only on the text in all its specificity but also on *"their responses as human beings"* (187, emphasis added). Clearly, among these critics the idea of a reader reading was not made to disappear, as is commonly claimed. However, the reader as envisioned was not naïve, uninformed, or uninterested in educated consensus.

New Critical attitudes toward authorial intentionality have also been somewhat oversimplified by those who have challenged the standards. The "intentional fallacy" (codified by Wimsatt and Beardsley in 1946 and revised by Wimsatt as Chapter 1 of *The Verbal Icon*) is typically portrayed as an unqualified insistence that nothing we know about the authors or their lives and times—i.e., nothing outside the texts—can be brought to bear on a reader's interpretation. The division between texts and their creators, however, is not so sharply drawn as this portrait suggests. In fact, the New Critical focus on close reading did not mean that nothing external to the text should play a role in the reader's interpretation. Wimsatt explains that "internal" and "external" are inextricably linked and actually implied in each other. That is, the internal is public in the sense that it is gleaned through access to cultural codes, "through our habitual knowledge of the language, through grammars, dictionaries, and all the literature which is the source of dictionaries, in general through all that makes a language and culture"; and the external—if by that we mean information gleaned from letters, diaries, the author's own commentary, or other such sources—is actually "private and idiosyncratic." In considering this counterintuitive perspective, we find that the "autonomy" of the text is expansive and elastic rather than narrow and rigid. Moreover, using biographical information is appropriate if it yields insight into "the meaning of [the author's] words and the dramatic character of his utterance" (10).

In what might be called an early set of instructions on how to read expertly with the grain, Brooks explained that while we need not embrace the values of a particular text, we are obliged to understand it in its contexts as best we can. He offered as an example Sophocles's *Antigone,* a play that George Eliot famously defended in 1856 against charges of irrelevance based on the antiquated (i.e., pagan) beliefs that shape the play's central dilemma ("The Antigone and Its Moral"). Brooks argues that while we may not share the attitude toward burial rites that underlies the drama, we must nonetheless feel and accept their meaning for the characters whose conflict informs the theme. More generally, we must "understand the language of the poem, including its ideas and allusions" (*Well Wrought Urn* 254). In a 1944 "brief for the defense" of the New Criticism, his exemplary interpretation of Alfred, Lord Tennyson's "Tears, Idle Tears" (selected purposefully for the lyric quality that would, according to opponents of the approach, make the poem unfit for a New Critical reading), Brooks reveals how much background knowledge his analysis took for granted—not only of tropes, irony, connotative language, and other linguistic markers of artful poetry—but also of such "external" fields as geography and Greek mythology as well as of lived experience, e.g., sea travel (288–89).

Such understanding, to be sure, was considered necessary but not sufficient; we must not allow literature to be reduced to cultural history (*Well Wrought Urn* 254). Also essential to understanding was a sensitivity to the text's "dramatic context" and "the play of the speaker's mind"—a sense of the occasion for writing inferred from the emotion unfolding in the words, lines, and stanzas as experienced temporally and also considered retrospectively as they compose, or are perceived to compose, a coherent aesthetic entity. The "critic's emotional reactions"—not completely free but constrained by "the "structure of the poem itself"—were implied in rather than banished from competent interpretation ("The New Criticism" 294).

Overall, skillful readers were assumed to bring perspective born of a broad cultural awareness, an understanding of the history of ideas, and a capacity for empathy with the writer's sense—inferred from the reading itself as well as from one's background knowledge—of what was at stake in the composition of the artifact. These contexts would automatically be brought to bear on the reading but they could not in themselves determine it. In sum, for the New Critics, rhetorical reading (including all of the "meta" aspects identified by Horning) was a sine qua non of "close" reading. To say so is not to embrace elitism or to elevate esoterica but to appreciate, as Brooks did, the claim of the humanities "to making a peculiar and special contribution" (*Well Wrought Urn* 235) entailing both critical judgment and "imaginative understanding" (74–75).

Thus it is a great irony that New Critical approaches have been cast as *antithetical* to the humanities—as absolutist, authoritarian, dismissive of cultural political contexts, detached from the experiences of individual human beings as shaped by personal influences and cultural structures. While their theories often did imply an "ideal" reading toward which skilled readers were expected to strive, they brought to their work a repertoire of expert understandings and practices that enabled them to take what Rosenblatt called a "stance" toward the text, helping them decide what to notice and what to make of what they noticed. They would no doubt agree with the cautions proposed by Tim Shanahan who, in his balanced appraisal of the standards, observes that text-dependency alone is not the determinant of a fruitful question, since many such questions might be "not very important within the universe created by that text" ("Letting the Text" 10) and that research findings on the role of background knowledge as an aid to comprehension have been oversimplified (7). Experts do not typically read in a contextual void, and if they are forced to do so they bring to bear the sorts of knowledge—of genre, of the terms of the conversation being joined, of likely authorial habits of mind—that traditional close readers have taken for granted. Above all, the New Critics attempted to read as members of the authorial audience—defined by Peter Rabinowitz as "a hypothetical construction of what the author expects his or her readers to be like" (Rabinowitz and Smith 23).

In this context we can see how the CCSS approach to close reading borrows the New Critical strict attention to the text but tends to ignore the knowledge and perspectives fundamental to playing the authorial reader. The result, to use Rabinowitz and Corinne Bancroft's apt phrase, is "Zombie New Criticism," a distorted and reduced version of the original, rooted in no theory at all (7). However, in associating close reading with "mechanistic inspection" (Gilbert 28), critics of the CCSS miss an opportunity to see the potential of the recommended pedagogies to help students avoid uncritical reaction and solipsistic interpretations. Effective close reading of any text (even the most apparently informative and objective ones) requires role-playing that entails engagement, background knowledge, and an understanding of genre and of disciplinary rules (Dobrin 1989). To the extent that the CCSS brand of close reading ignores or suppresses this kind of education by plunging students directly into the text with minimal guidance or framing, it is vulnerable to the charges of its critics and thus risks inviting the false binary of students' reactions versus textual meanings.

Close Reading and Distant Reading

> Our students are not engaged with their reading, and we educators, particularly at the postsecondary and secondary level, don't really know how to engage them. . . . Most students can't, won't, and don't do much if any required reading for their classes.
>
> —David Jolliffe and Christian Goering

Engaging students does not mean selecting texts that invite immediate identification with a persona or perspective. Robert Scholes makes the important point that close reading is actually "distant reading"—a way of temporarily relinquishing our identities in order to assume the viewpoint of another before reacting to it or judging it. "We, and our students, must learn to put ourselves into a text before taking ourselves out of it" ("Transition" 166). Such a move is a precondition of comprehension and even of an authentic personal response. This entry into the text is not the same as engagement per se, which can mirror the reader's already closely held beliefs or prejudices, a substitution for the role-playing inherent in an empathetic imagination. Scholes maintains, and many of us would likely agree, that "we are not good, as a culture, at imagining the other" (167).

A pervasive sense that this is true accounts for the fact that, even as "springboard" and "prereading" approaches became dominant in high school classrooms, the believing and doubting game introduced by Peter Elbow in the 1970s ("Appendix Essay") found echoes among scholars increasingly interested in translating critical theory into classroom practice. Drawing on similar pedagogic strategies, Scholes posited a double process for textual analysis—first of "listening and obedience" as a reader and then of "suspicion and rigor" as a critic (*Textual Power* 48). According to Doug Brent, reading requires "a delicate balance between sources of constructive freedom and forces that constrain meaning." The former include the reader's individual responses based on private associations, a particular knowledge base, and a stream of consciousness, while the latter entails traits of the author's imagined audience based on "public, communal and relatively stable aspects" of the communication context (44–45). James Seitz advocates writing assignments that ask students to impersonate authors based on the premise that "it is the existence of constraints that paradoxically creates the possibility of discursive production" (335). Wayne Booth and Rabinowitz further helped us to define the ways literary texts demand versatility in readers, showing us not only how to play the narrative audience (by being "taken in") and the authorial audience (by viewing the characters from the perspective of the implied author), but also how to step back, reflect on the cognitive and ethical power of the text, and consider whether to "reject the values of the story world [we] first 'took in'" (Booth, "Ethics" 49). This idea underlies the transactional process as described by Louise Rosenblatt beginning with *Literature as Exploration* in 1938 and elaborated in the ensuing decades. In summing up the evolution of her theoretical position, Rosenblatt emphasized that the reader must "learn to develop a guiding principle" for responding to a text, and be "selective" in deciding what in the text should be questioned, affirmed, or denied ("Transactional Theory" 383, 385).

Recent commentary by writing tutors and first-year instructors has reinforced these themes, emphasizing that faculty across the curriculum desire neither regurgitation of facts nor naïve reactions to an assigned text but rather a transaction with it informed by the relevant disciplinary moves. Experts in secondary and postsecondary composition and rhetoric are calling for more and better instruction in the distant aspects of close reading—in particular, playing the authorial audience as prior to other kinds of engagement with the text such as an aesthetic critique, a rhetorical evaluation, or a theory-driven methodological analysis. Such habits require a nuanced sense of the relationship between text and contexts. Good readers, it is argued, develop a repertoire of approaches and learn when to invoke the appropriate one: they learn to "read like a writer" (Bunn 55); to become aware of their reading practices and to adapt them as necessary to context, genre, and discipline (Carillo, "Creating"; Lockhart and Soliday); to practice paraphrase and analysis skills, including some "similar to what we would today call close reading," as preparation for argumentative and analytical writing (Kalbfleisch); and to use close reading not only as a way to learn content but as a means of acquiring skills in analysis, use of evidence, correct use of terminology, and question-posing (Tinkle et al.)—in sum, to develop different kinds of awareness of textual elements and contexts of various kinds (Horning and Gollnitz). These increasing calls for instruction in metacognitive skills suggest that the CCSS warnings against enabling students to substitute prereading information for the act of reading or to depend on undisciplined responses are somewhat misguided in their emphasis. While such warnings are an understandable reaction to high school practices deemed inadequate, they miss an opportunity to cultivate sophisticated textual engagement.

Background Knowledge and "The Text Itself"

The standards' insistence that teachers and students restrict attention to what lies "within the four corners of the text" (Coleman and Pimentel 4) is emphatic. Consider, for example, the following directives:

- "Student background knowledge and experiences can illuminate the reading but should not replace attention to the text itself" (7, 16).
- "Scaffolding should not become an alternate, simpler source of information that diminishes the need for students to read the text itself carefully" (9, 17).
- "Text-dependent questions do not require information from outside the text itself" (6).

Yet the role of background knowledge in comprehension has been well documented (see, e.g., Stanovich and Cunningham, "Studying" and "Where"; Bransford et al.; Hirsch; Willingham, "Critical Thinking" and *Reading Mind;* Wexler). The rhetorical frames constructed by experts comprise choices based on awareness of formal conventions and on inferred conversations in background derived from prior knowledge. As Kathleen Yancey has observed, "[R]eading is not some acontextual activity. Reading is about stuff, and your ability to read is in part dependent on how much you actually knew about the stuff to begin with" (Mallette et al. 16). This implicit contract between writer and reader is affirmed by current research on decoding and comprehension According to the noted cognitive psychologist Daniel T. Willingham, students striving to understand a text "need to know most of (but not everything) the writer assumes the reader knows" (*Reading Mind* 127–28).

This principle can be illustrated by the common complaint among instructors of high school and first-year college English classes that students don't get the irony of Jonathan Swift's "A Modest Proposal." As Stanley Fish pointedly illustrated in his summary of shifting interpretations of another work by Swift, irony is a function of assumptions one brings to a text, so the difference between the authorial voice and that of the narrator or persona cannot be assumed to be inherent in the text. Why, after all, couldn't Swift, in writing "A Modest Proposal," have been a madman offering his ideas in a serious way? Or, why need we assume—as a student of mine once asked—that cannibalism, a cultural practice, was necessarily being judged by Swift according to the standards of his own society?

If students are uninformed about Anglo-Irish history (many students understandably but incorrectly assume that Swift is addressing overpopulation or the potato famine of the nineteenth century), about Swift's career, about the role of "projectors" in the early eighteenth century, or about the generic constraints of parody, they can hardly be expected to read the "Proposal" as would the authorial audience solely by analyzing the argument. Even if the students are at first encouraged to read the text "cold," it seems necessary at some point to offer some essential information: that Swift was a Church of England clergyman who, while eccentric, was not likely to have advocated that babies born into poverty be used to feed the hungry of all classes and to enhance Irish prosperity; that the proposal begins with language typical of early eighteenth-century religious orations and closely imitates the opening sentence of one of Swift's actual sermons, thus luring readers of the time into expectations that would soon be shockingly upset; that the proposal's multipart rationale and quantitative reasoning invoke the practicality of social-problem solutions commonly recommended in Swift's time, thus offering a critique of inhumane policies based on the "political arithmetic" approach advocated by projectors such as Sir William Petty (1623–87). The rhetorical challenge for students in this case is to separate themselves from the narrative voice—to see how they were seduced for a time to read with the grain and then had to "correct" that early impression to get to the heart of the matter.

However, even with this act of resistance to what they first embraced, students will need help in teasing out Swift's take on the various objects of satire, some still the subject of discussion (e.g., the degree to which Swift was holding the Irish accountable for their own plight, his attitude toward "papists," i.e., Catholics, as shaped by the political-religious controversies of early eighteenth-century England, his conventional assumptions about social class, his conservative Tory sympathies, his acceptance of the noblesse oblige ethos). Here is where the close reading advocated by the standards would play an important role, as details easily glossed over in a summary or overview are brought into the analysis and used to both shape a coherent reading and expose unresolved tensions. Having learned or been told that the narrator is unreliable, students often don't do enough with the question of exactly what is being satirized and why. Given time and more historical contexts, students could then be guided in taking the next step: critically assessing the now informed authorial perspective on the problem and its solutions. What sort of person does Swift seem to be and who does he "pretend" to be? What audiences is he addressing and with what apparent purposes? (Typically, only in advanced college English or history classes would students have enough context to assess, based on historical evidence, the defensibility of Swift's particular attacks.)

To be fair, it should be noted that the importance of background knowledge is not entirely absent from the CCSS exemplars; in modeling strategies for teaching King's "Letter," Coleman does acknowledge how the text invites us to go beyond its immediate contexts by invoking historical analogies, Biblical allusions, and transcendent ethical principles. He also points out that the text is in dialogue with both the Declaration of Independence and the Gettysburg Address, "part of the great conversation in the United States" ("Bringing" 22). Despite such moves toward providing context, however, the frequent insistence that teachers ask only questions that "do not require information or evidence from outside the text" (6) and the cautions against excessive "scaffolding" discourage more expansive thinking by a student who has no way to bring the desired metacontextual awareness to the text.

Objections to the CCSS treatment of the text as an independent entity in which meaning objectively resides and can be extracted fall generally into two camps. On the one hand, critics such as Chris Gilbert and Daniel Ferguson are concerned that students' responses to texts are being disrespected; according to Ferguson, "Critical literacy argues that students' sense of their own realities should never be treated as outside the meaning of a text" (21), and Gilbert sees the standards as opposing a "holistic, personalized curriculum" (27) and prioritizing texts over students (28). For these teachers, the standards deny the importance for students of "having your own experiences, knowledge, and opinions valued" (Ferguson 21), a position at odds with Coleman's rationale for focusing on evidence-based interpretation and argument rather than expressive or personal writing: "people don't [care at all] about what you feel or what you think" ("Bringing" 10). Coleman's point is that the focus on personal and narrative writing does not demand of students enough rigor or enough serious effort to read difficult texts expertly, and his purpose, understandably, is to address the pervasive issues (weak comprehension and flat reading scores) that prompted the development of the standards in the first place.

Other critics are less concerned with honoring students' responses than with the limitations of acontextual reading, especially of historical documents. The notion of textual autonomy has been persuasively subverted over the past half century (see, e.g., Olson; Michaels; Warren, "Rhetorical Reading and the Development of Disciplinary Literacy"), and historical documents naturally invite such skepticism. Hence the critique proffered by Alan Singer, a professor of social studies education at Hofstra, who makes a good case that focusing on the text alone can be misleading: "A close reading of text without historical context promotes reading without understanding." From this perspective, some of the very questions teachers of the Gettysburg Address are told to avoid posing—"Why did the North fight the Civil War?" "Did Lincoln think that the North was going to 'pass the test' that the Civil War posed?"—are essential to an understanding of history and politics and thus to basic comprehension of the document under scrutiny.

Singer is appalled that students taught according to the CCSS will not be asked to undertake an ethical evaluation of the writer that depends on a knowledge of history. His own reading of the Gettysburg Address offers a harsh critique of Lincoln, recasting the honest and idealistic Abe of popular culture as a politician both compromising and compromised, a leader whose strategies worked more against Emancipation than for it. As evidence, Singer reminds readers of sentiments expressed by Lincoln—in his 1858 debates with Stephen Douglas; in an 1862 letter to *New York Tribune* editor Horace Greeley; in a message to Congress prior to the issuance of the Emancipation Proclamation; and even in the beloved conciliatory lines of the Second Inaugural Address, which, Singer argues, were addressed mainly to Southern whites:

> As I read Lincoln's Second Inaugural Address, I see a war-weary and politically cautious president who never believed

> in racial equality; who less than a month before finally issuing the Emancipation Proclamation, offered the South gradual compensated emancipation that would have extended slavery in the United States into the twentieth century, and who in the actual document sharply limited the scope of emancipation so that very few enslaved Africans out of the millions in bondage were directly and immediately affected.

As a historian, Singer makes an essential point. The stories we tell about canonical figures in history are often shaped by a desire for neat story lines and clear messages. However, instructors with specialized contextual knowledge and expertise in reading against the grain can leap too soon to expectations that students will enact such habits. Judging the implied author and conversing with the text can happen only after we know how to infer the authorial audience and to play this sympathetic, or believing, role. Thus the version of Lincoln that Singer sees in the text cannot be appreciated or evaluated until students have first been "taken in" by Lincoln's logic and rhetoric as situated from the point of view of the author. How that situatedness is to be established lies in the art of the teacher, whose own understanding of the challenge Lincoln set for himself, and whose informed professional judgment, enacted in real-time classroom exchanges, are key to success.

Coleman says as much when, in exemplifying a close reading of King's letter, he notes that the third paragraph is "dense with allusion" and might cause teachers to slow down to explain King's rhetoric: "I think one's always judging as a teacher when to pause in that way. . . . [I]t's perfectly appropriate to fill in some of those blanks" ("Bringing" 19). Yet the fear of substituting explanation—a "trivially summarized" version of the text—for actual reading is what drives the pedagogic guidance: Teachers, at least on a first reading, need only supply "enough [information] to keep moving through his argument" and take care "to not linger too long there and lose the force of the argument" (19). Here we see what I take to be an uneasy ambivalence in the standards between, on the one hand, a need to help students read "closely" and, on the other, an understanding that they can do so only when certain conditions of knowledge and perspective are in place (17).

Certainly, a central aspect of such knowledge is how and why particular words are used, so perhaps one area of consensus is that vocabulary is essential. But even here the pedagogic issues are somewhat more complicated than the standards suggest, as words themselves have histories and are often deployed by great writers to expand meanings and undermine certainties. As Walter Benn Michaels illustrated in his keen analysis of intentionality in legal decisions and in literary interpretations, the notion of inherent meaning is always based on an illusion, since the meanings we attribute to texts are derived from an interpretive consensus and thus are "institutional" rather than "formal." Writing more than four decades ago, Michaels was working to uncover the tacit formalist assumptions that he sensed underlay critical approaches to interpretation of texts literary and otherwise. His argument that ambiguity, clarity, and explicitness are functions of situations and contexts rather than of texts per se is one that the New Critics, even with their emphasis on textual unity and aesthetic integrity, would have found compelling. Wimsatt, for example, despite his cautions about the intentional fallacy, wrote: "The meaning of words is the history of words, and the biography of an author, his use of a word, and the associations which the word had for him, are part of the word's history and meaning" (10). Brooks noted that "we are always forced to go outside the poem for the unit meanings on which the poem is founded" (*Well Wrought Urn* 255), that "[i]n order to understand Shakespeare, we simply have to understand what Shakespeare's words mean." This is more than a matter of denotation, "far beyond the mere matter of restoring a few obsolete meanings"; on our understanding of words depends our interpretation of the text's larger meanings, including its conversation with a world of ideas: "Tied in with language may be a way of apprehending reality, a philosophy, a whole world view" (236).

While Michaels's project, in its insistence on the social construction of all interpretive criteria (even, his argument demonstrates, as applied to apparently unambiguous words such as *chicken* or *rock*), privileges skepticism over containment in ways that Brooks and Wimsatt would likely resist, the New Critical insistence on broad and deep contextual knowledge is consonant with Michaels's assertion that "the lexicon itself . . . has meaning only against a background of assumptions and information which it . . . can never contain" (33). On the surface, it appears that the standards, with their laserlike focus on having students understand words in context, comport well with such sentiments. Coleman's advice to help students understand "master words" such as *tension* in King's letter and *faction* in *The Federalist Papers* seems consistent with such a philosophy. However, as with the terms *proposal* and *projector* in Swift's notorious satire, such words—which ask us to embrace conflicting connotations—will not unfold their layers for any but the most astute adolescent (or for, that matter, adult) readers, and even they would need some historical context to fully join the authorial audience. Here again, even as the CCSS philosophy appears to recognize this fact, it seems not to have fully integrated the "distant" aspects of close reading.

This sort of limitation is also evident in the optional lessons offered to teachers who have time and inclination to include them. While every student is to be coached in working through the words and sentences "like a detective" (Coleman and Pimentel 16), an appendix suggests an additional assignment that takes readers outside the document to consider how its ideas might be critiqued. Under "Additional History/Social Studies Activities," we thus find a sample lesson that has students evaluate conflicting assessments of Lincoln's speech and especially his "reading of the Declaration of Independence into the Constitution" by examining two very different sources—(1) a furious 1863 editorial by the *Chicago Times* attacking Lincoln for advancing the notion of racial equality in opposition to specified clauses in the federal constitution and (2) Garry Wills's late-twentieth-century analysis of (and homage to) Lincoln's rhetorical and political accomplishment. Teachers are told that students might end with a debate about whether the text of the speech better supports the claims of the nineteenth-century editorial or the "pro-Lincoln thesis"—a passage of a few hundred words (one that, through an ellipsis inserted by the lesson planner, incidentally introduces a grammatical error)—excerpted from Wills's *Lincoln at Gettysburg* ("Common Core Unit"). The juxtaposition of opposites does hold the potential for lively discussion. But on what basis could a novice student defend either side?

This assignment, as I see it, is problematic for several reasons. First, it assumes incorrectly that once students have understood an argument on the level of diction, syntax, and logic, they are qualified to opine on its validity or persuasiveness, devoid of background. Second, it offers as material for such an assessment two short excerpts, presented out of context except for a passing reference to time period, from writers representing vastly different genres, historical moments, motives for writing, and kinds of interest. This decontextualization makes impossible the sorts of rhetorical framing habitually used by skilled readers and thus inhibits comprehension. Third, the excerpts themselves are written in complex language that would require as much unpacking as the primary text itself: the editorial quotes eighteenth-century legalistic language, and the excerpt from Wills, a master stylist, includes words such as *volatilized*, *macerated*, *prescinded*, and *transcendental*. A broader challenge lies in the sophistication of the arguments: Students are asked to appraise whether Lincoln violated the Constitution or whether, as Wills contends, he deserves kudos for choosing to focus on abstractions over particulars, so that "ideals are made to grapple naked in an airy battle of the mind" (37).

In a history or social studies class where time might permit, one can imagine a different sort of assignment. Rather than being thrust directly against the proslavery editorial, Wills's reverential exegesis of the address might be productively compared with the critique by Singer. Singer and Wills, both disciplinary experts, offer detailed contexts for the address but draw different conclusions and judgments—about the motivations and effects of Lincoln's choices, about the relation of his rhetoric to the policies that ensued, and about the character of the man himself and the legacy of his presidency. The *Chicago Times* editorial could be one piece of primary evidence among others, selected to give students a much fuller sense of the events, debates, and conflicting firmly held beliefs that Lincoln had somehow to accommodate and thus of the import of his rhetorical and political choices. The lesson for students here is not that we need to decide who is "right" but rather that defensible arguments about politics and historiography require more than a look at a few hundred words on the different sides.

The temptation to have students form judgments prematurely should be resisted both for students' sake and for our own. As Booth cautioned more than fifty years ago in a speech to the Illinois Council of Teachers of English: "[T]o make students assume a controversial pose before they have the genuine substance to be controversial about is to encourage dishonesty and slovenliness, and to ensure our own boredom" ("Boring"). A recent study by Karen Manarin et al. of students' reading in various disciplines confirms the unsurprising tendency of novice readers to fit arguments into already-held beliefs or feelings rather than take a stance of critical distance and analysis (a tendency earlier theorized and documented by Brent). While the authors of this study were disappointed that their "students jumped from understanding the text to taking a position," there is a strong implication that the understanding itself, because it was not based on an attempt to play the authorial audience, was thin and incomplete. Yet the easy appeal of superficial "debates" unfortunately retains its charm. By encouraging students to argue for positions they are ill-prepared to understand, the optional exemplar assignment unfortunately has the trivializing effect that the antecedent focus on close reading is carefully crafted to avoid.

That the CCSS, in moving "outside" the text, creates tasks for students that contradict its own principles of reading for depth and nuance testifies to the powerful urge to accommodate whatever causes cognitive dissonance by fitting it neatly into a familiar category. To debate whether it is more "correct" to condemn or admire Lincoln for his balancing of ends with means—his grasp of realpolitik—will not be educational for students with no sense of the historical milieu. This point is aptly made by Tim Shanahan, who appreciates the CCSS shift to text-centeredness but would like more recognition that different texts require different types of reading: "Lincoln's little speech is so clearly a historical argument that cries out for a historian's touch. And the disconnect is made even more striking because the Gettysburg Address is not just any historical document but the most sublime expression of American exceptionalism" ("How Bad?").

A worthy alternative to the CCSS exemplar is presented in the National Endowment for the Humanities (NEH) sample lessons for teaching the address. Students are given documents that enable them to read Lincoln in light of contemporaneous philosophical and political ideologies and are prompted to see his remarks as a purposeful response crafted to navigate these crosscurrents while keeping the ship of state on course toward a contested goal; that is, they are given the tools and guidance they need to read rhetorically. The CCSS exemplar suggests that the option of comparing the editorial attack on Lincoln with Wills's appreciative historical analysis might conclude "with an impromptu debate with students assuming one or the other side of the argument" ("Common Core Unit"). In contrast, the NEH lesson encourages role-playing. It asks students to use primary texts to imagine questions that might be posed by a prosecutor interrogating Lincoln on the charges in the editorial and then to imagine how Lincoln would respond, thus engaging in both close and distant reading, both inhabiting and resisting the role of authorial audience. Students are asked to work in groups and to engage individually in careful rhetorical readings of texts by the president and of objections by a forceful critic. They must not only decode statements accurately but infer questions arising therefrom as shaped by their growing understanding of the crisis at the time. Concluding the sequence is an assignment that cultivates argumentative writing based on nuance and careful evaluation rather than a stark either/or choice: "Ask students to rate Lincoln's response to the editorial on a scale of 1 to 5, with 1 representing a least favorable opinion of his ability to answer the criticism, and 5 representing a most favorable opinion. Then have students write a paragraph justifying why they chose the number they did."

The notion put forward by Coleman that fostering acontextual reading is a good way to address differences in student preparation might make sense if based on the idea that since readers are confronted regularly with unfamiliar texts, skilled readers must make sense of this material even if reading it cold. But this argument too is undercut by research that shows that the kinds of expertise deployed by skillful readers depend on positing a context where none is explicitly supplied, so that a plunge into the text includes the support of a procedural scaffold. Brent, in describing the act of reading as a process of "rhetorical invention," cogently sums up the limitations of narrowly text-centered strategies.

Meaning, he observes, is made "not just by the words of the text but by the place of that text in the larger epistemic conversation in which the reader is immersed, a conversation that generates certain questions about the text and places it in relationship to other texts based on those questions" (82). Rhetorical reading, a practice automatically enacted by experts, helps readers construct a kind of frame around the text by imagining such contextual aspects as the persona of the author, the occasion for writing, the intended audience, and the conversation being joined.

Moreover, instruction in rhetorical reading entails raised consciousness of disciplinary epistemologies. In his advocacy of teaching disciplinary literacy across the high school curriculum, James Warren not only posits instruction in rhetorical reading as a crucial approach to countering the "'the ideal of the autonomous text,'" but also, building on work by Elizabeth Moje, makes a compelling distinction between *strategies* and *practices*: The former are typically taught as generic and hence transferable skills, whereas the latter often entail moves that develop with disciplinary expertise. Some research suggests that such habits, while usually tacit, can be made explicit to high school students and thereby improve their reading in a range of subject areas (Warren, "Rhetorical Reading and the Development of Disciplinary Literacy"). By fostering such approaches, Warren claims, teachers can even help students do better on standardized reading tests, where passages have to be decoded completely out of context. The idea is that by seeing the passage as a rhetorical act rather than a free-floating set of signifiers, students are more likely to get the gist (7–8).

As many savvy students know, a rich repertoire of contextual and procedural knowledge can even enable us to write persuasively about a text we have not read. This is a point made memorably by William Perry's witty 1963 piece, "Examsmanship and the Liberal Arts," about a student who earned a high grade on an exam in a class he never took. The story goes roughly as follows: An undergraduate named Metzger who finds himself with unexpected time on his hands impulsively decides to sit for a social science exam about to be proctored in a nearby classroom. Unschooled in the discipline, and faced with writing an essay on one of two books totally unfamiliar to him, for each of which a positive and a negative appraisal has been supplied, he compensates for his dearth of text-specific data by bringing to bear a wide range of resources: information he has "heard" (e.g., that Margaret Mead is a social anthropologist), background linguistic knowledge (i.e., the likely cultural background of the other author based on his Anglo-Saxon sounding name), inferences regarding the general content of one of the books based on its title (*The American People*), his exposure to "table-talk" on concepts he correctly imagines to be relevant (such as cultural relativity and participant-observer bias), facility with "creative logic" and a basic understanding of rhetoric (e.g., the merits of appearing fair and balanced in an argumentative essay). Based on the excerpt we see from Metzger's essay, Perry might have added other competencies: his command of diction, syntax, and sentence rhythms (presumably honed by plenty of reading); his sense of discourse conventions (also probably cultivated by broad exposure to texts of various kinds); and his overall enjoyment of role-playing, as he assumes the persona of the serious student enacting discipline-specific expertise in an area he "knows" only in the most general and ambient way. Perry's point is that Metzger's A- on the exam (no doubt nettlesome to his friend who was enrolled in the class, had studied, and earned only a C) suggests the importance of what Perry calls "bull." Defined here as "relevancies, however relevant, without data," "bull" is normally punished when it is detected, whereas its reciprocal, "cow"—"data, however relevant, without relevancies" (6)—is rewarded as evidence of effort.

Metzger's grade reflects how much is tacit in the expertise we expect from our students: a disposition to inhabit the role invited by the assignment, alertness to textual cues and clues, linguistic fluency, inferential thinking, familiarity with the rhetoric of argument—in sum, knowing what the rhetorical rules are and how to play by them. Perry wants his audience of professors to acknowledge that in rewarding pure cow they hinder the intellectual and ethical development of students, while pure bull, though typically scorned, has its neglected merits:

> If a liberal education should teach students "how to think," not only in their own fields but in fields outside their own . . . then bulling, even in its purest form, expresses an important

> part of what a pluralist university holds dear, surely a more important part than the collecting of "facts that are facts" which schoolboys learn to do. Here, then, good bull appears not as ignorance at all but as an aspect of knowledge. It is both relevant and "true." In a university setting good bull is therefore of more value than "facts," which, without a frame of reference, are not even "true" at all. (8)

Perry thus reminds us that educating students according to the ideals we espouse means helping them see that even the most immediate and empirical examination of data, if it is to be meaningful, requires a thoughtful and considered frame of reference. In our current information age, this observation is more pertinent than ever.

Metzger's prank naturally disturbed the authorities but less because of his trickery than because he exposed the insufficiency of their common formulation. Clearly, his good grade, however embarrassing when his status was revealed, did depend on an act of successful reading: He had to decode the nature of the class, the assignment, the professor's expectations, and the basic premises of the discipline—a feat he was able to accomplish because he understood the opportunities and constraints implied in the occasion for writing. That is, Metzger's acculturation into the norms of academia had developed within a broad horizon of knowledge. Such an approach produced an essay that not only gratified the teaching assistant tasked with grading but enabled Perry to illustrate why and how we must "lead students beyond their concept of bull so that they may honor relevancies that are really relevant" (13)—and indeed, essential to the understanding and attitudes that are the aims of a liberal education.

Chapter Three

Reading, Fast and Slow

Connecting Parts to Whole

With so much emphasis on close reading as requisite for comprehension, it is striking to find one of the most compelling proponents of reading across the curriculum (RAC) making the case for a different sort of skill: "Effective reading is fast, not precise and not strictly or even mostly a visual activity" (Horning, "Reading Across"). This is an important claim that needs both elaboration and qualification. In fact, effective reading is sometimes slow and precise, depending on genre and purpose. Because of their aesthetic qualities and the quality and range of their transactional invitations, literary texts—novels, poems, and short stories, but also rhetorically complex and connotatively rich persuasive or expository texts such as, for example, Jonathan Swift's notorious "A Modest Proposal," Martin Luther King Jr.'s "Letter from Birmingham Jail," the Declaration of Independence, or James Baldwin's "Stranger in the Village"—do repay close, slow, and careful reading as well as rereading. Moreover, it is only by the close reading of challenging texts, particularly those that are opaque or call for an aesthetic response, that students can be attuned to the range and complexity of authorial roles and potentials. In noting the interdependence of sentence rhythms and meaning, Richard Lanham argues persuasively for making deliberate oral reading, currently rather neglected in first-year writing courses, a key practice for novice writers: "Every course in composition ought to be a course in Slow Reading" (146).

However, not all texts require or invite this sort of attention, and some actually discourage it. Lanham observes that the purposefully "neutral" style that is standard in scientific writing "is usually rhythmless, unemphatic, or cacorhythmic" (147). Moreover, As David Jolliffe has noted, the sorts of "strong" reading sometimes taught in first-year composition via texts such as David Bartholomae and Anthony Petrosky's *Ways of Reading*—i.e., the practice of approaching the text both as the imagined ideal reader and then as a thoughtful questioner or critic—are not generally expected across the curriculum, especially in general-education courses that tend to rely on informative texts ("Learning to Read as Continuing Education" 476, 479). And even texts to which we might, under ideal circumstances, devote a lingering engagement must be dealt with more summarily in the interests of practical constraints. Thus successful readers across the curriculum will acquire a repertoire of strategies that can be invoked in the range of textual qualities and occasions for reading.

Expert readers are able to read slowly and closely but also quickly and selectively as required by the context and purpose of their reading (Horning, "Where"). "Dutiful reading" as students conceive it will not in itself serve students well in college (Kegan 281). Gaining skill in the alternatives—skimming, fast reading, reading to answer a question—is equally demanding and in some ways more so, if those strategies are to be enacted expertly. Even the Common Core State Standards, with their emphasis on close-reading pedagogies, include a brief recognition that practicing close reading alone will not prepare students for the demands of college and the workplace: "Focusing on extended texts will enable students to develop the stamina and persistence they need to read and extract knowledge and insight from larger volumes of material. Not only do students need to be able to read closely, but they also need to be able to read larger volumes of text when necessary for other purposes" (Coleman and Pimentel 4, 15).

The potential drawbacks of a singular focus on slow and meticulous close reading have been illuminated by educational psychologist Robert Kegan's summary of the process by which students at Harvard in the 1960s and 1970s learned to recalibrate what it means to read (277–81). Overwhelmed by the amount of reading assigned by their professors and frustrated by their inability to digest it in the ways they thought necessary, the students sought assistance by enrolling in a course designed by William Perry to address this sort of problem. Central to the course design was a series of assignments that redirected students from what they thought of as close and careful reading to first skimming for an answer to a specified question and then, using a different source, gaining a quick overview of the material with the aim of posing their own question. The first task was enacted repeatedly with various texts, with the goal of decreasing the time required in each case to find the needed answer. As they undertook the second task, students were advised not to read sequentially but to scan as efficiently as possible, perhaps even starting with the conclusion of the text. While neither of these activities—skimming to answer a specific question or speedily gaining a sense of content sufficient to generate a meaningful question—was viewed by the students as "reading," such approaches were the ones they needed to deal competently with the copious material assigned across their courses. Some students were even disturbed by what seemed like the dishonesty of such techniques; however, Kegan attributes these feelings to a sense of loss (the deeply embedded sense of what "reading" means, or ought to mean) and to a fear that the self-direction required would put at risk their ability to be in sync with the professor (280).

Overall, the students in this situation who succeeded in dealing with the large amounts of reading in their coursework were enabled to make the transition to a new perspective. What most of them came to learn was that speeding up eye movement alone would not help without a greater sense of confidence in their ability to both answer and ask questions based on their transaction with the text. According to Kegan, this confidence requires not so much discrete skills as a kind of "courage"—to take charge of the task at hand, to "walk away from being subject to someone else's questions" (281). That is, the students in this context learned to think of reading as a self-directed activity, one that gave them the ability to construct meaning rather than try only to receive it as passive vessels. For these students, the assumption that reading is, most centrally, the ability to move one's eyes from left to right through sequential lines of text had to be replaced by an understanding that making meaning of any text depends on a sense of how parts relate to whole.

This skill requires the sort of flexibility entailed in "adaptive expertise," as explained in *How People Learn* (Bransford et al.). It must be deployed nimbly, adapted to the exigencies of text demands and purposes for reading. For literary texts, "distant" reading involves the ability to construct a coherent reading through attention to the interplay of multiple aspects of the text. Indeed, theorists of literary reading, whether New Critics or their successors, have attended with various emphases to the process by which readers combine discrete textual perceptions into a unified whole (Iser, *Implied Reader* 285, and *How* 65; Rosenblatt, *Reader* 90; Rabinowitz and Smith 97–102.) The title of Brooks's seminal text, *The Well Wrought Urn* (1947), suggests this thesis, although in literary contexts the ultimate effect of completeness or integrity is naturally not equivalent to the propositional logic of science and may be best defined as a "coherence of attitude" (246).

Certainly our experience of literature as art will, ideally, engage us in a rich interaction with the text both as we read and, in a different way, when we reread, with the overall movement being toward the harmonious integration of parts. Lecturing to undergraduates in the 1950s, Vladimir Nabokov maintained that "one cannot *read* a book; one can only reread it" because the temporal progression of our eyes across the page, a dynamic that predominates when we first read a text, is complemented—and complicated—upon rereading by a sense of "the whole picture" (571) enabling us to appreciate the way great literature combines "the precision of poetry and the intuition of science" (575). Peter Rabinowitz makes a similar point in his discussion of "reading against memory" (Rabinowitz and Smith 97): The linear aspects of story that take precedence when we read a novel for the first time recede upon subsequent readings, as patterns and relationships evident only when one has a sense of the whole begin to emerge and enrich both our experience and our appreciation of the writer's art. Louise Rosenblatt likewise connects her emphasis on the reader's readiness to engage the deeply felt experience offered by a work of poetry or fiction to the goal of integration: "only a reader in aesthetic transaction with the text can synthesize the parts into a 'whole' or structure which is a work of art . . . [and] build out of his responses to the patterned verbal cues a unifying principle" (*Reader* 90).

But it is not only literary texts that demand active pattern creation. As indicated in the lessons devised by Perry, a cultivated sense of what to notice and the habit of meaningful configuration are also essential to reading expository and argumentative texts. In such documents, even organizational cues such as subheadings may be perceived by novices as surface features signifying the apparent separateness of each section, whereas the inherent connection among the sections is tacitly evident to experts. In fact, experts in general, wherever they begin, move recursively between part and whole, data and concept, concrete and abstract, illustration and concept or general claim or theme. Donald Schön has elucidated how the principles of design in any profession require simultaneously an engagement with both individual elements and a sense of the whole: "Designing is a holistic skill. . . .Therefore, one cannot learn it in a molecular way, by learning first to carry out smaller units of activity and then to string those units together in a whole design process; for the pieces tend to interact with one another and to derive their meanings and characters from the whole process in which they are embedded" (*Educating* 158). Thus a coach, whether of architecture, teaching, or management, encourages a student to "'[w]ork back and forth between unit and total'" (164). The work of Linda Flower and her colleagues in uncovering composition practices suggests a comparable dynamic: Expert writers, they found, "built integrated networks of goals, plans, and criteria as they worked through the task" ("Taking Thought" 193) and alternated between details and abstractions (205). Similarly, in studying the revision strategies of novice versus expert writers, Nancy Sommers found that while the former focus on changing small semantic and lexical units, the latter are moving toward shaping an overall idea and clarifying the through line: "[T]he experienced writers often use structural expressions such as 'finding a framework,' 'a pattern,' or 'a design' for their argument" (384).

Just as the expert essay writers in Sommers's study focused in their revisions on clarifying overall patterns and connections, readers of all kinds of texts must be disposed to notice such patterns. Such a disposition requires what Rosenblatt has called, in the context of literary reading, "selective attention" (*Reader* 42, 163) or, in the framework offered by Bartholomae and Petrosky, "the assigning of significance" (*Facts* 20) to certain textual features, an action that will determine how the reader imposes order on a complex matrix of ideas or themes. In his characterization of reading for research-based writing as a kind of "rhetorical invention," Doug Brent emphasizes the obligation of students to refine and renegotiate a position on an arguable topic by playing the authorial audience with each text and then deciding which aspects of the new ideas encountered will be invited to transform their prior understanding of the issues at hand (105). Such moves require a sophisticated sense of cognitive and rhetorical designs: The reader "must be able to infer the patterns of assumptions that have led other writers to their conclusions" (104).

More recent work on information literacy affirms these principles. Sandra Jamieson aptly observes that the ability to understand how parts are integrated to produce a coherent whole is essential even to sentence-level understanding; syntactical awareness such as a sense of how main and subordinate clauses are related to each other affects basic comprehension. Critical reading as defined by Karen Manarin et al. entails "identifying patterns of textual elements" and "distinguishing between main and subordinate ideas" as a foundation for inference and evaluation (4). These researchers agree that while many students approach texts as static receptacles from which information is to be extracted, what is expected in college-level courses is instead an interaction or conversation with the text that requires an understanding of how the text *as a whole* is organized rhetorically, how its hierarchy of ideas might be represented, and what place it has in a larger conversation or process of inquiry. Central to this "construction" is alertness to sentence syntax and sentence sequencing. Thus the importance of the disposition to relate parts to whole cannot be overstated; the creation of coherence is, in essence, the nature of reading comprehension, regardless of the genre of reading and irrespective of whether it invites, to use Rosenblatt's terms, mostly aesthetic or mostly efferent readings.

Generally, nonliterary texts, such as academic articles or trade books that may be both argumentative and informational and thus demand a mostly efferent stance, require what Alice Horning has called a sense of "where to put the manicules," the drawings in medieval manuscripts of hands with pointing fingers marking important places in the text ("Where"). Horning demonstrates how she helps her students develop expertise in reading "extended informational prose on paper," which she calls "a kind of gold standard in a variety of disciplines, even with variations in genre, purpose and so forth." Such reading is often selective and nonlinear in nature; the identification of what is noticeable will depend on an ability to move rapidly through a text—and to infer when closer attention is necessary—rather than parse each line as one might do when taking an aesthetic stance. Like Perry and Kegan, Horning emphasizes rapid and judicious reading as a condition of both comprehension and persistence: "Novice readers often complain that they do not know how to highlight or mark a text because everything seems important. Meta-readers are . . . flexible: skimming, scanning, reading closely as the need arises based on what they are getting from the text and from their awareness of structure, context/purpose and language" (9). Horning's examples of pedagogy are drawn from her area of expertise, linguistics; however, she maintains that the principles she outlines apply in any discipline.

A Convergence of Research

Horning's claim is persuasive in the sense that, as noted above, expert readers are generally able to toggle back and forth between their understanding of discrete parts of a text and their deepening awareness of how the parts relate to the overall shape of the text as well as to the larger conversation it is joining. Moreover, the work of cognitive psychologists adds an interesting dimension to our understanding of proficient reading. Studies of how students make sense of informational text demonstrate that the interaction may be conditioned by factors we do not normally consider, revealing some surprising results. In 1996, Danielle McNamara et al. found that students with relatively high knowledge of a topic acquired deeper understanding when required to make sense of a text that was *less* coherent—one that required them to fill in apparent gaps in the exposition or argument—than when presented with a text with entirely explicit connections between semantic units. That is, texts that are explicitly coherent and thus do not challenge students to construct meaning are more likely to be processed superficially and therefore do not necessarily advance deep understanding because of the low cognitive demands they impose.

Such studies also affirm the limitations of approaching a text as autonomous. Whether or not *consciousness* of active meaning-making plays a role in comprehension, there is evidence that such activity both enhances and is enhanced by background knowledge and that this reciprocal relationship is key to deep understanding. By "deep," the researchers mean comprehension of how the text fits into broader contexts and thus how it relates to, and may modify, the concepts as already understood by the reader. Distinguishing for purposes of discussion between surface understanding of the literal text (the "text base") and the bigger picture given shape by the reader's existing knowledge (the "situation model"), the researchers emphasize that the two are not separated in the reading process. Low-knowledge learners are thus doubly hindered: they will struggle to make literal sense of texts in which logical connections between sentences and sections are not fully specified, whereas the "active inferencing" available to high-knowledge readers enables deeper learning than would otherwise be stimulated. As a result, college students, no less than those in elementary school, may experience an increasing divergence of skill levels, whereby the "rich" get richer and the progress of the "poor" is halting at best.

Ironically, this inequality would be increased by the assumption that students in need of remediation should be assigned texts with relatively simple logic and syntax (textbook overviews, e.g., rather than discipline-based arguments) that have already done the work of connection-making but on a superficial level. Counterintuitively, "one way to promote deeper understanding—the formation of a 'situation model'—may be to disrupt coherence at both the local, intersentential level and at the level of its global organization, or macrostructure" (McNamara et al. 4), thus requiring active attention to the work of meaning-making.

The role of constructivism in deep understanding has been reinforced by psychologists who study theory of mind, defined as "the capacity to identify and understand others' subjective states" (Kidd and Castano 377). In an intriguing study, cognitive researchers Joan Peskin and Janet Wilde Astington found that children who were read picture books requiring inferences with regard to characters' knowledge and expectations (the control group) improved theory of mind significantly more than students exposed to the same stories enhanced with explicitly metacognitive language (the treatment group). Most impressive was the ability of the control group to explain "false beliefs"; these children demonstrated notable improvement in their "understanding that a story character may be ignorant of a situation that the [reader or listener] knows to be true" (260). While the quality of the picture-book illustrations and their role in conveying states of mind was clearly a factor in the children's ability to understand various viewpoints, the general idea that delivery of information is less effective in literacy education than practice in active meaning-making encouraged by what is *not* expressed in the text is supported by a key conclusion drawn by the researchers: "The more direct, explicit condition may have produced less conceptual development precisely because it was explicit" (266). In related research, educational psychologists who study reading have offered evidence for the complex interplay between cognitive functions that are "memory based" (largely automatic) and those that are "constructivist" (requiring purposeful effort) (van den Broek et al.). Both functions depend on prior knowledge. Moreover, the activation of relevant remembered data is essential to, but not in itself sufficient for, the construction of a coherent reading, for which habits of metatextual and metacontextual connection-making are a sine qua non: "[A] significant component of comprehension is the identification of semantic connections between the various pieces of information in the text, and between this information and readers' background knowledge" (301).

What is especially interesting in light of students' struggles to effectively synthesize multiple texts is research suggesting that intra- and intertextual connection-making are variations of the same skill—i.e., expertise in connecting parts of a single text to one another requires a disposition and habits similar to those required for synthesis of multiple texts. There is evidence that students who fare poorly in integrating different texts to construct a "situation model" or "argument model" also struggle to build coherence within an individual text. According to Ivar Bråten and Helge Strømsø, "It seems possible to regard the reading of multiple texts as a special case of reading low coherence text. In both instances, readers must attempt to link concepts and ideas and build a coherent representation on their own" (464). Moreover, their study revealed correlations between students' assumptions about how understanding is constructed and their ability to meaningfully connect several articles on a given topic. Students who tended to see knowledge as fixed, unchanging, and comprising discrete facts located in authority struggled with textual synthesis more than students who viewed knowledge as subject to change based on rational inquiry methods and comprising interrelated ideas rather than separate bits of information. Bråten and Strømsø conclude that ideas about the nature of knowledge and its construction are as important to deep comprehension as the amount of knowledge brought to a text.

Understanding the interactive demands of informative texts can make a difference to how professors conceive the level of challenge offered by their courses. At the institution where I teach, Pamela Brown, who teaches communication law to students majoring in communication and journalism, shared with me what she called an "epiphany" prompted by her reading of a document that had been published in 2006, *Reading between the Lines: What the ACT Reveals about College Readiness in Reading.* This report, which links readiness for college with ability to understand complex texts, defines six aspects of complexity: relationships among ideas or characters, richness of information, textual structure, qualities of style, challenges presented by diction, and clarity of author's purpose (14–15). Frustrated by poor results on exams and having tried extensive study guides with limited success, Pam had, several years prior, given up the textbook and its many detailed cases in favor of what seemed like friendlier resources such as the trade book *Freedom for the Thought We Hate: A Biography of the First Amendment,* by Anthony Lewis. However, while the book seemed to her quite accessible because of its narrative structure and lively prose style, students struggled with it. For example, the following sequential sentences, from the decision by Oliver Wendell Holmes in *Whitney v. California,* 1927, were puzzling to many: "Fear of serious injury alone cannot justify suppression of free speech and assembly. Men feared witches and burnt women." Looking at the ACT table and its accompanying rubric, Pam realized that the relationships among the ideas and the structure of the language held hidden challenges for novices—there was indeed a "gap" between the sentences, with the logical links taken for granted, the knowledge of historical contexts assumed, and the connection inexplicit. Previously, she had noticed overall that students tend to ignore the import of small but key words in sentences—often logical markers defining contingencies, such as *only*, *not only*, *only if*—thus missing basic meanings. In the first sentence above, the word *alone* was often overlooked by students.

This novice tendency is confirmed by Robert Leamnson, who has noted that for many students, close attention to syntax and semantics, which can demand a deferral of closure, has not been cultivated as a habit of mind: "Sentences with conditional modifiers demand not just alertness, but a certain skill in holding one idea in a kind of mental buffer until those modifiers have done their work on it, at which point it is 'released' and becomes part of a complex concept" (27–28). It appears, then, that a key for meaning-making in all cases, whether the prose be fiction, creative nonfiction, or exposition, is the reader's ability to create connections within sentences, between sentences, and among the larger subdivisions, so as to develop a complete situation model based on an understanding of the text's "macrostructure" (McNamara 4). It is this expert move of recursivity—constructing intratextual coherence by filling gaps, moving between part and whole, and integrating the text at hand with prior knowledge to "place" it within a bigger picture—that challenges students most, as they struggle to make connections not only among texts of various kinds but also among the parts of a single text.

Certainly, college instructors cannot assume that this sort of reading will come naturally to all or even most students, nor that high school classes will have inculcated such a disposition. Yet, as more attention has been paid over the last several decades to how students learn in college, the research on reading practices in higher education has not been encouraging. Barbara Walvoord and Lucille McCarthy's 1990 study of students thinking and writing in four disciplines revealed the prevalence of unsophisticated reading habits, dubbed "text-processing," which deflected students from understanding the rhetoric and import of an individual text as well as its relation to other texts on the topic.

Fast-forward twenty-five years, and we find that such habits have been persistent. Manarin et al., in their 2015 study of students' reading and writing in four general-education classes across several disciplines, found that students rarely integrated even those sources assigned for the course and rather saw texts mainly as repositories of knowledge that could be mined for information (73): "In all four courses, the majority of reading logs did not contain evidence of any attempt to make connections among perspectives, disciplines, or even readings" (54).

These studies complement and extend Chris Anderson's advocacy in the 1980s for teaching students how to build meaning across apparent textual rifts by reading stylistically sophisticated literary nonfiction. Frequently anthologized writers such as Joan Didion, George Orwell, Lewis Thomas, and E. B. White exemplify the purposeful use of syntactic and rhetorical lacunae that intensify the reader's aesthetic experience as well as the efferent meaning derived. Drawing on Wolfgang Iser's theory of literary reading, Anderson demonstrates how students may improve their writing by using such texts as models—but only, he says, in advanced composition classes, after they have been carefully taught how to use strategies for achieving in their own writing the more explicit coherence usually demanded by instructors of first-year composition as a hedge against chaos. However, as I have been suggesting, the difference in the demand posed by texts deemed literary versus those that are mainly argumentative or expository may not always be as dramatic as is commonly assumed. The examples of reading passages given in McNamara et al. as well as the quoted sentences from Lewis Thomas's *Lives of a Cell* (Anderson 16) illustrate that even informative prose (the kind that would be considered "nonliterary" because its purposes are mostly instructive rather than aesthetic) can rely on readers to actively supply meaning across rhetorical gaps and, at its best, often does.

Faculty must do much more to address this challenge. Recent studies suggest that students are not being held accountable for actually reading entire texts and making sense of each as a whole, let alone relating it sensibly to other texts. The disturbing findings reported in the Citation Project are worthy of emphasis in this context. In this nationwide study, researchers found that the purported summary-writing of students tended to be based almost entirely on a few consecutive sentences of a text; more than three-quarters of the citations drew on the first three pages of the sources (regardless of their length), with nearly half of the citations referring to material on the first page of the cited source; and what passed for paraphrase was nearly always "patchwriting"—varying diction somewhat while relying on the source's syntax (Jamieson). Overall, it appears that the vast majority of college students conducting research in introductory courses rely on individual sentences rather than on sources to support their claims. Moreover, in choosing the sentences from the first page or two of a source, they are likely to misrepresent the argument of the text as a whole (Howard et al.; Jamieson and Howard, "Sentence-Mining" and "Unraveling").

The study by Manarin et al. of critical reading by students in foundational courses confirmed the Citation Project findings that students are not reading for understanding and those of Jolliffe and Allison Harl that students are not disposed to make connections even among assigned texts in a single course (612–13). Despite the fact that synthesizing perspectives was an explicit goal of the classes, Manarin and her colleagues found little evidence of progress in this area. While, as Jamieson has observed, many instructors "may not even imagine the possibility that students could produce effective researched papers without deploying advanced reading and writing skills" (2), the evidence indicates not only that work based on inadequate text comprehension is often judged satisfactory but also that when such papers evince the desired surface features, they may earn As. That is, while the integration of sources in the hands of students skillful at patchwork may convey the effect of thoroughness and competence, the reality can be very different. Thus the following scenario is likely to be much more common than we think: "One paper listing thirteen sources, including five scholarly articles, seemed to demonstrate [that] the student was interacting with her sources and developing an argument, until it was discovered that seven of the sources, including all five articles, were misrepresented" (Manarin et al. 62). Without reading the primary sources, instructors may err in assuming that students are reading carefully and engaging the actual arguments. Formally impressive papers are likely to be rewarded, while less graceful ones that reflect the writer's fledgling but authentic attempts to make sense of difficult material receive a lower grade. In effect, inadequate practices are unwittingly encouraged while genuine effort is penalized.

Such findings raise the question of the expectations we set for first-year writing and especially for "the research paper." Even campuses whose entering students are identified as underprepared design second-semester writing courses with the goal of having "students engage with an academic conversation (ideally within each student's field of study) and produce original research in relation to that conversation" (Young and Potter). Such a dramatic mismatch between student profile and expected outcomes is bound to lead to disappointment. Yet, while the drawbacks of requiring first-year students to produce full-blown, "original" research papers have become apparent, the alternatives have not been shaped to accord with research findings. In evaluating the composite skill of "information literacy," now a staple of higher-education learning objectives and assessment rubrics, we may too easily focus on form over content, with surface features rewarded over deep textual engagement. This tendency is natural when expectations are set unrealistically high. Indeed, many professors would be glad to see the stated objectives for original research-based writing approximated by advanced students in courses for majors. Data from the Citation Project suggest that skills typically addressed in first-year composition classes—summary writing, text connection, the development of coherent analytical prose—do not carry over into their research papers and thus cannot be "transferred" to assignments in other classes (Jamieson).

Currently, it seems, the pedagogies are inadequate to the needs, with remedies increasingly urged by worried researchers. Based on their comprehensive study of how students use sources, Jamieson and Rebecca Moore Howard insist on the importance of finding ways to teach the complex skills that must be practiced iteratively and expertly critiqued: "Teaching students how to summarize *and how to integrate that summary into researched writing* are compelling pedagogical mandates" ("Unraveling," emphasis in original). Their conclusions recall Leamnson's advice for realigning our pedagogic priorities: "[A]dvanced upperclassmen certainly need to be skilled in searching out sources. It is, however, a relatively easily acquired talent compared with deciphering and digesting the content when it is discovered" (124). Our failure to help students decipher and digest and to hold them accountable for summarizing accurately increases the likelihood that texts will be misconstrued. Overall, both classroom experience and systematic research affirm the assertion by Jamieson and Howard that the plagiarism often detected in first-year papers is, above all, a reading problem: "instructors should teach students how to read complex sources critically. . . . [P]lagiarism will inevitably occur if students can neither read complex sources critically nor conduct authentic researched inquiry. And our research reveals that they do not" ("Unraveling"). Chris Anson's humane and incisive analysis of the typically self-defeating approaches to plagiarism in the university helps us understand the importance of assignment design in fostering authentic learning, i.e., constructing tasks effectively to serve as teaching tools for students, not just assessments for instructors ("We Never Wanted to Be Cops" 148–49). In subsequent chapters I will address the details of assignment design. What follows here are contexts for that examination: variations in problem construction and analysis as reflected in expert reading and writing across the disciplines.

Disciplinary Epistemologies and "Transfer"

Ways of reading inevitably reflect ways of writing, which in turn reflect disciplinary epistemologies and the value accorded to various types of inquiry. Qualitative studies of rhetorical variations among disciplines reveal why. For example, the application by Jeanne Fahnestock and Marie Secor of classical rhetorical categories (stases and topoi) to the shaping of arguments in academic writing illustrates how the tacit principles underlying argumentation in science differ from those that inform literary criticism. A key point emerging from this study is that academic writing, even when it appears only to be building knowledge, establishes a rhetorical relationship with the reader and thus "can be seen as having implications of value and action . . ." (441). Such implications, however, are not likely to be understood by novices. The metacognition required to understand how different disciplines define appropriate questions and the nimbleness needed to "code-switch" among the relevant rhetorical conventions was elucidated in the 1980s by Susan Peck MacDonald, who meticulously charted the differences in problem-definition as typified by representative articles selected from *Child Development* (psychology) and *Publications of the Modern Language Association* (literature). She concluded that common types of assignments given in first-year writing classes at the time either limited students' understanding of problem-definition to the sort practiced by literary critics or offered few to no parameters for shaping a problem or a "vantage point" at all. In her subsequent studies of academic discourse, MacDonald identified four continua that proved useful as a way to distinguish thinking and writing in various disciplines: compactness and diffuseness, explanation and interpretation, concept-focus and text-focus, and degree of explicit epistemic self-consciousness (*Professional Academic Writing* 21–22).

Exposing qualities of academic writing not usually examined, MacDonald analyzed and compared stylistic choices (e.g., sentence structure and grammatical features) and related these to epistemological assumptions and to rhetorical elements that signify the author's putative relationship with both the intended audience and prior critics or researchers. Through this comparative study, she illustrated the qualities that define professional writing in the social sciences and humanities and showed how they reveal the emergence of subdisciplines or paradigm shifts within a discipline. The generic division between a historiographic essay and a piece of literary criticism, for example, is inevitably complicated by divergent approaches within each genre. It is worth taking a moment to consider how these implicit qualities of text (and disciplinary thinking), which are usually transparent to experts, make huge demands on the limited versatility and more rigid habits of novices. Thus while the question of whether skills in reading and writing are transferable across contexts and disciplines remains persistent, a deeper question is just what it is we are expecting students to transfer.

Building on Charles Bazerman's 1985 exploration of how physicists read in their field, studies have revealed that while all experts read metacognitively, there are important discipline-based differences in their reading habits. In the example of Perry's reading class described earlier, students were guided in starting from the end of some texts in search of the gist, rather than undertaking the linear, beginning-to-end, method they had assumed as a requirement of comprehension—a method often taught in English classes, where the experience of literature is primary or the unfolding rhetoric of an argument or exposition is subjected to close scrutiny. Scientists typically begin with selected pieces of a journal article, with differences found even within disciplines, e.g., between experimentalists and theorists in physics. In their study of reading by experts in three disciplines, Cynthia Shanahan and her colleagues found that chemists and mathematicians focus more on unpacking the internal logic of an argument or proof than on matters related to sourcing, which are critical to historians. Because historiography invites a wide range of narrative styles, experts automatically read to construct the rhetoric of the piece, in one case noting, e.g., that important points are typically found at the ends of paragraphs (Shanahan et al. 415). Mathematicians were found to be the "closest" of readers in a sense, intensely studying every aspect of an argument and even noting the ambiguities suggested by a wrong choice of preposition (420).

Also varying considerably among different kinds of experts was the perceived relationship between verbal and nonverbal information, with the mathematicians seeing equations and verbal texts as continuous, the chemists seeing graphic and textual elements as equally critical but separable and complementary, and the historians seeing graphical elements as subordinate to text (419). These findings illuminate how knowledge, rhetoric, and values are inextricably bound up with one another and how their holistic pursuit constitutes the work of the academy. As Fahnestock and Secor had observed, academic papers do not reside in a cloud of objectivity or ideological isolation: "[A]ll arguments involve a prior value argument that establishes the significance of addressing an argument in a particular stasis [rhetorical stance or mode of argument] to a particular audience." When questions of value are not explicitly addressed in an academic text, it is because the audience is presumed to understand the significance of the project at hand and its place in an ongoing debate or investigation (434).

The assumption of an ongoing debate or inquiry does not, however, automatically inform the reading of students, who are used to viewing assigned texts strictly as sources of information. In addressing students' resistance to the problem-centric nature of inquiry, knowledge-building, and meaning-making, Gerald Graff points to the inherently dialogic and sometimes adversarial nature of academic discourse: "To argue persuasively, you have to have an axe to grind; to want others to do something they are not already doing, if only to think differently than they do about something" (55–56). The idea that every academic article is addressing a problem and is therefore in some sense an argument seems strange and alienating to many undergraduates. Moreover, as MacDonald has suggested, in some fields the axe is double-edged, with the rhetoric serving oneself as much as the advancement of the field: disciplines such as history and English, which tend to be more diffuse and interpretive, with less convergence on problem-definition, may privilege originality over consensus building (197). Students who are not alert to such epistemic factors are bound to read naïvely and ineffectively, per Horning's distinction between the skimming habits of novices and those of experts: while novices may skate rather aimlessly along the surface of a text, more skillful readers bring the knowledge and contexts needed to skim selectively and efficiently and are automatically engaged in the recursive toggling that enables sense-making and analysis ("Where to Put the Manicules" 9).

First-year composition is not typically designed to give students an understanding of these differences, and instructors of such courses, often trained in literature and frequently focused on "basic" skills, are not usually inclined to focus on the varying demands of reading and writing across the curriculum. Jolliffe's comparison of the sophisticated implicit demands of many reading and writing assignments in the academy with the simplistic approach to reading improvement commonly offered in developmental courses highlights the mixed messages we give to students. The kinds of assignments most often given in first-year composition—read to find a prompt for discussing your attitude toward a general topic, read to imitate the rhetorical organization of a given text, read to find support or nonsupport for your opinion—constitute a "great, gray [curricular] middle" that is theoretically ungrounded and not particularly helpful to students ("Learning to Read as Continuing Education" 477). Assigned topics often assume either too much rhetorical knowledge and contextual understanding or too little (MacDonald, "Problem Definition"; Wilner, "Fostering Critical Literacy," "Asking for It"). Elizabeth Wardle has observed that writing assignments in first-year composition often call for the composition of "mutt genres," papers not identifiable with any authentic disciplinary genre and thus disconnected from any authentic sense of purpose. And indeed it is not surprising that skills such as "observation" or "persuasion" do not prove to be transferable.

Wardle's emphasis on the constraints and opportunities implied in genre development and use is crucial for thinking about the failure of transfer and thus the disappointing long-term effects of much instruction in first-year composition: "Genres arise when particular exigencies are encountered repeatedly; yet each time an exigence arises, people must be attuned to the specifics of the current situation in order to employ the institutionalized features of the genre effectively—or, in some cases, throw them out" (768). The subtleties of adapting to such conventions suggest why it is so difficult even for highly educated practitioners, let alone naïve students, to write competently in genres outside their own fields. In sum, what Gregory Colomb has said about writing in the following passage could apply equally to reading: "[W]hen we ask students to write in an alien discipline, we put them in a situation where they are unlikely to know what will count as a successful performance. And when we ask them to write in no discipline at all (as traditional composition is wont to do), we put them in an even worse situation, where even we have a hard time knowing what counts as success" (22–23).

Implications for First-Year Writing Instruction

While differing somewhat on the role of explicit teaching of generic conventions in fostering effective production by students of *writing* in a particular genre—especially in composition classes as opposed to discipline-grounded classes or workplace contexts—scholars have concurred on the value of having students attend to the aspects of texts that indicate intentionality, disciplinary epistemologies, and the overall interdependence of form, content, and purpose. Aviva Freedman, responding to an emphasis in English classes at the time to focus on reading fiction and on "personal and narrative writing," urged teachers to "stage-manage exposure to a wide variety of genres" (238) while resisting the temptation to reduce to "rules" the complexity and range of rhetorical features therein. Joseph Williams and Colomb observed the reciprocity of text and context that may be beneficial to novice students—"When we learn social context, we are also learning its forms; but when we learn forms, we may also be learning their social contexts" (262). Amy Devitt has argued for teaching genre *awareness,* so that students can "discern both constraints and choices that genres make possible" (198). Irene Clark and Andrea Hernandez, while cautioning that genres taught out of context can easily be oversimplified to emphasize form over rhetoric, nonetheless define genre as a "threshold concept" that students must master in order to read and write successfully across the curriculum (66). Ellen Carillo has argued that the potentially transferable habit worthy of our attention is not a particular strategy or skill but rather the tendency to recognize and adapt to conventions shaped by discipline, genre, and purpose and to the rhetorical demands of the moment ("Creating").

The value of teaching genre awareness in both reading and writing is also emphasized in John Bean's excellent handbook for college teachers, *Engaging Ideas,* which makes interesting connections between brain research and assignments that help students notice salient rhetorical differences among various genres of writing (59–65). And the need for attention to genre awareness as an aspect of reading comprehension has recently been highlighted by the finding of Manarin et al. that students, in writing synthesis papers, rarely notice the different demands of different sorts of texts and often do not consider genre as a category that might affect their reading. When genre is noticed, students tend to mislabel texts—e.g., they consider popular sources to be scholarly or subsume widely different kinds of texts such as speeches and memoirs under "articles" (51–53). Taken together, these studies should cause us to rethink our understanding of how students use sources and how to address their novice behaviors in deploying the words and ideas of others.

The systematically collected evidence we now have of the difference between our intentions and the learning outcomes they produce has prompted many in the field to advocate a major reboot of assignment design in composition, especially with regard to research-based writing. Moving away from the notion that first-year students should produce authentic research-based writing has proven to be difficult, however. As noted above, many assignment prompts continue to focus far more on formal correctness (the criteria for which often vary from class to class) than on in-depth engagement with content (Manarin et al. 64). While attention to this problem and suggested remedies have not been lacking (see, e.g., Fister; J. Nelson; Dirk), the assumption that first-year students should produce, with limited consideration of their reading skills, a thoughtful and original research-based synthesis and argument remains ingrained in practice. Surely, a reconsideration of this practice is in order. Jamieson and Howard concluded an analysis of findings from the Citation Project with a clear recommendation that, in light of the evidence, seems incontrovertible: teachers should "replace the end-of-semester researched paper with shorter papers that are source-based, but that use fewer sources and require students to engage with their arguments and build them into a conversation" ("Sentence Mining" 130).

Designing assignments that yield evidence of such engagement is a move that challenges conventional pedagogies. We know from studies of the different modes of reading enacted by experts in different fields that the role of discourse conventions as shaped by varying epistemologies is powerful enough to require explicit attention by instructors who hope to improve students' reading in their classes. Even the common practice of assigning annotated bibliographies in preparation for research-based arguments may offer a false impression of students' understanding if instructors are not familiar with the sources selected by students. In reviewing the results of one such assignment in a composition class, I found substantial evidence that what is taken for granted in designing such tasks—students' ability to recognize and digest material useful for their topics or questions—cannot be. The task of meaningful synthesis in such contexts is therefore unrealistic. As with the papers assessed by Manarin and her colleagues before and after examination of the source material cited, students' work was rewarded for possessing the outward signs of competency while actually reflecting inadequate reading and weak comprehension.

For example, a student writing about a short story chose a source that seemed helpful on the surface but was not: the author's intention was not to illuminate the story per se but rather to use it as a parable for some aspects of campus politics. Unprepared to infer the author's intended audience and purpose, the student was naturally led astray. Another student confused a critic's observation of a character's limited point of view (revealed through dramatic irony created by the fiction writer) with the critic's own perspective and was thereby led to an unsustainable interpretation of the story. Both sorts of misreading—failure to understand the intended audience and purpose of an argument and a misunderstanding of voice—are, of course, common among novices. But because we take reading comprehension too much for granted, such pitfalls are often glossed over in our evaluation of students' "research-based" work. Students' bibliographic annotations also reflect naïve notions about the genre of literary criticism or of scholarly studies in general. For example, I have seen claims by students that in offering a judgment of literary value, the author demonstrates "bias" and that a source is "reliable" if it uses evidence and quotations from the text under consideration.

Certainly the disproportionate attention often given to formal conventions over depth of content needs to be reconsidered. Wayne Booth, in his 1963 speech to a group of college English instructors, suggested as one remedy the assignment of great novels—he used excerpts from Jane Austen (*Pride and Prejudice*) and Saul Bellow (*The Adventures of Augie March*) as examples—to cultivate an ear for language and powers of observation that penetrate "beneath the surface of society's platitudes." Nonetheless, he acknowledged that studying such literary masters would not in itself turn students into good writers both because "it is not easy to impart ideas" and because "even the best-read student still needs endless hours and years of practice, with rigorous criticism." Booth considered and critiqued the then incipient and now well-entrenched emphasis on using popular media as the subject of composition classes, admitting the usefulness of such material as an adjunct to traditional texts but insisting on the unique and essential education in both ideas and attitudes afforded by "a steady exposure" to "the great narrative voices, ancient and modern" ("Boring" 256–57). Because of the increasing urgency today of exploiting the potential of first-year composition classes to introduce students to reading and writing across the disciplines, we might want to add to Booth's curriculum a sampling of great expository, reportorial, theoretical, and argumentative genres. But Booth's overall point remains compelling. Unfortunately, the persistent myth in composition pedagogy that we learn in a linear and incremental way remains hardy even in the face of all of the counterevidence. Like many "commonsense" ideas, it does not hold up in either theory or practice yet it is so persuasive in its apparent logic that it remains a strong obstacle to the needed culture shift. If effective writing depends on effective reading, and if expertise in "distant," "meta," and "recursive" reading is necessary for academic accomplishment, then we must design assignments and offer feedback that enable students to develop in this area.

Among prominent composition theorists we have begun to see some important moves in this direction. For example, Anson has lucidly explained the theory and practice of crafting engaging, low-stakes writing-to-read assignments ("Writing"). Carillo (*Securing* and "Creating") offers models of assignments that give first-year students practice in both close reading (passage-based papers) and cultivating a repertoire of reading strategies (reflective reading journals). Her recommended sequence of assignments for fostering source-based reading and writing in classes across the curriculum ("Engaging Sources") offers excellent advice and useful models for faculty who are motivated to rethink their assumptions about and strategies for supporting students' development in the disciplines. To these recommendations I would add a focus on the centrality of background knowledge to meta-reading, as discussed above. The content of a course—even a skills-based course—does matter. Therefore, the recovery of voices from the 1980s and 1990s that emphasized "*how* texts mean rather than *what* they mean" (Carillo, *Securing* 91) risks maintaining, especially for first-year students, a distinction that overlooks the value of building a knowledge base of significant classic and current ideas. Cognitive studies have suggested that a focus on process and self-awareness is not sufficient: "metacognitive strategies can only take you so far [because] [a]lthough they suggest what you ought to do, they don't provide the knowledge necessary to implement the strategy" (Willingham, "Critical" 13). Thus, reading about reading (Carillo, *Securing* 132–35) is likely to have the same effect on one's practice as reading about how to hit a home run, surf, or ride a bicycle. And there is an opportunity cost. Time spent on reading about reading is time taken from engaging with important ideas and questions—the sorts that are often explored in first-year honors seminars but not in mainstream or developmental classes—and, concomitantly, time taken from acquiring essential information.

Influential research on reading by Keith Stanovich suggests the consequences of subordinating *what* to *how:* those with greater knowledge (acquired by greater exposure to content-rich print media) are able "to acquire even greater expertise at a faster rate." Not surprisingly, these more highly skilled readers, because they read more, also have better vocabularies (37). Developing a general familiarity with enduring issues and questions can provide essential contexts for understanding the present. The costs of educational methods that overlook the importance of content knowledge are documented by education journalist Natalie Wexler, who has reported on studies that demonstrate how well-intentioned elementary-school pedagogies unfortunately deepen the Matthew effect. The evidence suggests that subordinating content to skills has not produced the desired outcomes, leading her to ask:

> What if the medicine we have been prescribing is only making matters worse, particularly for poor children? What if the best way to boost reading comprehension is not to drill kids on discrete skills but to teach them, as early as possible, the very things we've marginalized—including history, science, and other content that could build the knowledge and vocabulary they need to understand both written texts and the world around them? (23)

The drill-and-skill method, Sonya Armstrong and Mary Newman have observed, unfortunately persists in postsecondary courses designed to improve reading, with the effect of reinforcing misguided ideas about comprehension and learning (7–8). In their advocacy for using "intertextuality" (an assembly of core and supplementary texts of various genres that develop background knowledge around an issue) as a strategy for preparing developmental students for college-level work, the authors offer models of content and methods that have proven effective in a community college and in an alternative-admissions program at a public university. On the college level, content and skills coalesce in an additional way: most of the readings selected for significant content are likely to embody sophisticated stylistic choices that engage students in constructing meaning across the rhetorical gaps characteristic of writing that is artful and compelling.

While E. D. Hirsch's advocacy of a focus on specific knowledge as the sine qua non of the educated individual has long provoked a strong backlash, including accusations of authoritarianism and elitism, his insistence on "the paradox that you can successfully look something up only if you already know quite a lot about the subject" (2) deserves our attention. Deploring the tendency in education to disdain "mere facts," Hirsch observed at the start of this century that knowledge is what enables us to read with understanding and to learn: "Facts, like words, are rarely inert or isolated. A child's (or adult's) mind is in a constant flurry of subterranean integration and hypothesis-making. And a person's success rate in making sense of words and facts increases with a person's knowledge" (3). Such a claim (which coincides with the findings of researchers such as Stanovich, McNamara et al., and Walter Kintsch, as noted earlier) is not inherently exclusionary, nor must it privilege the status quo. In 2015, Eric Liu, co-founder and CEO of Citizen University, defended Hirsch's focus on cultural literacy, countering claims that Hirsch was reactionary and elitist and arguing instead that a widespread familiarity with "past forms, schema, concepts, figures, and symbols" is in fact needed to promote a progressive agenda. To illustrate, Liu cited Hirsch's example of the Black Panthers' use, in 1972, of ideas and language from the Bible and the Declaration of Independence as well as their mastery of academic diction and rhetoric (Liu, "What Every

American Should Know"). Liu was not, of course, valorizing the traditions of prejudice and structural discrimination that persist in American society. But he insisted that "we need a list." He noted that Hirsch's lists need to be updated, broadened, and deepened via the democratic process of crowdsourcing to winnow out no-longer-resonant idioms and to encompass the rich, complex, multicultural history that is the story of our country. This is a process of web-weaving rather than a substitution of one body of knowledge for the other. Liu's argument in defense of the oft-demonized Hirsch is a plea for common (though multifaceted and evolving) ground and reminds us that ignorance of the past and of its connection to the present is the opposite of empowering. Viewed in that light, the assumption that we should expose only our most highly skilled students to the texts, theories, ideologies, and conventions that have influenced our current social and political forms is inherently discriminatory and antiprogressive.

In this context I would like to consider briefly the ongoing conversation around reading on paper versus reading on a screen. So far, the research indicates that screen reading does not typically enhance comprehension and is more likely to inhibit it. The results of salient studies, summarized by experts in literacy and in higher-education pedagogy, suggest that both highly skilled and novice readers find it difficult to bookmark and annotate texts on a screen (Horning, *Reading, Writing* 174; Yancey et al. 53–54;); that screens are not conducive to the "immersive reading" that scholarly inquiry requires (Horning, *Reading, Writing* 175); that online reading tends to be more superficial and produces poorer comprehension than reading print on paper (Harris, 231–33); that the material qualities of paper texts may themselves aid understanding in ways not yet fully understood—due, for example, to spatial cues (Willingham, *Reading Mind* 163) and to the "kinesthetic" qualities of interacting with print on paper (Yancey et al. 54); and that "for the purposes of critical literacy in general, experts routinely and consistently go to paper" (Horning, *Reading, Writing* 176). These findings, I think, feel compelling not only because of the research that underlies them but also because they reflect our own experiences as habitual readers.

Reading on the web adds the additional challenge of constant distraction by the relentless invitation to leave one site and look at another. On the one hand, of course, hypertext offers prodigious opportunities to increase knowledge and to deploy skills unique to the information age. Summing up what I believe to be a large consensus regarding the wide range of literacies that students must practice, Horning observes that digital literacy entails skills traditionally associated with reading—"the abilities to analyze, synthesize, evaluate, and apply"—and additionally demands facility with spatial affordances such as bricolage (pulling together information from various sites to create new and original documents or artifacts) and juxtaposition (the arrangement of elements—often multimodal—on a webpage) (*Reading, Writing* 181). The visual aspects of such dynamics are evident, which is why visual literacy, including practice in multimodal composing, has become a staple of many FYC programs. On the other hand, one is left to wonder whether the promotion of competence in visual analysis comes at the price of auditory competence and what such a tradeoff means for reading. Reading, especially as one progresses past decoding, is far less a visual activity than an auditory one. Though hardly mentioned in discussions of textual analysis among experts in composition and rhetoric, the hearing-reading connection is well-known. Reading to babies and toddlers is universally recommended as a way to cultivate prereading skills. Research in K–12 settings has affirmed the strong connection between listening and reading, with evidence suggesting that as students mature, word recognition accounts much less for differences in reading comprehension than does listening comprehension and that "listening comprehension becomes the dominating influence on reading comprehension starting even in the elementary grades" (Hogan et al.) In one large longitudinal study cited by Tiffany Hogan and her colleagues in their review of the relevant research, "by eighth grade *all* of the reliable variance in reading comprehension could be explained by the listening comprehension factor" (200).

There can be no doubt that good readers can "hear" the flow of language and ideas as they proceed through a text and that good writers play their own audience by hearing the development of their ideas on the page. Understanding and appreciating a linguistic composition, much as one would a musical composition, generally depends on focus over time. The disruption of such focus, whether because of the constant state of distractedness inherent in the web experience or because, as Daniel Willingham argues, digital technologies foster "impatience with boredom" and an expectation of constant entertainment with little effort (*Reading Mind* 173), inhibits engagement in a sustained internal auditory experience that depends on language. Meanwhile, as multimodalism has become dominant, the art of classroom recitation, an exercise in the performance of sentence rhythms and a standard practice in classrooms throughout much of the twentieth century, has virtually disappeared.

While the emphasis on cultivating an ear for language through exposure to clear, polished, and engaging prose (as Booth recommended) may seem quaint in the digital age, its importance should not be understated; such an ear is a condition not only of effective reading and writing in the classroom but also, as Lanham has observed, of effective discourse in general, lending itself to "the ordinary uses of ordinary life" (186). And, as Liu's article on the persistent claims of cultural literacy makes clear, extraordinary uses are also enabled. The iconic rhythms of the King James Bible and the Declaration of Independence as deployed in the platform statement of the Black Panthers showed that "radicalism is made more powerful when garbed in traditionalism." The success of our students in mastering multiple literacies depends on their mastery of the old as well as the new. Given the inadequate outcomes of our customary approach to source-based writing, it may make sense, in considering best designs for first-year writing courses, to expect less from our students in some ways and, in other ways, more. The next chapter explores ways to address this challenge.

Chapter Four

Theory to Practice: Reading in First-Year Writing Classes

The Personal and the Political

Many years ago, as I was teaching a class of students placed into a developmental composition class that comprised students for whom English was a second language and also native English speakers, I noticed that the challenges for each group were quite different. While the former struggled somewhat with diction, idiom, and some contextual aspects of American culture, they nonetheless seemed to understand the assigned essays better than the latter group. They more often answered my questions correctly and were likely to write coherent essays responding to ideas in the reading. When I considered this difference, it occurred to me that the second-language students had been placed in a developmental class solely because English was not their first language and that the placement was misguided. In fact, they were competent in reading and writing in their native languages, whereas those for whom English was a first language had trouble with the sorts of recursivity noted earlier—detecting the overall organization of an essay, noticing how parts related to one another and to the whole, inferring a main idea when it wasn't explicitly stated. Class discussion and initial written responses had led me to this realization, but I had had no training in how to address it. That was probably the moment when I understood that I could not teach writing in any meaningful way without also teaching rhetorical reading.

Meanwhile, I had volunteered several years earlier to participate in a faculty-development project aimed at helping instructors of developmental writing classes teach their students some of the same texts included in the first-year honors seminars. The idea behind the project, funded by a state grant, was to address a system that seemed oblivious to the disparate effects it was unintentionally supporting in the design of remedial curricula, whereby those who have a solid base of skills and knowledge acquire further skills and knowledge more rapidly than those with a weak base, thus increasing the very gap that it is our mission to close. I was therefore prepared (and nervously eager) to teach to my "remedial" class such texts as Plato's allegory of the cave, the Declaration of Independence, the excerpt from Niccolò Machiavelli's *The Prince* on princely virtues and vices, and Martin Luther King Jr.'s "Letter from Birmingham Jail." All of these are part of the intellectual capital of liberally educated citizens, and the two that do not require translation from their original languages provide excellent opportunities for showing what happens when forms and intentions are perfectly married through linguistic and rhetorical genius.

However, as an English professor, I wanted to expose my students to a wide range of genres and stylistically excellent writing, and I had a sense that narrative would offer a friendly invitation into texts perhaps less daunting but equally rich in meaning and beautiful in craft. I therefore also included a sample of frequently anthologized personal essays selected for their depth and eloquence, the resonance of their descriptive details, their evocative imagery and syntactic variations, their ordering of narrative elements punctuated by provocative reflections. As I imagined it, we would savor together the nuances of E. B. White's "Once More to the Lake" (1941), Loren Eiseley's "The Brown Wasps" (1971), George Orwell's "Shooting an Elephant" (1936), and William Golding's "Thinking as a Hobby" (1961). The faculty-development project had not focused on such texts, and, mostly because of their narrative emphasis, I assumed they would be less challenging to teach than the "great ideas" texts.

This assumption, as it turned out, was flawed: I had not anticipated the level of demand that such texts make on young readers. I had not sufficiently accounted for their compositional complexity—their reliance on implication, metonymy and synecdoche, situational irony and the plural yet inseparable vantage points of the younger and older narrative personas—i.e., features that might be called "literary." Perhaps because of my experience with literature, such features seemed only natural to me. Since there is a common notion that personal essays or narratives are easier to teach or more accessible than theoretically grounded arguments, I would like to offer here some additional thoughts on why this distinction can be misleading. The elements I have called literary in memoirs often invoke a kind of nostalgia not easily accessible to the young, requiring the sort of imagination enabled by the habit of distant (or meta) reading. Each of the essays I had selected for study is a contemplative narrative, a philosophical trick of perspective cast by an older man on a younger, more innocent version of himself. Among the four essays, the meditations of Eiseley and White are more easily generalizable, capturing, as they do, the bittersweet insights of age, knowledge of what is gained and lost over time. The developing selves of Orwell and Golding, inflected by the seismic moral dilemmas imposed by empire and by war, crystallize moments that inspire the courage to be countercultural while taking the measure of the notable costs incurred. All demand not only close reading but also the sort of emotional engagement enabled by meditation over time—indeed a stretch for students in their late adolescence or early adulthood—as well as a feel for the truth of paradox.

What to make, for example, of the contrast in White's essay between "the deathless joke" observed by the narrator and the "chill of death" with which he leaves us? What does it mean to take "a firm grasp on airy nothing," as Eiseley does when he visits the site of his childhood home after sixty years—to be, along with wasps, pigeons, and field mice, powerfully bound to a place that has disappeared? What challenges and ironies reside in considering, as Golding does, the habit of critical thinking as a hobby? How can the position of the white man in the Raj be, as Orwell perceives, both outrageously cruel and outlandishly ridiculous—both powerful and, strangely, impotent? While the logic of the arguments by Plato, Machiavelli, Jefferson, and King could be teased apart and put back together, the essential aestheticism of the personal essays, along with the possibility of reducing them to mere "stories," hobbled my students' attempts to connect plot elements—or emotional resonance, if they felt that—to larger meanings.

Since the experience of that long-ago semester, I have worked hard to devise assignments that would give students practice in rhetorical reading—of individual texts and of paired or grouped texts from which commonalities might be inferred and synthesized in the service of a larger idea or insight. Like David Jolliffe and Allison Harl, I have found that students find it easier to connect text with world than text with text. Understandably so: abstracting and synthesizing ideas from multiple texts is generally more challenging than relating a text to one's own experience of the world. Presumably, this is why, of the following four topics offered to my students in a developmental composition course, the second has always proved to be the most appealing:

> Topic 1: Imagine you are Sonny or his brother, the narrator of James Baldwin's "Sonny's Blues," and that you have just read Jean-Paul Sartre's "Existentialism." Write a response to Sartre, explaining why his philosophy does or does not have relevance to your life, or which aspects seem sound to you and which unsound or inadequate. Use the details and development of your "own" life and the lives of those around you in Harlem in the years following World War II (as portrayed in the story) to provide a critique (positive or negative) of existentialism as explained by Sartre.
>
> Topic 2: In his 1963 "Letter from Birmingham Jail," Martin Luther King Jr. spoke of a faith that "we will be able to transform the jangling discords of our nation into a beautiful symphony of brotherhood." Imagine that you can communicate with King today, and write him a letter informing him of the ways you believe his dream has and has not been realized. You may use your knowledge of history and current events as well as your personal experience to support your opinion. In your response, incorporate ideas or thoughts prompted by *one* other reading we have discussed this semester. (For example, can you think of ways to bring in an idea from Plato's "Allegory of the Cave," from Sartre's "Existentialism," from the Declaration of Independence, or from Pinker, "The Moral Instinct"?) Remember to cite textual evidence from King's "Letter" and from your other selected text to support your claims.
>
> Topic 3: Write an essay in which you show how either or both of the brothers in "Sonny's Blues" develop in ways that are related to the experience of education and enlightenment as described in Plato's "Allegory of the Cave." Do your best to provide enough details from each text to prove your points to the reader while not allowing pure plot summary to dominate your paper and obscure your argument. Shape your paper around your thesis. That is,

organize your paragraphs to emphasize how the arc(s) of development portrayed in Baldwin's story demonstrate ideas from Plato's portrayal of the challenges, purposes, and rewards of moving from ignorance to understanding.

Topic 4: Imagine you are Sonny or his brother (the narrator of Baldwin's "Sonny's Blues") and that you have just read Sartre's "Existentialism." Sartre claims that "man is nothing else but what he makes of himself." He also claims that "in creating the man that we want to be, there is not a single one of our acts which does not at the same time create an image of man as we think he ought to be." Explain what Sartre means by these statements. Using one or more of Sartre's key concepts—"anguish," "forlornness," and "despair"—show how "you" (in the persona of Sonny or his brother) have developed, through your actions and decisions over time, a version of yourself that others might want to emulate. In what ways have your maturation and lessons from experience helped you "create an image of [humanity] as [you] think [it] ought to be"?

While all four topics require consideration of more than one text, Topic 2 seems friendlier to novice writers not only because it invites the immediacy of personal experience but also because it allows for a more linear method of organization (i.e., via a list of positive and negative developments in racial-justice policy and practice since King's death). Moreover, the requirement to "bring in an idea" from another assigned reading is often perceived as being satisfied by a perfunctory parallel, generally left to speak for itself. An advantage to such an assignment is that it engages prior understanding or at least perceptions, and offers to less-advanced students the opportunity for relative success in supporting an argument with some coherence.

However, students who choose this topic are shortchanged with regard to practice in textual synthesis. In comparison, students who choose Topic 1 or Topic 3 will be challenged to engage in "distant" reading and in "meta" reading even as they closely identify with individuals somewhat, or very, unlike themselves. Topic 1 entails inhabiting the identity of another as imagined from engagement with a rather complex first-person narrative and thereby inferring another person's responses to the real-life implications of a system of philosophy. It also specifies as the primary audience an individual whose ideas have prompted the response. Topic 3, while it does not as overtly demand direct impersonation or entail one-on-one exchange, does require the application of abstract ideas—in this case a developmental process—to particular experience. Practicing analogic thinking is a standard academic move, one that helps students see how one text can illuminate another. Students who choose Topic 4 often succeed in empathizing well with the selected character from Baldwin's story but tend to stumble in their use of the designated existential terms, somewhat familiar words that they must redefine in strange and unfamiliar ways per Sartre's explanations and illustrations; only rarely, for example, do students digest Sartre's reconfiguration of "despair" from hopelessness to pragmatic realism that can be a source of personal empowerment. But such difficulties remind us that background knowledge can inhibit as well as illuminate, and that the process by which emerging critical readers accommodate their understanding to include new ideas rather than assimilate the alien to more comfortable categories requires practice in ever-varying contexts.

To remedy the deficiencies of Topic 2, I devised a subsequent iteration, in a year when the shared first-year reading was Bryan Stevenson's *Just Mercy* (2014), a documentary narrative by a public-interest attorney of how biases based on race, class, and gender unconscionably distort the American criminal justice system:

> In his 1963 "Letter from Birmingham Jail," Martin Luther King Jr. spoke of a faith that "we will be able to transform the jangling discords of our nation into a beautiful symphony of brotherhood." Imagine that you are Bryan Stevenson and can communicate with King today. Write him a letter, from your perspective as a black man in contemporary society and a civil rights attorney, informing him of the ways you believe his dream has and has not been realized. Remember to cite textual evidence from King's "Letter" and from your "own" book to support your claims.

While the first drafts of compositions written in response to such prompts are often far from clear and polished, they show signs of grappling with the desired higher-order thinking and reading skills. Such assignments cannot be fulfilled through mere data mining in support of an opinion, and they avoid the pitfalls of the springboard approach (Jolliffe, "Learning to Read as Continuing Education" 477). That is, they foster deep engagement with the perspectives of others and, in some cases, encourage rhetorical imitation through the posited roles.

It might be argued that assigning readings on topics far from the experience of young students handicaps them unnecessarily. Richard Haswell et al., for example, in their replication of a 1988 study by Christina Haas and Linda Flower, found that students assigned a text on a topic to which they could relate with relative ease (in this case, a complaint by a student unhappy with the education provided by her all-girl high school) tended to invoke strategies for reading rhetorically (i.e., with a conscious sense of genre, audience, and purpose) more often than when given a more highly specialized text: "When the topic is familiar to the reader, rhetorical background—history, writer motive, reader response—and personal experience emerge from the same matrix" (18). The authors recommend, therefore, "using familiar topics as a first step" toward helping students write on unfamiliar topics. However, I am skeptical of this claim for two reasons. First, I would argue that too much familiarity breeds what Gerald Graff and Cathy Birkenstein have called "the closest cliché syndrome," the tendency of novice readers to convert a nuanced point into a (generally simpler) version of a commonly held idea (ch. 2). Second, there is little evidence to support the assumption that the strategies invoked by students engaged in reading on familiar topics will transfer when, as is inevitable, they are confronted with texts on subjects to which they cannot easily relate. It is the rhetorical demands of the text itself that students must become adept at noticing. This is a lesson I learned many years ago when, in an attempt to engage a developmental composition class in a topic that would not seem too alien, I assigned David Guterson's "Enclosed. Encyclopedic. Endured: The Mall of America."

This essay, published in *Harper's Magazine* in 1993, takes a gloomy sociological look at a nearly ubiquitous American experience, advancing the thesis that our modern culture has deprived us of the traditional benefits of the communal marketplace while offering us the sad illusion of salvation via material goods. I had asked students to write a two-page paper "explaining why you agree or disagree with some aspect of Guterson's argument." But I soon regretted that plan. While students could all relate to the mall experience, Guterson's essay was too long and, like the personal essays I had previously taught, too demanding in its structure, language, and assumption of background knowledge to enable students to discern the forest from the trees. Reminded to include references to the text, almost all of them used the example I had supplied in the rather elaborate assignment instructions, thus revealing that they were struggling with the genre of the essay *assignment* as well as with the essay itself. Topic familiarity, I concluded, is less important than helping students improve their meta-reading habits, and that would have required much more scaffolding than I had provided. Similarly, the challenges for novice readers of "Once More to the Lake" and "The Brown Wasps" are not so much the unfamiliarity of their topics (feelings upon revisiting a place remembered from a long-ago encounter) as the conventions of the expert personal essay, which gives heft and weight to an individual experience, invites readers to inhabit an intensely felt world, and, even in its most lyrical incarnations, provokes confrontation with excavated and often difficult truths.

The personal essay, since it requires, as much as does any genre, an awareness of how parts relate to whole in rhetorically sophisticated compositions, fits well into a first-year reading-and-writing syllabus that includes a range of text types. One way to help students move from reading only for "story" to considering elements that forge a theme—to be a meta-reader, to read rhetorically—is to make this task the subject of the assignment, which was my intent in the following:

> ***Assignment 2: Exposition of Themes in Narrative Essays or: How Stories Mean More Than the Events They Describe***
> Readings to be considered (from *The Norton Reader,* shorter 13th edition):
>
> Langston Hughes, "Salvation"
>
> Edward Rivera, "First Communion"
>
> Mordecai Rosenfeld, "Genesis, Chapter 22—A Respectful Dissent"
>
> George Orwell, "Shooting an Elephant"
>
> Alice Walker, "Beauty: When the Other Dancer Is the Self"

> Your second formal essay assignment is to do the following:
>
> *Choosing one of the essays listed above, show, in an essay of about six hundred words, how the author uses details of personal experience to convey an important theme or thesis.* You will need at least one very well-developed paragraph that makes clear *what* the theme or thesis is. And you will need to show *how* the writer uses details of personal experience to reach the reader.
>
> What kinds of observations can you include in your essay to show how a personal narrative conveys an idea? Here are some suggestions: [Reminders of possibly relevant rhetorical features—e.g., organization, figurative language, narrative voice, and use of examples—are noted here]. Remember, however, that your overall purpose is to relate these specific aspects to the larger idea you think the author means to convey to the reader.
>
> Finally, offer your own response to the essay, indicating how it affected you and why. Be as specific as you can in giving reasons for your response.

Asking students to relate narrative details to overall ideas in a personal essay is comparable to the demands of moving, in literary study, from plot to theme and, in informative articles, from examples to claims—all require consideration of how the concrete relates to the abstract, the particular to the general. When assignments are designed to support rhetorical reading, the variety of genres addressed can be used to foster practice in the kinds of abstraction and synthesis required for success in source-based writing across the curriculum.

Building Intellectual Capital

Teaching the classic texts that encourage thinking on big, enduring (i.e., open-ended or controversial) questions provides additional opportunities for practice in sophisticated rhetorical reading. Such reading can provide a foundation for source-based papers in discipline-based classes not only because of the potential to foster meta-reading habits but also because of the knowledge base that is thereby fortified, enabling further cognitive development. To illustrate, here is a topic I have offered to developmental classes later in the semester, following our discussion of Plato's cave allegory and of Machiavelli's definition of princely virtues:

> For an essay on "The Morals of the Prince," excerpted from Niccolò Machiavelli's book *The Prince* (1513), imagine the following situation:
>
> Some students in your former high school are studying the European Renaissance in World History. You have been asked by your high school to return as a guest speaker in the World History class in order to share what you know about Machiavelli's philosophy. Because you would not feel comfortable speaking only from notes, you have decided to write a paper that you will read to the high school students.
>
> Your paper will explain Machiavelli's ideas in language the students will easily understand, even though they have not read anything Machiavelli wrote. Because these students have already studied Plato's "Allegory of the Cave," you refer to Plato for purposes of comparison or contrast. In order to make sure they understand how Machiavelli's ideas are relevant to more recent times, you decide to include in your paper two examples drawn from your knowledge of history and/or current events. One example will illustrate political behavior that you consider "Machiavellian"; the other will illustrate leadership that you consider "Platonic." You end by offering your own assessment of the relative value of the two perspectives.
>
> Be sure to include an introduction that makes the *purpose* of your paper clear, and try to write a conclusion that raises an interesting question for your audience to consider.

Topics like this, which demand role-playing along with comparative analysis, require both "close" and "distant" reading, as discussed in Chapter 2. While we read each text closely, I avoid reinforcing the "autonomous text" myth by alerting students to historical periods, sociopolitical contexts, and—to the extent we can know, infer, or speculate—each author's motives for writing. Exposing such factors allows me to help first-year students consider audience and purpose and thus to read rhetorically, both with and against the grain. And the responses among students who had placed into a developmental composition class showed incipient moves toward the desired skill development. One such student, for example, found *The Prince* "intriguing because it really introduces the idea of utilitarianism to a ruling class that needed it" and posited that in history one can hardly find a ruler "that didn't put the needs of the nation before the needs of the individual." Another student, seeming to prioritize the demands of national security in his sympathy with Machiavelli's ideas, nonetheless asked a big question—"Can a bad person who is rather unjust and clever exercise all of the qualities of a good leader and keep the nation on a steady path?" A third student noted that had Adolf Hitler been more successful in taking Machiavelli's advice, i.e., in demonstrating more of the qualities of the fox, "there is no telling what could have happened." While such comments by first-year students are, understandably, not firmly rooted in the disciplinary perspectives of history or political science, they are nonetheless encouraging examples of how apprentices can begin to enter intellectual conversations. Overall, the thinking throughout my students' essays demonstrated some encouraging moves: abstraction of main ideas, synthesis, and evaluation, as well as an acknowledgment that ideologies, while shaped by historical contexts, can have more generalized application, for better or for worse.

To be sure, some students' essays demonstrated, even toward the end of the term, less than satisfactory coherence in juggling the various demands of the assignment; still, the practice seems worthwhile, and one senses the potential for authentic development of ideas, not least because important and influential ideas have been at the center of the course. While not immediately "familiar," the question of what makes a good leader and how to balance ends with means is the sort of topic that can indeed prompt the authentic expression of attitudes grounded in some understanding of what, based on a theoretical or philosophical framework, is at stake. And students, of course, will benefit because the questions they are engaging with are relevant to every culture and every generation. Another advantage accrues to instructors: In reading such papers, even with their naïve assumptions and faulty rhetoric, faculty are less likely to be ground down by the sorts of formulaic expositions or "opinion" writing so often expected of entering students. And, since Wayne Booth's observation in 1963 that "any teaching that bores the teacher is sure to fail" ("Boring" 248) is equally pertinent now, it is not irrelevant that such texts decrease the chances of boredom.

Reading and writing assignments of this type can also set a tone of mutual respect between student and instructor. Challenged to connect abstract ideas, mapped out in complex texts, to concrete situations, students generally work hard to effect the synthesis, and those who have never been assigned such a task are often pleasantly surprised, even if a bit daunted at first, to be considered eligible for such high expectations. In the same class as the one that produced the excerpts above, I also assigned Steven Pinker's "The Moral Instinct" (2008) and Sartre's "Existentialism" (1945)—texts that address highly abstract questions while illustrating their claims with examples and anecdotes. While the task of unpacking the texts required close and sustained attention, I found that even students who were least experienced in skills associated with rhetorical reading were able, with support and encouragement, to see how Pinker's definitions of *community*, *authority*, and *fairness*, as well as Sartre's definition of *freedom*, could prompt deeper thinking on a culture-driven dilemma. It is difficult to assess without richer contexts the following examples from their essays on Amy Tan's "The Red Candle" (a chapter of *The Joy Luck Club,* 1989) or on George Orwell's "Shooting an Elephant." Yet one can sense from such excerpts that these beginning students are stretching to inhabit perspectives other than their own default ones—trying to see, with the aid of theoretical lenses such as the ones provided by Sartre and Pinker, another culture's values and another individual's choices from the inside out.

"Lens" assignments have the additional benefit that might be deemed ethical: They foster an empathetic imagination in the contexts of cultural diversity. One student noted that "by understanding the culture she lived in, Lindo Jong was able . . . to prevail without requiring the community to redefine its values." Another observed that freedom is conditioned by responsibility: "In the beginning of the short story, Jong speaks of the importance of promises in Chinese culture and that is why she chose her 'freedom' the way she did." A student who analyzed Orwell's position in Burma under the Raj through the lens of the moral spheres as defined by Pinker invoked both empathy and critical distance: Thoughtfully gauging the narrator's miserable position as conditioned by cultural demands, the student felt keenly the dilemma of the young colonial policeman and, in considering the terrible choice, was comfortable with uncertainty: "In the grand scheme of things, the elephant is not the main problem here; the problem is [that] Orwell loses a little bit of himself while making this choice. . . . Did he do the right thing or was he just part of a system, forced to do this duty?" The interrogative mood of this student's essay reflects his attempt to grapple with the text and the relative sophistication of his approach.

Of course, not all students learn in one semester to deal successfully with abstract and unfamiliar ideas (such as Sartre's exposition of the relationship between freedom and constraint). Some continue to rely on bromides that reveal weak comprehension of main ideas, and some fall back on too much plot summary as a substitute for analysis. In some cases syntax breaks down under the weight of cognitive confusion. In a skills-focused class, however, instructors can make the cultivation of more sophisticated reading (and writing) a curricular focus through judicious text selection and artful assignment design. Variations in skill level are to be expected, since students are beginning at very different levels of reading comprehension and writing competency. The ethical imperative to strive for an effective balance of challenge with support is therefore all the more urgent.

Rethinking Remediation

Because I had pushed my students so hard and had met with varying levels of resistance, I was reluctant to read the anonymous student evaluations that are made available to instructors after the final grades are submitted. However, the comments by students who had placed at the developmental level confirmed what I had first learned when I diminished the difference between how I taught honors classes and how I taught "remedial" ones, offering me some grounds for encouragement. One student warmed my heart by indicating curiosity and initiative but was willing to sacrifice the practice in writing: "I enjoy the readings and do take a lot out of them. As I was looking through the book I saw many other readings that would have also been interesting. So maybe just an idea is to read more and have more quizzes vs. only essays." Another wanted the reverse: "I think the readings were a little too challenging. I think that made the focus shift from writing skills to explanations of the readings which was not the purpose of the class." One student indicated a consciousness of skill transfer: "I'm making a lot of progress in the field of reading other books." Most of my students understood and appreciated the reciprocal relationship between reading and writing, as reflected in the following sorts of comments:

"I liked reading various essays and stories. The essay questions were well constructed to help apply the stories/essays."

"I think this class has challenged me a lot but I learned a lot about my writing."

"I feel I grew a lot as a writer. This course definitely laid the foundation for success in the rest of my college writing courses."

"I have learned a lot in this class, not just on writing but on other topics as well."

My experience in general has been that as long they feel supported, students tend to be more appreciative and gratified than angry or resentful at being asked to play the various roles demanded by important and enduring texts.

And beyond their immediate reactions lies the ethical dimension of how we sort and teach students. In light of the role of the Matthew effect, why should the very students most in need of enriching their intellectual and cultural capital be the ones least likely to be given the opportunity to do so? Why *not* use the forty class hours plus homework time to increase their repertoire of strategies for thinking about ideas that matter by unpacking polished, provocative, and influential texts, making such texts and ideas their own, to be deployed in ways that will then enable further enrichment? In foregrounding the question of equity in higher education, the Association of American Colleges and Universities has defined learning outcomes for all students that require faculty to reconsider assumptions about the separation of skills from content. Among the learning goals that faculty are urged to support are the development of "broad and integrative knowledge of histories, cultures, science, and society" and "well-honed intellectual and adaptive skills, including analytic inquiry, communication fluency, quantitative fluency, engaging and working across difference, problem solving, and ethical reasoning" (*Committing* 7). Such goals can best be met if students are offered, from the beginning, structures for engaging in authentic conversations with texts that express important and nuanced ideas and demonstrate sophisticated command of language.

It is not just that increased reading deepens and broadens one's knowledge base but that reading "can make you smarter" (Cunningham and Stanovich, "Reading") by enabling deeper, more efficient, and more lasting learning. Research by Keith Stanovich and Anne Cunningham has made a strong case for the role of exposure to print media (as distinct from general cognitive ability) as the dominant factor in the acquisition of general knowledge: "The cognitive anatomy of misinformation is one of too little exposure to print; to a lesser degree, of deficiencies of general ability (as indicated primarily by mathematics test performance); and to a small degree, of overreliance on television for information about the world" ("Where Does Knowledge Come From?" 225). Written before the ubiquity of computers and the existence of social media, the report does not address students' dependence on new technologies. However, it seems fair to speculate that Neil Postman's commentary in 1988 on the effects of television—that TV exposure fosters "knowledge *of* many things but *about* very little" (qtd. by Stanovich and Cunningham 224)—has been made more salient by Google and hypertext, by Facebook and Twitter. If indeed "there is a consensus in cognitive psychology that it takes knowledge to gain knowledge" (Hirsch 2), then relying on data-mining from the internet is not in itself a strategy for success: "[T]o be able to use that information—to absorb it, to add to our knowledge—we must already possess a storehouse of knowledge" (3).

Studies of expert versus novice thinking show quite conclusively that the ability to frame and solve an unscripted problem depends heavily on prior understanding of the relevant variables to be accounted for; that is, "you can't think critically about topics you know little about or solve problems that you don't know well enough to recognize and execute the type of solutions they call for" (Willingham, "Critical Thinking" 12). Thus, as E. D. Hirsch observes, without deliberative educational interventions, the internet will "exacerbate the 'Matthew effect'"; those who are already more knowledgeable will learn more and at a comparatively rapid rate, whereas those already lagging in knowledge "will face . . . a frustrating confusion of information that they will be unable to sort, evaluate, or absorb" (5). This is why relegating students pegged as developmental or remedial to classes where content is watered down and demands for skill development remain basic, classes whose instructors may believe that "discussion [of readings] could be superfluous when students need to know how to use commas and write introductions" (Bosley 297), is bound to increase the disparity between the relative haves and have-nots.

One criterion I have suggested in considering whether to include a particular text in a composition syllabus is its helpfulness to students trying to understand the ideas behind current events and, more specifically, the allusions in journalistic commentary. As David Kaufer aptly observed thirty years ago in his constructive critique of Hirsch's *Cultural Literacy,* and as affirmed by Eric Liu in the more-recent contexts of cultural diversity, it is our task as instructors to help students see how the present is conditioned by the past, thus broadening their notion of "relevance." Frequently I am able to assign an ad hoc reading of an op-ed piece or item of analytical commentary in the *New York Times* related to our class discussions, and my students even smile a little when I proclaim that I have found "'great ideas' in the news!" In the spring of 2015, for example, David Brooks's opinion column "Goodness and Power" provided excellent fodder for bringing up to date the ideas of governance advocated by Plato and by Machiavelli. While those names were not explicitly mentioned in the column, students could see their ideas resonating in Brooks's central question—"Can bad people be good leaders?"—and in his very language noting the role, in leadership, of fairness, empathy, and honesty and the need to balance private morality with savvy pragmatism, since it is essential "to react against unprincipled people who want to destroy you." Not incidentally, Brooks explicitly invokes the wisdom of the serpent and the innocence of the dove, thus inviting another influential text into the discussion. One need not have embraced Brooks's assessments of current political figures to have understood his argument, but a basic knowledge of Plato's and Machiavelli's ideas on leadership would have provided a dimension for thoughtful critique.

Later in the lead-up to the 2016 presidential campaign, the *Times* published, on the eve of the Fourth of July and shortly after the Brexit vote, a ragged-edge column by Jim Rutenberg on the front page of the business section, deploring the increasingly politicized and therefore fact-challenged media environment and its hugely consequential effects for national policy and international relations. Using as a hook Ben Franklin's statement on the power and urgency of a free press—"It is a principle among printers that when truth has fair play, it will always prevail over falsehood" (B1)—Rutenberg asked, "What happens to the balance between truth and falsehood when an important portion of the national news media hands the political debate over to partisan operatives who, as a rule, skew the facts—or abandon them—in the service of their own political ends or business interests?" (B5). Deploring the British media's representation of issues on Brexit before the vote, Rutenberg noted that "the partisan press climate meant all facts were up for debate. Nothing could stand as Platonic truth" (B5). American cable news, he argued, was not far behind in its failure to help the public distinguish fact from spin or from total fiction. The issue of a free and responsible press in a democratic society is current, historical, and enduring, and it is likely that most students could get the gist of Rutenberg's commentary and caution. But why should an understanding of the allusion to "Platonic truth" and its implications for how theories of knowledge affect structures of governance and public policy be available only to honors students?

In this context, it is also worth considering the request from some students that more class time be spent on grammar. Debates about whether and how to "teach grammar" in college classrooms are long-standing. Professors across the disciplines are wont to complain that their students "don't know how to put a sentence together," and they wonder why the English department doesn't fix the problem once and for all. The answer is that attempts to enhance students' command of grammar, syntax, and mechanics through drills focused on memorization of rules have not proven very effective, and better solutions are difficult to codify and to deliver. Our individual and collective experiences affirm this. Early in my career, I was required to teach reading-based writing in first-year composition while students were required to study and pass quizzes on grammar in "labs" independent of the class. Thus, it was reasoned, grammar deficiencies could be rectified while professors could use class time for the more sophisticated (and presumably more interesting) aspects of first-year composition. Students dutifully studied the rules, and many did very well on the quizzes. However, there was little transfer of that "knowledge" to their compositions, an indication that being able to recite and perform the rules acontextually is a woefully limited skill, separate from understanding when and how to apply them or makes choices about how to deploy them with conscious purposes in mind.

The concept of knowledge that is conditionalized, i.e., that is retrieved and used appropriately (see the contributions to Bransford et al.), is typically associated with problem-solving in STEM disciplines, but it also has relevance to liberal arts and humanities domains. While grammar is commonly reduced to errors in form or mechanics (e.g., subject-verb agreement, use of apostrophes, comma placement), it is more aptly thought of in its broader connotations, with special emphasis for purposes of pedagogy on syntax, the juxtaposition of phrases, and the construction of sentences to create meaning. The uncertain phrasing sometimes demonstrated by students who are asked to read out loud complexly constructed sentences and passages reveals difficulty in processing how the parts of the sentence relate to each other. As noted earlier (see Jamieson, "Reading"), identifying a main clause versus a subordinate one in order to understand the connection between them is not a mere matter of demonstrating knowledge of "correct" English but rather an indication of reading comprehension. What we think of as teaching grammar must therefore be considered an aspect of teaching rhetorical reading, and students who have not been heavily exposed to the type of print culture that dominates academia deserve pedagogies that effectively address their needs.

Students at all levels need to be shown how expert writers construct sentences not with the aim of avoiding errors per se but with rhetorical effectiveness in mind. And such lessons can be engaging. In my experience students are interested to learn, for example, how Thomas Jefferson uses the rhythms of a polished periodic sentence in the opening of the Declaration of Independence to establish the snap-shut logic of his argument and also his ethos. When I ask where the main clause is and what its grammatical subject is, we can thus consider why Jefferson would have used the word *respect* (for what, for whom, and why?) as a rhetorical focal point in his call for a violent revolution. Later, in reading Martin Luther King Jr.'s "Letter from Birmingham Jail," we can revisit the idea of sentence periodicity as a way to engage both hearts and minds, with particular attention to the long why-we-can't-wait paragraph written in response to those who say they share the movement's goal but counsel "gradualism." This textual connection illuminates the persistence of a syntactic strategy through centuries as a rhetorical device more common in formal written prose than in speech and also its variability depending on context and purpose.

Noticing such structures is a natural bridge to short focused lessons on the design of simple, compound, and complex sentences and the virtues of using many kinds of sentences to achieve one's desired effect. Then positive examples from students' writing, as well as an analysis of before-and-after constructions, can serve as reinforcement and motivation to press on, as students are encouraged to see composition—by themselves and by expert writers—as comprising particular choices. Moreover, I emphasize in all of my classes, whether introductory or more advanced, that rules are not ends in themselves, but conventions that one must master in order to know when and how they might productively be broken. No one strategy, of course, will work miracles in a semester or two, which is why my larger argument entails instruction in reading as a reciprocal to writing across the curriculum. (I also recommend that students beyond the first year be offered courses in rhetorical grammar, reading, and writing. I have developed two such courses at my institution—one primarily for preservice K–8 teachers and one for English majors.) In any case, whether or not we sort students into classes labeled "developmental," we need to get over the idea that we must first deal with "the basics" before engaging our students in the more sophisticated aspects of college-level work, while at the same time avoiding the opposite trap of setting challenges without designing sufficiently expert scaffolding.

Balancing Challenge with Support

An idea gaining currency in closing the achievement gap is to rethink the value and purpose of so-called developmental courses altogether (Relles and Tierney; Hassel and Giordano; Martorell and McFarlin; Attewell et al.). On my own campus, as increasing proportions of incoming students were being recommended for a nine-credit (three-course) composition requirement as opposed to the traditionally typical six-credit (two-course) requirement, the question arose of what, if any, advantages were being conferred by the additional semester. To find the answer, we began a pilot that would enable comparison of students taking the three-course sequence, which included an initial developmental class, with those of similar initial academic profiles placed, along with students who had been exempted from the developmental class, into a two-course sequence. Thus the pilot sections were heterogeneous in terms of skills, each comprising in close to equal numbers developmental and mainstream composition students. To diminish the potential for bias, students' initial placement scores were not available to instructors. Several thematically related readings of different genres were taught in all the pilot sections, and the focus in writing assignments was on synthesis. The common readings across all pilot sections (all related to the theme of obedience to authority) were George Orwell's "Shooting an Elephant," Amy Tan's "The Red Candle," and Stanley Milgram's "The Perils of Obedience." Instructors were individually responsible for complementing these texts as they thought best. Since "The Perils of Obedience" was written as a "popular" description of scientific experiments, I decided to include one of Milgram's earlier, more specialized reports on his research, anticipating some unusual opportunities for instruction in rhetorical reading.

Below is a list of topic options I offered for their third essay assignment. Because of the importance of enhancing students' genre awareness, my reading list included a nonfiction book, a short personal memoir, two iconic political documents, a report of a now-classic social-psychology experiment, and a subsequently published version of the experiment rewritten for a more popular audience and published in *Harper's*. I was able to include the book

Just Mercy (attorney Bryan Stevenson's wrenching account of the challenges he faced as an advocate for victims of institutionalized prejudice in the criminal justice system) because it had been assigned as summer reading to all incoming first-year students, and I focused in class on several excerpts especially relevant to our themes.

Topics for Essay 3 (1200 words)
Texts:

Bryan Stevenson, *Just Mercy* (2014)

Langston Hughes, "Salvation" (1940)

Martin Luther King Jr., "Letter from Birmingham Jail" (1963)

Stanley Milgram, "Some Conditions of Obedience and Disobedience to Authority" (1965)

Stanley Milgram, "The Perils of Obedience" (1973)

Thomas Jefferson, the Declaration of Independence (1776)

Note: Whichever topic you choose, include enough of a summary of "Some Conditions of Obedience and Disobedience to Authority" to make your argument intelligible to a reader unfamiliar with the study.

A. According to Stanley Milgram's 1965 study of the conditions in which people choose to disobey authority, "Many subjects [could] not find the verbal formula that would enable them to reject the role assigned to them by the experimenter [an authority figure]. Perhaps our culture does not provide adequate models for disobedience" (67). Write an essay in which you apply Milgram's findings to the situation of either Jefferson or King. Explain: How did Jefferson or King, in his respective document, offer the "verbal formula" appropriate for his time that would embolden people to disobey long-standing and extremely powerful forms of authority? How did Jefferson or King help people rethink the "conditions" that might affect their choices?

B. Milgram published his article in the 1960s, and some have claimed that his results reflect aspects of that period—that people today would react differently. Based on your reading of one or more episodes in *Just Mercy,* consider how Bryan Stevenson would assess the contemporary relevance of Milgram's experiments. In your essay, show how Stevenson's experience relates to the psychology and behavior revealed in Milgram's study. Try to smoothly integrate a summary of Milgram's main findings and speculations within your argument.

C. With particular attention to the section on "tensions" within subjects in Milgram's experiments, apply Milgram's ideas about the conditions of obedience and disobedience to authority to the behavior of the young Langston Hughes in "Salvation." What were the *conditions* that created the tensions within Hughes? Use Milgram's *speculations* about human psychology to account for the young boy's behavior and his ensuing feelings.

D. Compare the two versions of Milgram's study that you read—"Some Conditions of Obedience and Disobedience to Authority" and "The Perils of Obedience." Notice the important differences, keeping in mind our class discussion of rhetorical strategies. How do the differences reflect the different intended audiences and purposes, and what are the advantages and drawbacks of each approach? Explain which one you found more interesting and why. Support your argument with detailed evidence from both texts.

Deep comprehension of the texts was supported with frequent small but challenging assignments—summary and paraphrase, completion of "empty outlines" (Angelo and Cross; Bean); says/does analyses (Bean et al.); discernment of logos, ethos, and pathos—that move students beyond "information gathering"; through such tasks, students can learn to distinguish rhetorical subsections and relate these to a controlling idea as well as see how and why writers make choices in style and structure. The small class size (capped at fifteen) made individual attention possible. From the first week and throughout the semester, students grappled with big ideas and complex arguments. Like my honors students—and like the classes of "developmental" students I was also used to teaching—they read Plato, Sartre, Darwin, and Baldwin. They applied existential thinking to the character development portrayed in "Sonny's Blues" and looked at the choices made by Orwell's persona and by Amy Tan's protagonist through the lens of the moral categories explained by Steven Pinker.

The range of genres offered frequent opportunities to locate texts in formal, cultural, and historical contexts and to discuss different motives for writing. Juxtaposing two versions of the Milgram experiment showed students how an individual author can reshape information and argument to accommodate different intended audiences. Moreover, the topic proved particularly engaging; even students who were already familiar with "the Milgram experiments" from the 1960s were interested in revisiting them. As a hook, I showed a video of the original experiments (so uncomfortable and so fascinating). Then, after carefully unpacking the targeted conditions of obedience and disobedience and Milgram's conclusions in the 1965 scientific report, we compared the rhetoric of this article written for scientists with the "popular" and rather pandering version published in *Harper's* in 1973.

This comparison proved even more valuable than I had anticipated, for several reasons.

Raising genre awareness: The two Milgram texts discussed here illustrate how instruction in genre awareness can work in a first-year composition course. By virtue of both feature and function—imagined audience and intended purpose, site of publication, selection and organization of content, character of the authorial voice, and cognitive demands on readers—the two texts beg to be considered as different genres composed at different times for distinct occasions. One is a scientific report subjected to peer review by disciplinary experts, the other a spiced-up feature-type article, replete with stereotypes of selected subjects, tidy moralizing, and a format designed for "human interest." Their titles alone ("Some Conditions of Obedience and Disobedience to Authority" in *Human Relations,* "The Perils of Obedience" in *Harper's*) hold clues to genre, audience, and purpose. The 1973 version includes data from follow-up experiments in different countries and from iterations that include women—mentioned in the 1965 report as a type of variable to be studied in "further experiments." In the *Harper's* essay we have heroes, villains, and "peculiar" cases: the "attractive" young German émigré, Yale medical technician Gretchen Brandt, who is the epitome of moral integrity (not to mention "courteous behavior"); the none-too-sharp Bruno Batta, "robotic" son of Italian immigrants, whose behavior creates a "brutal and depressing scene"; the "impressively fluent and intelligent" Morris Braverman (a character out of Malamud), whose willingness to inflict pain under the conditions of the experiment causes his wife, in a fit of hyperbole, to compare him to Eichmann—whose trial was being televised as Milgram was conducting his early studies.

The version written for the more general audience, preferred by most of the pilot-class instructors, certainly has its appeal. However, the scientific report shows how a research project is developed and conducted and may be useful in helping students understand discipline-based writing. The line graphs—and the accompanying explanations—demonstrate the role of graphic information in scientific reports and are simple enough to be easily accessible; my students enjoyed interpreting these, perhaps as a change from so much verbal analysis. We discussed how and why the scientific report does a better job of raising meaningful open-ended questions; the *Harper's* version appears to want to simplify the conclusions by offering a neater explanation. Thus students could clearly see how authorial choices with regard to genre are constrained by contextual factors and both reflect and influence readers' expectations and perceptions.

Dispelling the myth of the autonomous text: It is a cliché that students today are notoriously ahistorical; these texts were an ideal medium for demonstrating the relation of text to contexts—historical, social, ideological, commercial. We discussed, for example, how the original experiments published in 1965 were begun in 1961 and reflect a 1950s culture (I briefly introduced touchstones such as Sloan Wilson's 1955 novel, *The Man in the Grey Flannel Suit,* and William H. Whyte's *The Organization Man* [1956]). Milgram's own prior research (including his dissertation) entailed studies of conformity. Hannah Arendt's argument for the "banality of evil" appeared in 1963. Interestingly, the *Harper's* article, while adding a historicist (Marxist) explanation based on division of labor and alienation from the total human experience, does not mention the protests and civil disobedience in the 1960s. On the other hand, it is notable that in 1970 Seymour Hersh had published in *Harper's Magazine* his explosive exposé of the My Lai Massacre, and Milgram did allege a connection between the Vietnam atrocities and his studies. One might speculate that *Harper's* reached out to Milgram for reasons that, if probed, would cast a light on the popular chord touched by Milgram's methods (subsequently found to be ethically suspect by some psychologists) and conclusions (universally disturbing and especially to Milgram himself, as he notes at the end his report), on the zeitgeist of the 1960s, and on *Harper's* interests in particular. Including such contexts in discussion helps to dispel the myth of the autonomous text and encourages rhetorical reading by raising awareness of how writers shape content for targeted audiences.

Having worked hard to analyze the nuances of the scientific report, students were alert to and rather surprised by the stereotypes and simplified lessons in the magazine article. Overall, students responded to this lesson with enthusiasm, and several brought in the relevant historical contexts they had learned about in high school (the Holocaust, the Eichmann trial, post–World War II culture and sociopsychological concerns). It might be inferred, then, that in reading the texts based on the background schemata (Hirsch 39) or "situation models" (Bråten and Strømsø), the students found them more accessible and more engaging than might otherwise have been the case.

Fostering meta-reading: Differences in contexts for text generation naturally enable different strategies for reading. Milgram's article published in *Human Relations* ("Some Conditions . . .") reflects the basic conventions of scientific writing in its subdivision into sections that enable nonlinear reading. These include, e.g., "Terminology," "The Subject Population," "The General Laboratory Procedure," "Pilot Studies," various conditions that were studied with regard to the question of obedience to authority, and "Further Studies." Results reported under the condition "Immediacy of the Victim" contain, in a smaller font, a further subset of commentary—hypothesized reasons for the outcomes, using terminology and concepts from psychology with which readers are expected to be familiar. Text is sometimes broken up with representations of quantitative data, and several pages include discursive footnotes that add information, explain methods or results in more detail, and sometimes argue for a particular inference.

Applying the categories developed by Susan Peck MacDonald, we can see how, in its rhetoric (e.g., use of passive voice, use of hedges, preponderance of sentences that foreground in their syntax the phenomenon being studied), and in its organization according to the principles of scientific inquiry, the article in *Human Relations* represents a central feature of "epistemic" prose and thus lends itself to the kinds of selective reading (skimming and scanning some sections, slowing down for others) research tells us are common among scientists. In contrast, "The Perils of Obedience," with its narrative structure (including heroes and villains among the "characters"), use of active voice, and explicit evaluations of individual behaviors among the subjects, has more of a "verbal" style that invites the audience to read it as a story and draw from it the lessons of a cautionary fable. The subdivisions here are fewer, and they seem calculated to encourage both dramatic suspense and moral judgment: "An Unexpected Outcome," "Peculiar Reactions," "Duty without Conflict." As students compared the two articles, they could see how the report in *Human Relations,* in complying with the epistemological rigors of scientific method, offers sections that can be considered discretely both to yield insight into factors affecting human behavior in conditions of stress and to enable methodological and interpretive critiques. The *Harper's* article, in slightly sensationalizing the experiments, portrays individuals as culturally representative types and ends by suggesting closure (i.e., by identifying fragmentation of individual identity as "the most common characteristic of socially organized evil in modern society") rather than raising further questions or, as the article in *Human Relations* does in its postscript, broadening the significance of the issues to encompass questions that the study itself does not directly address.

Purposeful Teaching for Cross-Disciplinary Awareness

The assignments I have offered as examples are intended to encourage the sorts of advances in reading skill demanded by texts assigned in classes beyond English. However, a somewhat different course design could even more explicitly help students practice a range of strategies for reading across the curriculum as well as gain an incipient understanding of the range of disciplinary habits practiced by experts. A junior colleague of mine whose teaching I was asked to evaluate made rhetorical reading across the curriculum the focus of her course. Organizing her syllabus around readings from three disciplines—sociology, biology, and literature—she focused her assignments on rhetorical analyses of texts, directing students to develop arguments about how and why texts are written as they are and also to compare rhetorical strategies used in texts representing the same discipline but directed to different audiences (as my students did with the Milgram essays). Formal writing assignments included a comparative rhetorical analysis of two science articles, a social-science white paper on a criminal-justice topic, and a literary analysis of a novel. Prior to these assignments, students were given directed practice in meta-reading skills, as appropriate to the text at hand. In the class I observed, students practiced decoding a rather technical article from the *Journal of Animal Ecology,* "Unravelling the Annual Cycle in a Migratory Animal: Breeding-Season Habitat Loss Drives Population Declines of Monarch Butterflies" (Flockhart et al.).

This article, obviously written for trained scientists with a background in both animal ecology and mathematical modeling, seemed at first a rather daring and perhaps even foolhardy choice for a first-year composition class. When I sat down to make sense of it, I struggled somewhat and had to read very slowly and very carefully. In this way, I had much in common with the students to whom it was assigned, and I found myself wondering how in the world the class of diverse first-year students representing different majors would deal with such technical material. I was further perplexed when I realized that the research described was not itself a direct report of empirical observations (which is what I had anticipated) but a meta-analysis based on a projection matrix model (a concept not exactly in my wheelhouse) that synthesized and analyzed data from prior studies to define correlations, assess probabilities, and make predictions.

My limited training in statistical analysis made it impossible for me to fully understand, much less evaluate, the researchers' methods, and I relied much more on verbal explanations of graphical figures than on the visuals themselves. I was most interested in the "So what?" aspect of the research, which did not appear in the article's five-point introductory summary and in fact did not emerge until the end of the essay without, it seemed to me, adequate emphasis. The question was addressed primarily in a sentence on the penultimate page of the article and again in a sentence on the last page, each beginning with the word *Ultimately* and relating the findings to broader issues of conservation planning, including "legal implications for conserving threatened wildlife that migrate between countries that classify and protect species-at-risk differently" (162, 163). Perhaps most important, it took a second reading for me to recognize that this was not an observational study per se but rather one that used prior data to construct a predictive model to explain the factors affecting population declines of the subject species. Having found the text quite challenging, I was more than curious to see how the students would deal with it and was half expecting a disaster.

As it turned out, the class was remarkably effective. The professor, who had carefully charted the use of class time, made clear that their work in this session would help prepare them for their rhetorical comparison of a specialized journal article with a somewhat less specialized piece by sociobiologist E. O. Wilson, which they had already analyzed. That is, they would not be responsible for an in-depth understanding of scientific data and methods as reported for experts but would be expected to infer rhetorical differences between texts written for different purposes and contexts. She started by asking the students to recall points from their prior discussion of the Flockhart article's introduction and results sections. They then turned to the (more difficult) multipart methods section. After analyzing the first methods part with them, she assigned each of the remaining sections to a group and asked each group to compose a single sentence expressing the key idea of "their" section. She had each group articulate its sentence, helped them refine where necessary, and wrote the findings on the board. She then turned, in the last quarter of the class period, to helping students use their understanding as a basis for shaping summaries of the article, with an eye toward the formal comparison that would follow. She noted that they would be moving from questions of "what" to questions of "how" in relation to the texts. To this end, she asked students to articulate differences between the approaches taken by Wilson and by Flockhart. During the last few minutes of class, students were asked to write down their observations on a rhetorical analysis worksheet prepared by the instructor and, as the class ended, told to bring these back for continued work at the next meeting.

Students responded much more favorably to these challenges than I had expected. I chatted informally with several of them after class and found that even those with little background in science were comfortable with the tasks assigned. One especially helpful aspect of the pedagogy was that the instructor, a specialist in literature and herself untrained in the subject matter and methods of the article, was able to work with students in deciphering specialized writing containing elements (e.g., arcane vocabulary, complex statistical methods, and technical visual data) that she herself found difficult. In this way, she served as a role model and guide for beginning students, who must navigate among multiple courses and ways of reading and thinking. Such an approach coincides with John Bean's advice for helping novices make sense of difficult texts by preparing reading guides that focus their attention on key takeaways rather than having them struggle with technical data or methods that require prior knowledge to understand. In sharing one such first-year seminar guide for an article related to gender identity from the *Journal of Child Psychology and Psychiatry,* Bean notes: "I wanted to assure students that it was okay to understand only, say, 20 percent of the article and recognize why the other 80 percent was accessible only to experts" (*Engaging* 176). Moreover, as Sheridan Blau has observed, the ability of more advanced students to engage productively with an unfamiliar text even in their own field cannot be taken for granted: Many secondary-school English teachers are "fearful of teaching any text they haven't been taught" or for which they do not have a publisher's lesson plan (271–72). Instructors who demonstrate how to meet such a challenge, whether in their own discipline or in others, and who scaffold the practice for their students are therefore reinforcing their own meta-reading skills and offering a valuable model to undergraduates.

The rhetorical focus of my colleague's course was reflected in her assignment sheets and in her classroom strategies, which emphasized that she expected students to focus on understanding texts, not on voicing their own points of view. Their thesis-driven papers were thus more likely to closely approximate writing in the academy, in which experts are entering an informed conversation, than, as is more frequent among novice students, expressing personal opinions in response to familiar issues. By backward-designing the course as she did, she aimed at helping students develop confidence that they, too, could make sense of unfamiliar and perhaps intimidating material by identifying genres, understanding common discourse conventions, and reading strategically. At appropriate points in the semester, she assigned a key reading or video on how research is written up in the disciplinary area in which students were reading at the time.

While I have often heard composition instructors claim that they cannot teach academic articles not in their field (which is almost invariably English literature or composition), this class was an excellent demonstration of how a motivated instructor who understands the practice of rhetorical reading across the disciplines can make such a curriculum work. If it is true, as has been argued, that "the development of expert reading practices can be accelerated through explicit instruction" (Warren, "Rhetorical Reading and the Development of Disciplinary Literacy"), the effects of such instruction and a focus on assignment design would be worth investigating further, especially with regard to their potential for "vertical" connection throughout the undergraduate years. It is with the aim of exploring such potential that I show in the next chapter how instructors across the disciplines can build on the foundations of rhetorical reading as laid in first-year composition classes.

Theory to Practice: Reading Across the Curriculum

The importance of building rhetorical-reading instruction into classes across the curriculum was illuminated by Christina Haas's 1994 case study of the reading habits of Eliza, a biology major, across the four years of her undergraduate curriculum. Encouraged in her first-year English class to see discourse as comprising context-bound conversations, Eliza lost this "scaffolding" in her sophomore year and "again seemed content to view texts as autonomous." Haas's analysis of this student's approach to a vaguely defined "research paper" assigned in her sophomore biology class revealed that "at this point, reading and writing were seen as the work of school, not of science" (68–69). While Eliza did acquire sophisticated meta-reading skills as she progressed through her junior and senior years, we know from our own experience, from an increasingly compelling body of research-based evidence, and from the urgent pleas of a wide range of scholars and practitioners that Eliza is more the exception than the rule—that many students do not acculturate without consistent and expertly designed scaffolding.

Proponents of teaching reading across the curriculum see such instruction as vital not only to disciplinary understanding (Leamnson; Bain; Horning, "Reading Across") but also to overall success in college (Rhodes; Young and Potter; Jolliffe and Harl). In his argument for "deep reading" (engaging big ideas and grappling with difficult material) as a threshold concept in composition studies, Patrick Sullivan calls us to recognize the across-the-curriculum consequences of an academic culture that all too often rewards the appearance of learning ("surface learning, answer-getting," "gam[ing] the system") rather than the real thing ("Deep Reading" 151). As a result of her study of how students conduct research for source-based papers, Sandra Jamieson concluded that we need to "entirely rethink our pedagogy and expectations across the curriculum" and proposed that "pro-active pedagogies" in rhetorical reading could help us "avoid the necessity of developing reactive pedagogies to respond to patchwriting and other misuse of sources" (18). The essential move that is needed has perhaps been stated best by Karen Manarin and her colleagues, who, having studied evidence of the reading habits of first-year students in a range of foundational general-education seminars, advocate assignments that require more systematic attention to reading and note the need for fundamental shifts in attitude throughout the academy: "[R]eading needs to be framed not as a basic skill, but as a complex process worthy of study and reflection itself before we will see large numbers of faculty taking up our call to pay attention to critical reading in their classrooms and their disciplines" (103).

Such reform depends on a recognition among faculty that the intellectual and professional autonomy so rightfully cherished in academia, an independence critical to the free play of ideas that sustains a democracy, must be complemented with a commitment to teamwork in ways that are often counter to professorial and institutional culture. Manarin and her coauthors have pointedly summed up the issue: "We understand our own resistance to change, with both the effort involved in creating something new and the grief of letting go what has been . . . yet we cannot afford to continue the status quo. We need to work for change together" (104). Historian William Cronon's compelling essay on the meaning of a liberal education reminds us that freedom and responsibility are mutually implicated: "It is the community that empowers the free individual, just as it is free individuals who lead and empower the community" (77). Yet a vision of teaching that, like scholarship, is "community property" (Shulman) remains elusive. Faculty must feel confident that to capture, publicize, and critique best practices and illustrative artifacts is not a move toward standardization but part of a process of self-reflection in service to an archive and record from which others may learn and borrow, adapting particulars to their unique contexts.

The need for such a shift is the thrust of Richard Arum, Josipa Roksa, and Amanda Cook's *Improving Quality in Higher Edu-*

cation, which documents the cross-institutional work of faculty representing six disciplines to define learning goals and develop guidelines for assessing student progress toward achieving the specified outcomes. According to the authors, engaging faculty in this way is an important corrective to strategies that may seem more efficient and more likely to produce easily quantifiable data but are less likely to yield authentic and productive insights: "Bringing faculty together to engage in these kinds of efforts is crucial not only to help avoid the narrow focus on outcomes over which colleges have only limited control (e.g., early postgraduation wages) but also to steer the conversation to the core of higher education: teaching and learning" (21). In their afterword to the book, researchers Natasha Jankowski and George Kuh, members of the National Institute for Learning Outcomes Assessment, reinforce the importance of faculty teamwork in reflecting on disciplinary epistemologies, defining desired student-learning outcomes, and determining authentic assessment techniques; such collaboration, they maintain, enables a consensus that benefits students and the institution overall as well as meeting expectations of external stakeholders (241). In my experience as a faculty-development leader, the opportunity for faculty to work in collaborative groups on teaching and learning challenges has indeed proven effective in facilitating the kinds of reforms now vigorously advocated. And while exchanges among practitioners of the same discipline (the project described by Arum, Roksa, and Cook) is central to program improvement, my work has led me to conclude that multidisciplinary faculty-development groups offer unique opportunities for insights and can motivate important curricular changes. The following section offers evidence for this claim, with emphasis on how classroom-inquiry projects illuminate the potential for vertical integration of reading skills within and across disciplines.

Collaborative Theory in Practice: The Benefits of Faculty Learning Communities

For fourteen years, inspired by my training as a fellow of the Carnegie Academy for the Scholarship of Teaching and Learning, I led a cross-disciplinary program called BRIDGE (Bridging Research, Instruction, and Discipline-Grounded Epistemologies), in which a group of six to eight faculty members annually engaged in a series of workshops organized to support their forays into the scholarship of teaching and learning (SoTL) through focus on a classroom challenge each had selected. Since the groups were multidisciplinary, our meetings provided ample opportunity for creativity and analogic thinking and also revealed cross-curricular synergies (Wilner, "Multidisciplinary"). Among the most striking parallels was the imperative to support students in reading specialized texts with expertise and for specific purposes. A theme that emerged from repeated iterations of the faculty-development seminars was that students can benefit not only from attention to meta-reading in a particular class but also from faculty alertness to skill development required throughout the undergraduate curriculum and thus the importance of vertical curricular coherence. This experience affirms Chris Anson's contention that carefully crafted "writing-to-read" assignments can improve students' academic achievement in any discipline while dispelling the notion that attending to reading in college classes is a remedial activity ("Writing" 37). The examples that follow are intended to demonstrate how such a valuable effect might be achieved as courses build, over time, a hierarchy of skills.

I have indicated in the previous chapter how the types of scaffolding recommended by John Bean (*Engaging*) for a first-year theme-based seminar were deployed by one of my colleagues in a composition class to help students discern the broad outlines and key ideas of a fairly technical scientific study. Thus first-year students learned they could be selective in their reading of an article outside their comfort zone, using strategies keyed to the rhetoric of the discipline to infer the purpose of the inquiry, the results, and the implications thereof. In comparing this approach with reading-comprehension strategies used by a psychology professor in a laboratory class for which a course in statistics and research design is a prerequisite, and with those designed by a chemistry professor in Biochemistry II, for which a one-semester survey of biochemical topics is required, we can see not only that students are expected to adapt their reading strategies as the situation requires but, crucially, how professors can cultivate this agility.

Learning to Read Psychology

In her course Research in Human Cognitive Neuroscience, one of several upper-level laboratory classes offered to psychology majors, Stephanie Golski, using backward-design principles, had identified "increase professionalism" as a key goal for her students. In practice, that meant they needed to develop proficiency with primary sources, improve their presentation and summary skills, and effectively apply course concepts to real-world problems. Among several interventions, Steph included strategies to support students' ability to read rhetorically in the discipline, specifically *one-sentence summaries* (an idea adapted from Thomas Angelo and Patricia Cross's *Classroom Assessment Techniques*) and *article dissections.* Steph prepared written prompts for each task. The one-sentence summary assignment instructed students to answer basic text-based questions before class each time they were asked to read a research report: Who does what to whom? Where, when, how, and why? In class, students worked in pairs to derive a clear statement that accurately and succinctly addressed all the questions. Both individual and group statements were graded on a four-point scale. Steph observed that the parameters of this assignment naturally influenced her selection of assigned articles, and she found that grading students for both individual and group work strengthened comprehension. Moreover, repeated iterations gave students crucial practice in the relevant reading and writing skills: "This is definitely an assignment that should be done more than once to evidence a learning curve. . . . [O]nly with feedback were students able to assemble [their responses] into a succinct summary sentence that captured the main point of the article."

The article dissections stretched students a bit further by requiring them to identify, summarize, and critique peer-reviewed studies. They were directed to look for primary sources with sections labeled *introduction, methods, results,* and *discussion,* using resources such as PsycINFO, ScienceDirect, and PubMed. After providing a bibliographical citation in APA format, students were asked to "dissect" the chosen article by identifying elements through effective meta-reading. Such elements included basic content (the research question, background findings that led to the inquiry, primary methodology, results and their significance, and questions identified for further research); evaluation (potential biases, clarity of presentation, internal and external validity and reliability, lingering questions), and connections ("How does this study relate to other content we have studied in this course? Identify concepts, and include explicit explanations of the connections you see").

As with the one-sentence summaries, repetition and formative feedback proved essential. In this case, after receiving the first dissection back with comments, students were required to accompany subsequent dissections with the previously graded work in order to demonstrate their progress: Steph called this requirement "the single most important aspect of this assignment," noting that "performance improved greatly on submissions following feedback when resubmission (as an attachment) was required, versus previous semesters when students may only have scanned my comments enough to find the grade." In addition, the brevity required by both the one-sentence summaries and the dissections reduced "tendencies to plagiarism and to copying without comprehending." The final element of the dissection assignment "yielded some wonderful examples of synthesis."

Support for synthesis was enhanced by the professor's use of another technique included in the Angelo and Cross book—recall, summarize, question, connect, and comment (RSQC2), which asks students to recall and rank-order main concepts and terms from a unit of work (including material presented orally), compose a prose summary capturing the big ideas or points emerging therefrom, conceive of questions that remain, connect the unit ideas to others in the course in terms of both methods and content, and write an evaluative comment directed to the unit takeaways as a whole and/or their own approaches to digesting and connecting it. This exercise gave students practice in relating details to ideas and abstractions, a hallmark of effective meta-reading, and Steph observed some encouraging outcomes: "As was true for the one-sentence summary, students improved in their ability to demonstrate holistic thinking. Initially the terms selected as most important from the unit and used in the summary sentence disproportionately emphasized details and specifics, but student abilities shifted towards a more expert understanding of the key themes of the discipline." A collateral benefit was the professor's improved ability to offer constructive formative feedback and assess evidence of learning outcomes based on more finely distinguished tasks, as indicated by the range of grades, from A to D. Steph notes, "In previous semesters I would have worried about assigning a grade lower than C in a seminar class since there was so little to document performance" (*BRIDGE Participant Examples/Stephanie Golski*).

Especially relevant to the vertical curricular integration goals of RAC is the significant overlap between the first-year-composition task described in Chapter 4, involving instruction in the reading of a fairly complex science-journal article, and the article dissections described here. Both assignment sequences are aimed at helping students sharpen awareness of what to notice, as shaped by genre, audience, context, and purpose, and accurately discern main ideas and their connection to data, details, and examples. The psychology assignments, however, as is appropriate for the focus and level of the course, not only require more elaborate and more formalized evidence of such understanding but additionally ask students to evaluate the quality of the argument presented. The higher expectations for what students will absorb from reading with the grain in a more specialized class are evident in assumptions that students can write knowledgeably about discipline-specific research methods, with understanding of concepts such as external and internal reliability and validity and the meaning of terms such as *controlled experiment* and *correlational study*. Expectations for reading against the grain—i.e., providing a critical evaluation—reside in the task to identify "potential biases, confounds, unclear presentation, [and] at least two lingering questions." Since scientific advances depend on such critique, offering repeated practice in it as part of regular reading assignments—individually, in groups, and with professorial feedback—would aid in deepening mastery of disciplinary epistemologies.

Learning to Read Biochemistry

Understanding the subject matter, methods, and rhetoric of a scientific research article well enough to provide a persuasive critique of the argument or findings is a hallmark of expertise, and this precise ability was targeted as a pedagogic goal by an instructor of Biochemistry II. In this case, Bryan Spiegelberg's assignment sequence was motivated by his desire to develop in students the skills and confidence not just to articulate the substance of a study but to evaluate its strengths and weaknesses in design, execution, and presentation. His own experience had been buttressed by survey data showing that students habitually rely on researchers' interpretations of their data and routinely fail to test verbal explanations against graphical representations. Further, he "realized that many reading assignments tend to enable this tendency to avoid struggling with complex data" ("A Focused Assignment" 1–2).

The biochemistry interventions, like those in the psychology class, entail careful structure and multiple iterations. In this case students must not only understand a paper's overall problem, hypothesis, methods, and rhetorical strategies but must practice deep analysis by closely critiquing the representation of and explanation for a single figure in the paper. Like the instructions for the article dissections in the psychology class, the questions provided by the biochemistry professor offer students a scaffold for building comprehension of how parts of the paper relate to the whole and also the relationship of the text to a larger conversation (Spiegelberg 3). Hence the meta-reading aspect of the assignment is prominent: "Rather than diving in to the interpretation of the figure, students are first asked to take a step back and describe the logic of the experimental strategy itself," a step that requires "deep" reading and is "often the most difficult part of the assignment," sometimes prompting further research or consultation with the professor.

The sequence begins with each student addressing the "So what?" question (per Graff, *Clueless* ch. 8) by using "review articles and, perhaps, popular scientific literature" to identify a protein of interest, describing its importance and potential significance. Students also identify three research articles relevant to their selected protein and must thus focus on the difference between primary and secondary literature. Once they have reached the stage of delving into the figure analysis, the part-to-whole connections remain prominent, as students must carry out the following tasks:

- Paraphrase the experimental strategy chosen by the researchers and show how and why it is applied in this instance.
- Explain all the variables and their representation on graph axes and account for variations among different panels in a visual display.
- Use their own analytic skills as well as the authors' explanations to interpret data.
- Identify and evaluate the experimental controls, using this information to identify "alternative explanations . . . being tested."
- Close the loop by explaining how their interpretation of the experiment "fits in the hypothesis or overall thrust of the paper that they described in their analysis of the 'introduction'" (4).

Repeated iterations of this assignment, using papers related to the syllabus topics and complemented by oral presentations to the class, had two sorts of positive effects: students performed better on test questions requiring analysis of data not previously encountered, thus suggesting increasing expertise in a discipline-specific skill, and students reported high satisfaction with the structured reading-analysis assignments, calling it, e.g., "very useful," a "great experience," "helpful [in teaching me] how to efficiently read and interpret scientific papers" (4). One student, a science major in the honors program, told the professor that these exercises were truly eye-opening and wished they had begun in lower-level courses.

In looking at all three sets of assignments—in first-year composition as taught by my colleague, in psychology, and in biochemistry—we can see their hierarchical connection. Each, in its way, is teaching students what might be considered "generic" skills deployed by scientists in gaining information from research papers, but at different levels of specificity and expertise. The stepped assignments provided by all of the instructors redirect students from what might be a more familiar type of close reading invited by narrative genres and commonly used for literary analysis, moving them instead toward the kinds of selective reading performed by scientists. Interestingly, the specific data-analysis and evaluative skills that are the focus of the biochemistry course are consonant with the findings of Cynthia Shanahan and her colleagues that chemists tend to see "the graphic and prose elements as usefully separable in science text" because these elements "include overlapping but different information, and that to read such material properly it [is] essential to be able to cognitively 'translate' or 'transform' the information from one form to another" (419). While the same students might not take both the psychology course and the biochemistry course, a first-year grounding in genre awareness with practice at the appropriate level, supplemented by additional exposure to the relevant practices in the major's prerequisites, could provide a strong meta-reading foundation for all students. In such a context, students are likely to experience later upper-level challenges as a reinforcement and extension of prior habits rather than as an introduction to something new.

Learning to Read History

In considering the learning objectives for Biochemistry II, Bryan not only listed the "what" of the course, i.e., the topics to be studied—"including bioenergetics, DNA metabolism, protein synthesis and degradation, and basics of signal transduction"—but also pondered the "how," which meant focusing on high-level reading skills. While the textbook would serve to introduce subject matter, he made clear that the course "is focused on reading and interpreting data" and the "deeper learning" to be gained from expert analysis of primary and secondary literature in the field. Since such learning outcomes are desired by many instructors across the curriculum, it did not surprise me to find that Brooke Hunter, a professor of history, defined her classroom challenge in similar ways:

> In Seminar in Historiography, an upper-level class for majors, students must learn to read as historians do. This means not only identifying and evaluating the thesis, but also recognizing the author's purpose and methodology, situating the work in the larger body of scholarship and using the work to provide ideas

> for further research. This kind of critical reading is required for successful capstone work. Yet students struggle with the basic identification of these key elements of historical scholarship. How can I teach students to "read like a historian" more effectively? (*BRIDGE Participant Examples/ Brooke Hunter*)

Although this seminar was intended to foster competence in senior-level research projects, assessment of the capstones revealed widespread weaknesses in students' ability to engage in the specified aspects of reading. As a result, Brooke modified her seminar, introducing measures to increase students' accountability for the necessary sorts of critical analysis. These included the following assignments:

- a 250-word précis of an article, perhaps using very minimal quotation but preferably none;
- an 800-word book review in which students summarized the writer's main argument and methods for supporting it, explained the writer's contribution to an ongoing area of inquiry, and evaluated the persuasiveness of the argument based on the use of evidence;
- article worksheets focusing on the same skills and including a table keyed to each section of the article with boxes for main ideas, evidence (not just sources), and comments about evidence or approach.

Questions to be considered included some that transcend traditional close reading and invite reading against the grain:

- Could the same evidence be used to support a different conclusion?
- Is the argument weakened by questionable or inadequate evidence? What makes it questionable? Why is it inadequate?
- Can the conclusions of this study be generalized? If so, how far? If not, why not?

Overall assessment of the interventions was conducted via a pretest and a posttest. For the pretest, students were given the introduction and conclusion to an article from the *William and*

Mary Quarterly, "The 'Tragicall Historie': Cannibalism and Abundance in Colonial Jamestown" by Rachel B. Herrmann, and asked to annotate this excerpt for specified elements—topic, significance of the subject and the author's purpose, evidence of relation to other relevant sources, method or approach (study design), and thesis, i.e., the answer to the central research question—and then to write up their analysis. The posttest asked the same questions based on a different article, with the addition of a requirement that students show how subsections relate to the overall argument of the paper and consider whether and why the evidence as presented is "convincing."

Identifying Disciplinary Challenges

These elements are strikingly similar to those in the scaffolding supplied in the psychology and biochemistry courses discussed above, but with some important differences relevant to discipline-based practices that are not intuitive to novices in the given field. Budding scientists might not be in the habit of thinking of a scientific research report as a kind of argument needing interrogation. The issue for novice historians is more contextual: when confronted with different representation of the same facts, they are likely to overlook the role of cultural frames, individual values, and varying philosophies. In the seminar, ten out of thirteen students, despite prior work in history, said they had "no" or "basic" knowledge of the term *historiography*. Some "had no idea," "had never heard" the term, or had heard it but were never asked to practice the expert moves entailed. As might be expected, therefore, selection and use of sources were central considerations in Brooke's scaffolding, and questions related to choices of historiographical approach required that students infer quite a bit from the rhetoric of the article rather than pursue further research on the topic at this point.

Readers of history, as Timothy Shanahan and Cynthia Shanahan ("What Is Disciplinary Literacy") have observed, must focus more on the potential bias of the author than do readers of scientific literature: "Our interviews with chemists have shown that they do rely on author but more as a topical or quality screen when determining which texts to read. . . . Once reading begins, unlike the historians, however, scientists try to focus their attention specifically on the text" (11). Because there is less consensus on historiographical approach than on scientific method, students in the history seminar needed to be alert to the kinds of arguments being constructed and take cues from the text to build a rhetorical frame of the sort described by Haas and Linda Flower, so that they might even "*recognize an important claim that was never explicitly spelled out in the text*" (180, emphasis in original). Brooke's instructions to students demonstrated awareness of this challenge. In asking for an explanation of how an article assigned for analysis fits into an existing scholarly conversation or body of research, she noted: "As a beginning researcher you may feel that you lack the experience and knowledge to make such judgments. But a careful review of the article should enable you to comment on many aspects of a scholarly work. Focus on the author's aims/claims in the introduction and notes." The mention of footnotes is also an indication of disciplinary epistemologies, connected to sourcing and uses of evidence. In advising students on how to undertake the critique aspect of the review, Brooke again emphasized the relation of historical argument to evidentiary choices: "Focus on whether the thesis is supported by the evidence[;] . . . use specific examples to support your claims. Do not neglect the notes!!" Results, while encouraging, were mixed; trend lines were positive but indicated a need for additional work. For example, "Two-thirds of the students failed to articulate the thesis on the pretest, while one-third of the students still failed to identify the thesis on the posttest." Some students continued to confuse historiographical claims with a paper's primary argument, indicating that they were still struggling to identify the research question.

Teaching students to read like disciplinary experts is best regarded as a team effort that requires the vertical integration of skills within the major. To such a project Brooke's individual efforts have made a great contribution, inspiring her departmental colleagues to help students "practice 'reading like a historian' in every course and not just in seminars [since] only through repetition and practice will 'reading like a historian' become a habit of mind for our majors" (*BRIDGE Participant Examples/Hunter* 5–6). Exemplary in this regard is the work of Anne Osborne, chair of the History Department, who has composed detailed instructions for critical reading and accurate summary-writing—guiding students in developing a "map" of the text's rhetorical structure, and helping them compare the demands of textbooks with those of historical scholarship as well as distinguish "description" from "interpretation" and "scope" from "theme." In moves that recall some elements of Mariolina Salvatori's "difficulty papers" ("Reading"), Anne prompted students in her 200-level course The Craft of History to confront challenges rather than avoid or dismiss them:

> If despite a genuine attempt to grapple with the piece, including reading it at least twice, you do not understand it, bring in as much of the required information as possible together with specific questions on the aspects you do not understand. Be prepared to show what you understand and precisely what points are still unclear to you, and show how you have grappled with possible meanings.

At a workshop designed to help faculty imagine an integrative curricular approach, Brooke outlined departmental learning objectives for history majors at various stages. For example, in a 100-level course, students should "be introduced to historical questions" and "read and summarize historical scholarship, making explicit connections between evidence and argument"; in a 200-level course, "identify historical questions" and "practice historiography skills by assessing and evaluating scholarship, identifying arguments and use of sources"; in a 300-level course, "develop own historical questions" and "locate and select appropriate primary and secondary sources to construct an argument in a mini research project"; for a capstone project, use all of the previously practiced skills to "select a historical problem to study," define strategies for addressing the question, and "use [discipline-grounded] methods to gather, sift, analyze, order, synthesize, and interpret evidence in support of an argument." Clearly, the benefits to be derived from teaching reading across the curriculum can be multiplied within departments by collaborative efforts at scaffolding meta-reading, and the writing to which it is essential, at every level of course challenge. (For examples of Anne Osborne's reading-support instruction sheets for two history course levels, see Appendix 2.)

Using Textbooks in Science, History, and Law: Helping Students Take Charge

Professors in all of the disciplines discussed so far use textbooks only minimally or as adjuncts to other materials—naturally so, since their intent is to increase disciplinary expertise in deep analysis of authentic sources in the field. Textbooks typically distill knowledge without accounting much, if at all, for its derivation, thus masking the rhetoric and epistemology of the discipline being "covered." As literacy specialists have noted (see, e.g., Haas; Warren, "Rhetorical Reading as a Gateway"), textbooks are written as if anonymous and autonomous and thus do not invite meta-reading (Warren 394). Textbooks are often seen by students not as the products of human agency—i.e., as written by real people who made decisions that might differ from those of other experts about what to include and how to organize the material for novices—but rather as products of a nebulous, objective, impersonal "they," "the book," or "it" (Haas 46, 60–61). In their influential summary of research on how expert meaning-making differs from that of novices, John Bransford et al. note that "texts often present facts and formulas with little attention to the conditions under which they are most useful" (49). The arhetorical reading thus encouraged can have only minimal value in advancing important aspects of disciplinary expertise. A professional learning center tutor on my campus observed that by depending on textbooks, students "learn how to make lists, not how to read academic discourse."

And textbooks themselves seem increasingly designed to be marketable products rather than learning tools. I was amazed when, several years ago, the tutor showed me two CCSS-aligned high school textbooks—one for biology and one for English literature. In trying both to satisfy government guidelines and appeal to the imagined needs of a hypertext generation, the books have become enormous tomes (barely liftable, let alone conducive to study), chock-full of distracting apparatuses and elaborate graphic designs that overwhelm the page, scatter attention, and deflect focus from the core elements of a discipline. Using such texts in digitized forms would address the issue of heft but could amplify the potential for distraction and fragmentation. In contrast, the assignments detailed here, by giving students practice in reading primary literature as an expert would, expand the subject of the course to comprise not only the "information" aspects of the discipline but also how and why meaningful questions are determined, pursued through particular methods, and represented to target audiences—an emphasis long advocated by campus experts in SoTL and increasingly by external groups that focus on accountability (e.g., the Carnegie Foundation, the Lumina Foundation, the American Association of Colleges and Universities, and governmental accreditation bodies).

Another drawback of textbooks reported to me by BRIDGE participants is that textbook chapter divisions are often seen by students as bright dividing lines, inhibiting essential connection-making among topics. For example, Reed Schwimmer, a professor of geosciences, defined his main teaching challenge as overcoming the shortcomings of traditional textbooks as the basis for introductory classes:

> Earth science textbooks are generally weak at illustrating the connections both within and among chapter topics, and students tend to treat each chapter separately, not relating new material to concepts already covered. I don't want to enable this fragmentation by teaching to the artificial divisions of the book. How can I increase students' motivation to learn actively (not just memorize) and deepen their real understanding of interrelationships among Earth processes by changing both my course organization and my assessment methods? (*BRIDGE Participant Examples/Reed Schwimmer/ Project Question*)

To address this challenge, Reed created concept maps to illustrate for students the salient connections among parts of a chapter, among chapters of the book, and between the course concepts and the larger implications of the disciplinary matter, thus addressing the "So what?" question. As a next step, he designed exercises with various levels of scaffolding aimed at giving students practice in creating their own concept maps. Thus students were encouraged not to use the textbook as a series of discrete chapters to be read in a linear but disconnected way and to instead achieve the more complex, holistic perspective predicated on teasing out connections not immediately apparent to them but enabled by meta-reading strategies.

Phil Lowrey, a professor of biology, similarly defined his teaching goals as helping his students not only to distinguish the forest from the trees (i.e., understand the difference between concepts and data) but also to connect the two levels of content in the way that experts do. At the beginning of his project, he summarized the challenge this way:

> Biology Department faculty who teach the BIO-117 course [Evolution, Diversity, and Biology of Cells] use the same text and cover the same topics. We have all noticed that students tend to learn each topic in isolation rather than asking themselves, for example, how a topic covered in Week 2 of the course relates to a topic covered in Week 6 of the course. The major problem addressed by my BRIDGE project has been to find a way to help students make connections from one topic to another throughout the course[,] . . . to recognize that ultimately all of the topics covered are important in understanding the normal functioning of cells. (*BRIDGE Participant Examples/ Philip Lowrey*)

Influenced by "How Experts Differ from Novices" (in Bransford et al.), Phil then selected key principles to guide his assignment redesign and articulated strategies for enacting them. These principles included the expert habits of pertinent pattern-seeking, application of knowledge as conditionalized by contexts, and ability to communicate ideas clearly to peers. An important early intervention was the change from Angelo and Cross's one-sentence summary classroom assessment technique to a short answer integration and summary question (SAISQ), which encouraged the habits of applying concepts learned earlier to new material and considering how ideas currently being addressed relate to prior coursework. For example: "In class you have recently learned how glucose is broken down (oxidized) to form CO_2, NADH, $FADH_2$, and ultimately, ATP. As the energy currency of the cell, ATP is necessary for many processes. Use your knowledge from topics covered thus far in the course to describe at least *two* specific cellular processes dependent on ATP."

However, as the semester progressed, it occurred to Phil that he could gain additional insight into his students' evolving synthesis skills by designing a variation on the SAISQ. He therefore introduced an assignment that entailed reading an excerpt from a recent scientific paper and answering questions that tested basic comprehension, ability to apply course concepts, and understanding of implications. "My hunch," he wrote, "was that those students who had successfully synthesized information up to that point in the semester would do well, while those students who simply attempted to master information for the next quiz or exam would have difficulties." The example in Figure 1 is provided in his project summary. The abstract (on the left) comes from a paper published in the *Proceedings of the National Academy of Sciences.* The three questions on the right (labeled A, B, and C) require that students recall and explain specific biochemical concepts and processes included in the course, gather additional data from the article, and use prior knowledge to explain the new discovery and its significance. Because of its holistic nature—its integration of skills that aid "cold" reading comprehension—this task not only assesses students' essential competencies in key course objectives, but also helps them unpack the elements of an effective abstract.

As a nonscientist, I found the choice of article and excerpt particularly apt for two reasons: (1) The topic is fascinating and the finding surprising—the possibility of photosynthesis in deep-sea environments where there is virtually no light, and (2) while I could understand the general concepts rather well (i.e., the writing is clear and accessible to nonspecialists), I could not, without the expertise provided by Phil's course, answer any of the questions (except to speculate on what the findings mean for life on other planets [exciting!], since the writers give this away). Thus, the assignment seems beautifully calibrated to the level where students are expected to be at this point in their disciplinary education and designed to assess the application of cumulative knowledge and skills. With reference to the problems that David Coleman and Susan Pimentel aimed to redress via the CCSS, effective teachers will be able to mentor students in such reading without "preempting," "replacing," or "translating" the "contents" of the text (8).

In introductory history classes, the challenges will be somewhat different. If learning outcomes entail understanding of how

The abundance of life on Earth is almost entirely due to biological photosynthesis, which depends on light energy. The source of light in natural habitats has heretofore been thought to be the sun, thus restricting photosynthesis to solar photic environments on the surface of the Earth. If photosynthesis could take place in geothermally illuminated environments, it would increase the diversity of photosynthetic habitats both on Earth and on other worlds that have been proposed to possibly harbor life. Green sulfur bacteria are anaerobes that require light for growth by the oxidation of sulfur compounds to reduce CO_2 to organic carbon, and are capable of photosynthetic growth at extremely low light intensities. We describe the isolation and cultivation of a previously unknown green sulfur bacterial species from a deep-sea hydrothermal vent, where the only source of light is geothermal radiation that includes wavelengths absorbed by photosynthetic pigments of this organism.	A. This team of scientists uses the phrases "reduce CO_2 to organic carbon" and "oxidation of sulfur compounds". *Explain* what these phrases mean. B. Where are the organisms described here obtaining light? C. Using your knowledge of photosynthesis and other information that we have covered in the lectures on metabolism, explain what this team has discovered, and offer an explanation of the significance of their findings.

FIGURE 1. *Sample assessment of student comprehension of an abstract. (Abstract from Beatty, J. T., Overmann, J., Lince, M. T., Manske, A. K., Lang, A. S., Blankenship, R. E., Van Dover, C. L., Martinson, T. A., & Plumley, F. G. (2005). An obligately photosynthetic bacterial anaerobe from a deep-sea hydrothermal vent.* Proceedings of the National Academy of Sciences of the United States of America, 102, *9306–9310.)*

historical accounts are constructed, students must realize that textbooks themselves are interpretations and are thus subject to evaluation based on disciplinary criteria. Thus while textbooks as a genre are not naturals for critical reading, they can be fruitfully subjected to it as part of an introduction to historiography. This is why, in her design for the second half (1500 to the present) of a general-education course in world history, Brooke Hunter highlighted source evaluation as a central skill; created assignments and assessments requiring use of primary, secondary, and tertiary sources; and included two exercises called "Opening up the Textbook" (a strategy developed at Stanford University). Here is an excerpt from her syllabus, which makes clear that each text must be read in the context of others and that different genres require different sorts of reading:

As an introduction to the discipline of history, this course will help students learn to identify and evaluate three types of sources historians use to interpret the past: *primary* (direct evidence produced at the time being studied), *secondary* (interpretation of the past using primary sources), and *tertiary* (overviews synthesizing information gathered from secondary sources). Time is a defining element in differentiating between the types of sources.

Examples:

Primary	Secondary	Tertiary
World War I diary Photograph of life in the trenches World War I casualty list	Book on a World War I battle Journal article on trench warfare	Textbook chapter Encyclopedia article Website listing battle sites

Emphasis will be placed on:

1. The critical reading of *tertiary sources* to debunk the common misconceptions that textbooks are the final authority and that history is a set of known facts to be memorized. Putting textbooks in their rightful place, as one interpretation among many, is a key move for students.

2. The exploration of a range of *primary sources* in terms of form (e.g., written, visual) and cultural perspective to develop students' knowledge of the past, historical thinking skills, and global awareness. Beyond textbooks and document readers, the Web is a great resource for free materials.

3. Experience with *secondary sources* (e.g., journal articles, books) to introduce college students to reading and writing like historians.

[Exercises requiring critical analysis of the textbook include the following:]

1: Opening Up the Textbook on the Slave Trade (inspired by the National History Education Clearinghouse)

Read the 2015 *New York Times* article about a controversy over slavery in a Texas high school geography textbook. In the outrage, no one noted that the sentence [quoted] contained several more historical errors. Your task is to: (1) Use the map and quantitative data to identify three historical errors not mentioned in the article in the statement: "The Atlantic slave trade between the 1500s and the 1800s brought millions of workers from Africa to the southern United States to work on agricultural plantations." Your response should form a well-developed paragraph with a clear topic sentence and supporting evidence, which must include quantitative data. Use parenthetical citations, e.g., "(Strayer 672)." (2) Now that you have identified the errors, draft a new, historically accurate sentence to propose to the publisher. Include a paragraph addressed to the publisher with an explanation of your reasoning for what you included and what you left out of your sentence. (3) Final reflection: Based on this activity, explain the limitations of textbooks in a paragraph.

2: Opening Up the Textbook Document-Based Question on the Invasion of Nanking (from the Stanford History Education Group)

Write an essay explaining how and why Japanese and Chinese textbook accounts of the same historical event differ.

Rather than watering down the course, attention to the "how" as well as the "what" of a subject can, as the examples above illustrate, inspire faculty to create tasks for students that engage deeper understanding than would otherwise be harnessed. Using a textbook as one resource among many, showing students how to identify and evaluate the limitations of the textbook, and putting the book in explicit dialogue with other sources are among useful strategies for dealing with the drawbacks of a teaching tool one does not wish to entirely abandon.

Textbooks in "Applied" Courses: The Case of Business Law

In preprofessional or vocationally oriented courses, no less than in traditional academic courses, the notion that students will use the textbook effectively as a resource rather than as a collection of data can easily lead instructors astray; specialists habituated to the tacit expertise behind real-world practice may make unwarranted assumptions about the skills of students who are advanced in the major but entirely unschooled in the specialized focus of a required course. Such was the case with Susanna Monseau, an experienced attorney and professor of business law, who found that she had initially overestimated the ways that students would automatically adapt their reading habits to the constraints and frameworks of the discipline. Assuming at first, based on struggles in class discussion, that students were not reading the textbook before class, she administered mini-assessments, drawing on suggestions from Angelo and Cross such as "muddiest point" and one-sentence summaries to test comprehension, as well as "spot the principle" to test application of a legal principle in a new context. The responses revealed that students were not so much avoiding the reading as failing to understand it in ways that would allow the expected abstraction, synthesis, and application. Like her colleagues in other disciplines, she found that "once a topic had been covered in class, students appeared to consign it to an area of their brain that would only be reactivated shortly prior to any exam for cramming purposes" (533).

A disconnect between preconceptions or basic instincts, on the one hand, and legal principles, on the other, also hampered learning; for example, even after instruction in the relevant legal terms, concepts, and reasoning, "students would use 'gut reactions'" to assess liability and "would continue to assess and explain negligence based on their own opinions of the 'guilt' of the parties involved, rather than using the legal test" (534). Feedback from students revealed that novice reading habits were at the center of the problem. Crucially, the professor had wrongly assumed that students would use the textbook as a resource to support their inquiries; instead, as with the adult students who sought William Perry out for help in digesting all the assigned reading (see Chapter 3), they were reading in a linear, indiscriminate way, uncertain about the hierarchy of ideas. "The students . . . tended to read the book cover to cover, . . . since they did not know (as nonexperts) what were the important questions" (*BRIDGE Participant Examples/Susanna Monseau 3*). Having diagnosed the problem, Susanna crafted changes to encourage students to read and think the way lawyers do. First, she found a textbook organized thematically around legal issues related to a single industry so that students could more easily make connections among different aspects of the law. Then, attending to the meta aspects of reading like a lawyer, she provided advice on "active reading," wrote open-book quizzes to help students use the book efficiently before each meeting, and assigned case-summary drafts for use in class (534–35).

Liberated from the constraints and complications of a compendious textbook, Susanna could more effectively foster the critical skills of abstraction of big ideas and recognition of their relevance in new contexts. Because the new textbook comprised fewer cases, she took the opportunity to have students learn how to locate and summarize cases on their own, using their growing knowledge of legal citation and the federal court system. She selected cases with assignment design in mind, i.e., to enable increasingly complex and iterative tasks requiring discipline-based reading and writing. For example, *Ashcroft v. ACLU* (regarding availability of some internet sites to children) was used, in sequential assignments, to teach students to understand the logic of case citations, how to brief (summarize) a case, how a case moves through the court system, the role of the Supreme Court vis-à-vis the legislative branch, how precedents work, and how legal principles are applied to particular cases. Later in the semester the same case was used to illustrate principles of constitutional law regarding First Amendment rights and its value as a precedent when considered in different contexts. According to Susanna, "the beauty of using one case for the whole set of exercises was that students appreciated that the law was not a set of disparate concepts but [that] there were links between many legal areas and concepts . . . which could be embodied in the application of one decision" (535). In a sequence based upon another decision that had been appealed, students were guided in practicing legal reasoning in steps, e.g., drafting a well-supported complaint, using a fact pattern that they later learned was based on a real case; considering the basis for the actual decision and locating the appeal, which enabled them to compare the reasoning in their own documents to that in the real-world case; and, since the parties preferred not to return to trial court following the appeal decision, comparing the merits of litigation versus alternative dispute resolution.

To help students avoid drawing conclusions based on preconceptions, she assigned short readings on a controversial topic related to their study of each of three units and had students use these, along with independent research, for debates, with "sides" designated rather than chosen. Whether minds were changed or not, arguments had to be supported with legal reasoning. This multistage assignment helped students deal productively with controversy rather than evading it: "Previously . . . [they] would appear to accept either the instructor's views or those in the textbook in class, and would then revert to their own opinions, whether substantiated or not, in written assignments" (537).

While at first glance these exercises might seem too specialized to have relevance across the curriculum, I would argue otherwise. As I see it, the instructor's astute evaluation of students' needs dovetails precisely with commonly cited issues in both first-year writing classes and various discipline-based courses. In the context of my argument for RAC, what is most notable about this project, an exemplar of classroom research as explained by Angelo and Cross, is that the effort to increase disciplinary expertise was made manifest in a set of sequenced assignments focused on the varied aspects of meta-reading that I have addressed in earlier chapters and that are useful in courses across the curriculum. These aspects, which require re-envisioning the traditional role of the textbook as a source of information to be extracted, include:

- selecting the stance appropriate to the text at hand, per Louise Rosenblatt, by recognizing its genre and the contexts for its generation
- reading with a defined purpose and therefore possibly in a non-linear way, as advocated by Robert Kegan and Alice Horning, thereby using a text as a resource to be consulted rather than as a narrative or a list of facts to be digested indiscriminately
- distinguishing concrete evidence or examples from big ideas and guiding principles, i.e., deciding "where to put the manicules" (Horning, Jamieson)
- discerning the hierarchy of ideas in a text—connecting parts to one another and to the organizing principle of the document as a whole (many theorists—e.g., Iser, Rabinowitz, Horning, Kegan)
- using role-play or a lens (in this case, legal principles and precedents) to frame arguments not based on naïve opinions or gut reactions (Booth, Scholes, Perry, Wilner)

These skills also align perfectly with those specified in the most recent (2014) Council of Writing Program Administrators' "WPA Outcomes Statement for First-Year Composition," under "Critical Thinking, Reading, and Composing," as "foundational for advanced academic writing": Students should learn how to "separate assertion from evidence, evaluate sources and evidence, recognize and evaluate underlying assumptions, read across texts for connections and patterns, identify and evaluate chains of reasoning, and compose appropriately qualified and developed claims and generalizations."

It is notable that Susanna combined what might be regarded as low-level support exercises or even "spoon-feeding" elements, such as reading questions and low-stakes content quizzes, with rehearsal of sophisticated professional practices, such as writing briefs and applying precedents to new fact patterns. In balancing challenge with support, she helped students gain some confidence in grappling with unfamiliar content and rhetoric "so that class could be devoted to acquiring higher level thinking skills" (5). Without understanding the nature and effects of this instructor's interventions, casual observers of this class might consider the choice of a friendlier textbook merely a way to make the class simpler. However, it is apparent that the opposite was true—that in fact students were able to succeed in complex and authentic tasks that would not have been possible without the scaffolding designed to support discipline-grounded meta-reading of both the textbook and primary texts.

"Close" Reading Redux: Learning to Read Fiction

As noted in the earlier discussion of the Common Core State Standards for literacy and their association with New Critical interpretive approaches, the question of whether the text should be read as "autonomous" has been especially fraught in the field of literary studies. I have argued that students who are encouraged to practice close reading so as to focus only on "what lies within the four corners of the text" (Coleman and Pimentel 4)—as if the page were produced in a cultural and historical vacuum—are unintentionally deprived of practice in acquiring disciplinary expertise. College instructors of literature, even if they do not explicitly teach literary theory, often find they must devise ways to encourage reading that transcends a focus on themes, character appraisal, or personal connections. English professor Terra Joseph, who undertook a BRIDGE project designed to address this challenge, defined her students' novice tendencies as follows:

- *Assimilation:* Students want historical literary texts to say things with which they can agree. They then "rewrite" the ideas of the text to reflect their own ideological investments.
- *Rejection:* Students recognize historical difference and find it alienating. They struggle to fully understand how literary texts attempt to establish sympathetic identification to convey ideas.
- *Simplification:* Students generalize, assuming all writers of a given era must share similar views. Thus, they miss the complexity of ideas. (*BRIDGE Participant Examples/Terra Joseph*)

As Doug Brent persuasively illustrated in his study of how students undertake research-based writing, such tendencies inhibit a question crucial to critical reading: "When should I change my mind?" (13). Although the potential of literature to enhance critical analysis is often hobbled by the ease with which it can be used as a tool for engagement via easy identification with familiar characters or reduction to comfortable "themes," the study of literature actually offers especially rich meta-reading challenges and opportunities (an idea elaborated in Appendix 1).

However, its particularities as a discipline are perhaps more difficult to define both because the field of English studies as it has evolved over the past half century comprises a wider range of theory and epistemological practice than other disciplines and also because the texts that are the objects of study are evaluated not primarily by their consonance with events or natural phenomena but rather by the complexity and power of the experiences they are able to evoke. In the sciences, primary literature typically refers to research reports, and secondary literature to a range of other genres including review articles, popular translations of technical material for nonspecialists, and textbooks. Brooke Hunter's syllabus shows how historians distinguish primary, secondary, and tertiary literature. In literature classes, the focal point is the creative work, and secondary texts typically refer to interpretations and critiques. While rhetorical reading in any field requires an openness to having one's mind changed and thus to playing the role, even if unconsciously, of the author's intended audience, the difficulty of doing so is compounded when the text is not only historical but also itself an imaginative construction with a persona or narrator who cannot be identified with the author.

When students are naïve with regard to the demands on them that the rewards of reading good literature entail, their resistance to reading itself can be amplified. Many years ago, a difficult classroom experience forced me to deal on the spot with this reality. My challenge began when I assigned my composition class to read David Leavitt's "Territory," a short story about a gay man who brings his partner home to meet his mother. Some of the male students adamantly refused to read the story because they found its subject matter (previewed in an editor's note) offensive. I have detailed elsewhere my response to this unexpected rebellion against what I had imagined to be the authority of my syllabus ("Confronting Resistance"). What is important in this context is that it was through explicit role-playing that my students were able to cross the threshold from seeing literature as needing to be transparently affirmative of their closely held but largely unexamined beliefs to understanding the pleasures and psychic benefits of being taken into the world of an unfamiliar other. The key move I made, inspired by my training in a WAC program, was to ask the students—after I had persuaded them that the mere act of reading the story would imply nothing about their attitudes toward the events or characters portrayed—to assume the persona of either the protagonist or his mother, writing in a letter to the imagined character the thoughts and feelings that were too difficult to express face to face. The freedom to impersonate another human being whose conflicts and suffering are made real through artistic choices enabled students to play the narrative audience as they otherwise would not have been able to do. Peter Rabinowitz is surely correct in his assertion that "fiction is different from nonfiction, not because it has a different relation to literal truth . . . but because it calls on different conventions of reading" (Rabinowitz and Smith 24).

To foster expertise in these conventions in her Victorian literature class, Terra defined *close reading* as comprising the following:

- The ability to understand *what* is being said
- The ability to understand *how* a text may attempt to shape an intended reader's perspective using literary conventions (point of view, tropes, genre, motifs, etc.)
- The ability to understand *why* the text says what it does given its historical, cultural, and social contexts. *What is a text's intervention in an ongoing conversation?*

Her signature assignment, conceived to address these goals, is described below. In terms of meta-reading, this task was intended to give students practice in *synthesis,* defined by the professor as "the ability to position the writer's viewpoint in relation to the range of available perspectives in a given historical moment," and *evaluation,* defined as "the ability to anticipate historical readerly responses to a text given the same range of available perspectives."

> Creative Synthesis Assignment
>
> 1. Read the first installment of a serialized novel.
> 2. Write a 3- to 4-page *review* of the installment from the point of view of a *specific* Victorian reader. This reader may be (a) a writer we've read or (b) a character who appears in a work of fiction we've discussed.
> 3. Write a 3- to 4-page *rationale* explaining the choices you made when writing the review.
>
> In a brief prefatory note before your review, you should clearly identify who you imagine *your target audience* to be. Is this a private letter to a friend, family member, or fellow writer? Are you writing directly to the author of your serial novel? Do you intend to publish this review in a popular magazine for like-minded readers?

To prepare students, Terra modeled the process and devised ways for them to rehearse the steps. For example, she had them work together in class on developing a character analysis of Sissy Jupe from Dickens's *Hard Times* and then imagine, from Sissy's perspective, an evaluation of a character from another novel they were reading, Lady Audley from Mary Elizabeth Braddon's *Lady Audley's Secret*. The time spent on this collaborative effort proved worthwhile: "I was able to then and there critique impersonations that lacked some element of understanding." The next task for students was to work in groups to analyze another character, from whose perspective they would write a letter to Braddon. In line with my much earlier experience in a first-year class, the combination of role-playing and letter-writing encouraged a move toward reading that was both empathetic and yet detached enough to foster necessary critical distance.

In this case, because Victorian literature typically enrolls upper-level English majors, an added benefit was the creation of a *conversation between texts* (an intellectual move that we know is habitual to experts though usually not to students), including practice in a relevant literary style, which deepened understanding that in literature form is not separable from content. "I was quite impressed," Terra wrote,

> with the quality of writing in many of these letters, as in many cases [students] imitated not only types of arguments and perspectives of the selected characters/writers, but also the tone and style. This was an important activity for showing students how tone and style contribute to characterization, and thus the way language is inextricable from textual meaning.

Terra concluded her course with a project intended to sustain the kinds of independent and connected thinking encouraged by the creative synthesis assignment: Students were asked to identify a topic of interest emerging from the course (e.g., Victorian fiction and science, empire and adventure fiction, the industrial novel and Marxism) and write a proposal for an independent study with rigorous specifications. The proposal had to include a four- to five-page rationale (supported by secondary texts) for the topic choice as well as an annotated bibliography, comprising at least five sources, of the relevant primary literature. Students also had to provide a justification for the selection, including the anticipated learning outcomes.

Literacy experts emphasize that reading in all disciplines always already implies the construction of a rhetorical frame that depends on understanding content and methods that transcend the four corners of the text at hand. Whether a scientific report, a work of historiography, or a novel, "a text may draw from, extend, or refute a myriad of other texts, whether those texts are directly cited or not" and "a text may also be supported by situational, cultural, or historical contexts" (Haas 48). In the area of academic discourse, we would be justified in replacing the contingency of "may" with "will." With that cross-discipline commonality granted, however, we must not lose sight of the way classroom assignments that support rhetorical reading reflect particular discourse conventions. Many assignments in the humanities aim to preempt the novice habits identified by my colleague Terra Joseph: assimilation, rejection, and oversimplification. As important, they cultivate toleration, and even appreciation, of irresolvability; in this, perhaps, lies their essential underlying difference from the science-based assignments discussed above, which presume the progress of knowledge toward increasing understanding of natural laws and interactions. The discipline of history, it might be argued, lies somewhere between the sciences and the humanities on a continuum of "closure," since the discovery of new evidence might enable a reevaluation of a particular historiographical account relative to another. The legal training fostered by Susanna Monseau, which developed in students the capacity to compose differing yet compelling arguments based on the same fact patterns, similarly depends on elements of narrative bound by rules and information.

Content Coverage and Critical Thinking

Students' nimbleness in adapting to the wide range of readerly and writerly roles expected across the curriculum is a quality that will serve them well throughout their undergraduate careers and into the world of work. To the extent that professors can nurture this dexterity, we will be doing students an essential service, and much of the nurture lies in the possibilities of formative feedback. When each assignment is part of a sequence designed to build skills over time, students who receive constructive evaluations can improve over the semester. On the instruction side, professors find that they can more effectively distinguish among levels of student performance, identify particular areas of strength and weakness for each student, and tie the rationale for their evaluations more clearly to course objectives; as important, they can learn where and how the assignment sequence or other aspects of their curricula need to be refined. In considering outcomes in her psychology class, Steph Golski noted that "in those instances where performance fell short of expectations, the various assessments ensured [that] such performance could be appropriately distinguished from best practices." In biochemistry, Phil Lowrey used the somewhat disappointing initial responses to his summary-and-integration questions to reflect on possible reasons for his students' relative weakness at these tasks—"Perhaps this in part owes to my first attempt to write these types of questions (question-design issues), or maybe students have not seen similar questions in their other courses (novel, unfamiliar question format)"—and, rather than retreat from the challenge, redoubled his efforts: "This suggests to me that students need more assistance/practice in making connections among the topics as the semester progresses." Terra Joseph, realizing that she had overestimated her English majors' background and expertise in research design, decided to revise the assignment prompt for the independent-study proposal "to be clearer about the use of secondary sources and about the types of primary sources that should appear on the list of readings." In business law, Susanna Monseau did not see as much improvement as hoped for in students' ability to connect legal principles with fact patterns but attributed this outcome partly to her inclusion of too much material in a single course (a common tendency in first iterations of course revision): "So many interesting and relevant legal cases could be found to illustrate topics and concepts that the course probably still contained too many staged, case-based assignments" (538). However, the sequence of exercises she assigned, particularly the role-play entailed in the debate assignments, indicated a significant advance in critical thinking, as students wrote more than the required minimum in explaining how and why their study of affirmative action had caused them to rethink prior beliefs and perhaps change their minds on an issue about which they had previously held strong (if unexamined) opinions (538).

Overall, the assignments designed by these faculty members reflect a keen awareness of disciplinary epistemologies, reinforcing research findings that domain knowledge is essential to critical thinking (see, e.g., Hirsch; Willingham, "Critical"; Wexler). Somewhat paradoxically, such instruction requires not only humility, patience, and an authentic respect for students, but also a willingness to relinquish a prior understanding of what "course content" means and how much content a course must comprise. Professors of all disciplines who undertake the challenges of assignment redesign to cultivate expert practices and habits of mind are likely to experience increased tension for a while: in focusing on disciplinary epistemologies, they will be unable to "cover" as much material. This tension afflicts not only instructors in STEM and preprofessional courses, which are often conceived as hierarchically related such that one course must explicitly prepare students for more advanced concepts in the next, but also those who teach liberal arts and humanities classes. In reflecting on the benefits of her meta-reading assignments in Victorian literature, Terra admitted that the sense of discomfort is not easily resolved: "I suspect I will always struggle between the desire to emphasize content knowledge and the need to think less about the [amount of] reading and more about what students will *do with* the reading." However, if privileging content per se (usually defined as the amount of material or number of topics for which students are responsible) over the inculcation of expert habits were such a good idea, there would be little limit to what we could or should try to stuff into a syllabus. As biologist and SoTL expert Craig E. Nelson has argued, the presumed "tradeoff," regardless of discipline, is "actually illusory" ("On the Persistence"). We must remind ourselves that being subjected to as much information as possible in as short a time as possible is not how people learn (Zull). In my experience, faculty do often come to see, especially through assignment design that supports meta-reading, how less can be more. Each of the professors whose work is excerpted here, and many others who participated in the cross-disciplinary workshops, came to appreciate this insight, aided by the support and encouragement of colleagues pursuing similar objectives.

Each project was pursued independently, but the collegial feedback given at every stage (through the monthly seminars) proved vital. Such workshops, where faculty are asked in collaborative settings to think purposefully about how their curriculum design conveys the relationship between content and habits of mind, are bound to be stimulating and useful. While semester- or even yearlong programs like BRIDGE offer the luxury of recursive experimentation and the formation, over time, of a faculty learning community, programs that are condensed and concentrated can also make a difference. Several years ago, as a supplement to BRIDGE, I designed a three-day workshop called Diving Deep in the Disciplines, which entailed a before-and-after exercise intended to surface the generally tacit assumptions made by academic experts, as follows:

> **Preworkshop Exercise** (Time will be set aside during the workshop for individuals to share their thoughts, first with disciplinary partners and then with the whole group.)
>
> *Identify the following:*
>
> - Epistemological and conceptual assumptions for practitioners of your discipline
> - Methodological assumptions for practitioners of your discipline
> - Fundamental questions for practitioners of your discipline
> - Tacit habits of mind for practitioners of your discipline
> - Common misconceptions/novice habits of mind

The idea was to help faculty backward-design and scaffold their assignments so that a focus on content coverage would not trump attention to students' learning. To help jump-start my colleagues' thinking, I shared my own attempt to articulate ideas and assumptions usually left unspoken. In Appendix 3 I have juxtaposed my list with a document produced at the end of the workshop by chemistry professor Danielle Jacobs Duda. Unexpectedly, Danielle's list led to a fascinating discussion of how terms such as *theory*, *hypothesis*, *law*, and *model* are used in various disciplines and of the challenges for students who must infer any variations on their own. Like Brooke Hunter's definition of student learning objectives at each level, brainstorming lists such as these, even if generated in a cross-disciplinary setting, could then be used to inspire discussions *within* departments. And since understanding the concept of disciplinary epistemologies, as discussed in Chapter 3, is essential to reading in college, I would suggest that this sort of work, in its melding of individual and collaborative elements, has the potential to benefit students at all levels. In this way instructors from all campus domains can work together to redress the unconscionable equity gap that may otherwise be inexorable.

Chapter Six

The Ethics of Teaching Reading Across the Curriculum

Equity and Excellence (or, Why Is Change So Hard?)

In considering how to persuade faculty members that instruction in rhetorical reading is critical in every discipline, one is led to contemplate the history of writing across the curriculum (WAC) and writing in the disciplines (WID). As documented by David Russell in his curricular history of writing in the disciplines, the strains of resistance to incorporating writing instruction into classes across the university have entailed a sense that skills, as opposed to content, ought not to be the subject of instruction beyond the first year. Noting the "gatekeeping" function served by general-education composition courses for much of the twentieth century, Russell cites the role of increasing specialization and professionalization as a dynamic inimical to the integration of discourse conventions in disciplinary pedagogies: "Disciplines never acquired a conscious knowledge of the rhetorical conventions they used daily and expected their students to use, for these conventions were so bound up with the activity of the discipline and were acquired so subtly in the learning of the discipline itself that they were rarely thought of as writing instruction" (17). Aspiring to excellence in higher education, it was assumed, required weeding out students who might make it through the first doors of academia but could not unconsciously acquire the tacit habits of experts.

Those who delivered this sort of curriculum naturally found appealing the notion that writing is a generic skill and could therefore be taught separately in a foundational course, thereby addressing remedial needs. The necessary skills, according to this assumption, would naturally be transferred and adapted to disciplinary cultures, an idea that, as noted earlier, has been debunked by both research and experience. Yet it has always been easier to foster the fiction than to address the reality, and, because of this "myth of transience" (Rose 355ff.; Russell 7), inequities have often been reinforced rather than mitigated. It is indeed easy to see how such a myth, based on elitist assumptions about the university's mission as well as a conveniently defined role for rhetorical instruction in the curriculum, would enhance the Matthew effect. While acknowledging the obstacles to reconfiguring higher-education pedagogies as sites where writing is "structurally linked to the values, goals, and activities of disciplines" (301–07), Russell argues for the continued development of WAC as a means of reform.

Needless to say, the tension between equity and excellence continues to play out vividly in the current environment of higher education. Gerald Graff has helped define the inadequacies of the mixed messages conveyed to students by a curriculum that is fractured and disparate within an environment that demands, without necessarily teaching, an understanding that arguments of specific types underlie all of academic discourse and a meta-understanding of disciplinary similarities and differences (*Clueless* ch. 3). Like the "disciplinary secrets" addressed by Gregory Colomb's illustration of how evaluation of students' writing is shaped by sophisticated yet unspoken discipline-based expectations, the culture of academia as analyzed by Graff highlights the distance between theory and practice in pedagogy and emphasizes how this discrepancy amplifies the achievement gap among our students. While rejecting the "cynical" argument that academic structures are designed to sustain elitism—"to maintain high levels of social inequality [in order to] keep the cultural capital of literate public discourse out of the grubby hands of the riffraff"—Graff argues that it is up to faculty and academic administrators to demonstrate the inaccuracy of this claim by reconfiguring their policies and practices (14). As one such desirable change, Graff proposes composition classes taught by faculty across the curriculum to foster students' sense of the connection between discourse and epistemology as well as a sense of convergence and divergence among various fields (78). We now know that the success of such an across-the-curriculum effort would entail an equal focus on reading.

Given such a strong confluence of evidence regarding the ways in which we could better address the needs of our students, why is the distance from theory to practice seemingly insurmountable? Why, we might ask, given the trends of the last four decades—the rise of composition and rhetoric as a distinct field of study and credentialing, the increasing respect on many campuses for the scholarship of teaching and learning, the proliferation of journals dedicated to higher-education pedagogy, and the increasing recognition that traditional methods will no longer be adequate—do we still seem to be engaged more in hand-wringing than in consensus building regarding next best steps? I would like to propose several answers to this question, using as a lens the theories expounded in the 1970s by Chris Argyris and Donald Schön (later elaborated; see, e.g., Schön, *The Reflective Practitioner*) to explain why strategies for addressing the issue are not intuitive and how progress might be pursued.

The nature of professional practice in general does not foster the needed research or the systematic application of theory to practice. Often, professional practice has not been theorized at all, preventing systematic investigation; this is as true of the professoriate as of other professionals and perhaps even more so because complete autonomy in the classroom is so highly valued. Thus "professionals often function without considering what they have learned from previous situations" (Argyris and Schön 144). I would add that even when professors do consider what they have learned, they are often uncertain, in the absence of a working theory or structure for responsive intervention, about what the next steps should be. As Chris Anson has argued, this challenge may be especially acute in the field of rhetoric and composition, and his analysis of the problem, while directed at writing pedagogies, is equally pertinent to the support of rhetorical reading. Without more, and more systematic, research, as well as an openness to change based on what we discover, we will never move toward what all professional fields require: "some common understandings based on what we can know, with some level of certainty, about what we do" (Anson, "Intelligent Design" 12).

The culture of academia inhibits the necessary collaboration. It is a striking irony that many faculty members who deplore what they regard as their students' failure to make important connections within and between courses are themselves great defenders of their own isolation from and independence of their peers and of other disciplinary approaches. Eschewing in the domain of pedagogy the traditions governing the pursuit of the empirical sciences, professors have not valued public peer review with regard to their teaching practices; rather than tested, shared, and critiqued, pedagogic practice is widely regarded as "private, tacit, and ephemeral" (Argyris and Schön 144). As a result, reports of findings can appear to be not so much cumulative and accretive as incidental and anecdotal. Despite the proliferation of teaching-and-learning centers over the past decades, the "pedagogic solitude" that Lee Shulman deplored in 1993 has not been sufficiently remediated. In this and other ways, "norms for behavior substitute for knowledge" (Argyris and Schön 28), and the potential for collaboration is undermined by competition (e.g., for high student ratings on course evaluations). Conventional institutional practices thus often work to sustain the untested status quo, inhibiting the very kind of classroom experimentation required for improvement.

Testing theories in practice can feel too risky to undertake. The demands of "action research" are counter to the training of many academics, and because of the need for both skepticism and commitment, such inquiry is often resisted. Action research means dealing with a complex of variables, many uncontrollable, and can therefore feel uncomfortable as a methodology. In the 1970s, Argyris and Schön described "double-loop learning," in which one not only learns from experience but also reframes the assumptions and theories governing one's behavior. Such learning does not come naturally, however: "The inherent variability of the behavioral world gives us more information than we can handle, so we value a stable world-picture, being predictable, and being able to predict. We work at maintaining the constancy of our theories-in-use" (Argyris and Schön 16–17). Thus familiar routines are privileged over needed changes.

Motives for maintaining a theory-in-use may include more than the structural elitism discussed by Russell and by Graff, more than a desire to evade the complications of addressing messy multivariate problems, and more than a natural tendency to affirm the goodness or at least adequacy of one's current practices. To better understand the nature of resistance to change in this context, it is worth considering the seeming paradox identified by Richard Arum and Josipa Roksa in their 2011 study of "limited learning on college campuses": that the institutions whose stated mission is to advance learning and understanding are stymied by a culture that inhibits such a purpose. The reason is that each set of stakeholders—students, parents, professors, administrators, government funding agencies—can fulfill their goals (whether a diploma, social experiences, research, retention numbers, financial solvency, advancement of knowledge that supports selected interests) without making student learning primary. "Limited learning on college campuses is not a crisis because the institutional actors implicated in the system are receiving the organizational outcomes that they seek, and therefore neither the institutions themselves nor the system as a whole is in any way challenged or threatened" (125). In recent years, however, looming pressure exerted by external stakeholders such as the federal government and regional accreditation agencies, along with increasing employer dissatisfaction with the skills offered by many college graduates and rising tuition costs that mean burdensome long-term debt for many graduates, has intensified the threat and the challenge.

Teacher as Student

No less than students, faculty need to continually ask themselves, "When should I change my mind?" The classroom-intervention strategies summarized in Chapter 5 offer examples of faculty open to changing their minds and their habits and to reconceiving truths that no longer seem to be serving them so well. This move requires of faculty what we desire in students—an empathic imagination, the ability to inhabit the perspective of others. Such agility, often honed in scholarly pursuits as one enters ongoing dialogues that require a fair restatement of alternative viewpoints, is not always as habitual in the teacher-student relationship. Often only vaguely discernible in the background of graduate training and of many campus cultures, including those of institutions labeled "teaching universities," the practice of assuming the persona of novices can make important differences for learning, as exemplified by the sample SoTL projects derived from the BRIDGE faculty-development program. In rethinking their assumptions about what students know and can do as apprentices in a field, faculty envisioned themselves in the students' position, thus demonstrating the intellectual versatility and spirit of inquiry they wanted to encourage in their classes. Here we may be reminded that William Perry's course in reading (originally designed for adult students) did not "aim to improve their reading as they had defined it but to suggest a whole different idea of what reading is" (Kegan 280). It may not be too much to say that the changes the faculty made in their syllabi and assignments reflected a change in their fundamental conceptions of what teaching is, a shift that depended not merely on tips for improvement but on a reconfiguration of their pedagogical identities. Helping our students gain a sense of their possible selves depends on instructors doing likewise.

While many colleges have programs designed to enhance the first-year experience, I have found that special attention given to faculty involved in the academic aspects of that experience can be an excellent investment of institutional support, enhancing pedagogic know-how, morale, and collegiality. For several years I facilitated a three-day summer workshop for faculty who frequently teach first-year students (FFTF), in which participants (both adjuncts and full-timers, some relatively new to teaching, others quite experienced) discussed assigned readings and planned course and assignment redesigns to be implemented during the fall or spring semester. Feedback from faculty participants reflected appreciation for both the content of the "course" and the opportunity to collaborate across disciplines:

> I found Leamnson's point about imagination particularly relevant: "Doing hypothetico-deductive reasoning requires a suspension of disbelief—imagination. . . . Part of our job will be to reinvigorate the imagination if we expect new students to understand arguments based on contingencies" [46].

> I have rethought the balance between accountability and support, and have reworked my model of scaffolding in the hopes of increasing confidence and empowering my students. . . . Some of the more valuable ideas that I am borrowing from the readings and from the group are: "less is more"; developing effective reading skills and teaching note taking strategies ("notes are something they make not something they take" [Leamnson 62]); providing an audience for the assignments I create; . . . the idea of "entering the conversation" and locating controversy in the field; the asking of essential questions that promote independent thinking and expression of ideas; . . . and, to sum it all up, the "Why can't they just give me what I asked for" [presentation] pushed me to look at my syllabus, course content, assignments and expectations and to revise them.

> [To] borrow the idea of generalization that we work so hard to foster in our students, I think that the faculty that participate in the workshop should, on at least a quarterly basis, reflect, share and brainstorm with faculty in their respective department to foster a university that prides itself on "best practice."

These observations reveal how much commonly remains undeclared or even unconscious in our formulation of what students need and expect from us. In his valuable conception of a holistic developmental theory and its application to teaching and learning, Robert Kegan has observed the fault lines between what our assignments specify, what we really mean, and how adolescents and young adults are likely to interpret our instructions and advice:

> We would like them to understand that when we told them to think for themselves, we did not really mean "be sincere, use your own opinions," but that's what it means to them. We want them to hear "think for yourself" as something more like "take charge of the concepts of the course and independently bring them to an issue of your own choosing." They suppose that, too, would be more what we call "self-directed." But as far as they are concerned, every single thing they are doing that we would prefer they do otherwise is highly self-directed! It is just that the "self" they are directing is not the one we want! (285)

It strikes me that this analysis also has relevance to contexts of faculty development. As the comments quoted above suggest, a stimulating, respectful, and collaborative environment can offer the conditions for meaningful reconception of purpose and design. Teachers, no less than students, must be supported in crossing bridges that seem to lead to unfamiliar and therefore uncomfortable places. In the spirit of Kegan's challenge to be a better reader of our students' needs, I now return to the moments described earlier—classroom reading responses that left me dismayed, and surprised at my dismay—and attempt to see them through a different set of lenses.

Rereading Scenes of Reading

Scene One: A First-Year Composition Class

In reflecting on the student who defined *candid* to mean "fake," I regret pressing for clarification of an answer that was so evidently off base. I might have realized that, for this student, reading was still a matter of decoding and defining words, and that the habit of doing so acontextually was so strong that it prevailed even in the presence of explicit instructions to try to infer the writer's intentions based on audience and purpose. A prospective major in digital media, this student might have been fairly well attuned to the discursive requirements of everyday communication platforms. But higher education requires more, and the deepened expertise does not come naturally. Noting "the powerful ways that young people already use to negotiate multiple discourse communities and literacies in their lives," Elizabeth Moje reports results from her own research suggesting the limits of this adaptability: "[Y]ouths' transfer of proficient skills from popular texts that interest them—and for which they have constructed extensive domain knowledge in practice—is compromised when they find themselves confronted with texts for which they have little sophisticated domain knowledge and for which they have little context or purpose" (104). As teachers respond to this need, insight and understanding must temper the impulse to unpack naïve habits on occasions that might take even experienced instructors by surprise. So my pursuit of the student's thought process in real time was not my finest teaching moment. Nonetheless, there was benefit to be derived from the content-rich curriculum and the assignments designed to stretch deep-literacy skills. As I have argued, such students (of whom there are many) especially need and deserve exposure to difficult texts from the beginning of and throughout their college careers, with explicit support in rhetorical reading. And by choosing enduring and influential texts, we help them develop sophistication in the domain knowledge and contexts necessary for success in the academy and in the kinds of careers they seek.

Scene Two: A First-Year Honors Seminar

With regard to the student who dealt with Frost's "Design" unsatisfactorily, I have earned a different sort of mea culpa. Aware that because of campus demographics this class often enrolls students of deep religious faith, I should have known that a poem written as a provocation to personal and community convictions might be too much for a first-semester student to contend with. Indeed, I had reason to know this from papers submitted in prior semesters. I got what I asked for. Frost's poem not only raises existential questions already answered by mainstream religions (is the universe governed by a divine intelligence and, if so, is such a power both omnipotent and benevolent?) but further provokes readers by suggesting that the evidence darkly opposes conventional answers and also intimating that the truth remains elusive. It is not surprising that young students may struggle with this sort of uncertainty and especially with the prompt to reexamine articles of faith, whether religious or epistemological. Perry speaks of the profound psychological effects that accompany a move away from dualism—the notion that questions have a single right answer—calling this "the loss of Eden": "The Fall consisted of man's taking upon himself, at the serpent's suggestion, the knowledge of values and the potential for judgment. In our records the serpent appears in the form of the university" (*Forms* 67). Certainly the serpent was lurking in the texts assigned for the first unit of the course: "Genesis" 1–3 (King James Version) and additional creation narratives, Plato's cave allegory, Sartre's "Existentialism," and two essays by Stephen Jay Gould ("Nonmoral Nature" and "Sex, Drugs, Disasters, and the Extinction of the Dinosaurs").

In retrospect, I can see how my assignment Option 1, in its caution against naïveté, is itself rather naïve, asking that beginning students detach themselves from their own beliefs:

> Although the texts in this section vary widely in time period, genre, point of view, and purpose, several address the following question:
>
> *Is there a design to the universe and a Being or Force that creates and/or governs it?*
>
> Assuming the position of a "naïve" reader (i.e., one who brings no preconceived ideas to the subject), argue that two or more of these works offer answers to that question. Include in your discussion an implied or explicit comparison between or among the texts you choose. (Keep in mind that you are *not* being asked to explain your own personal beliefs.)

Instructors who conceive such assignments ignore at their peril the caution offered by Perry: "A salient characteristic of [unquestioning trust in authority], and the source of its innocence, is its lack of any alternative or vantage point from which a person may observe it. Detachment is impossible, especially regarding one's own thought. A person cannot explicitly describe such an outlook while embedded in it" (*Forms* 69). In this light, another option offered to students would have been, had they selected it, less devilish:

> Write an essay in which you compare and contrast two texts (selected from the list above) as provocative statements intended to "rewrite" history or "tell new stories" in the interests of truth or justice. How does each offer a critique of a prior "story" (prevailing ethos) and why was this revision or addition considered imperative?

But this topic tended not to be chosen by students intent mainly on affirming their closely held beliefs. How, then, to make the most of a potentially powerful teachable moment? In a class where openness to a particular disciplinary epistemology is a condition for success, such a question must be confronted. Nelson, in an expert and compelling narrative, has described his strategies for helping students in introductory science courses overcome automatic rejection of the theory of evolution ("Teaching Evolution"). However, because my first-year honors seminar, although it addresses epistemologies, has a more expansive focus than a discipline-based course, I have decided for now not to lead students unnecessarily into temptation and have eliminated Option 1. A small retreat is sometimes the best way forward.

Scene Three: Another First-Year Honors Seminar

The first-year honors student who insisted on the democratic equality of all "interpretations" of a literary text, including her imagined backstory for Ophelia, obviously touched a sore point in me. I believe I sputtered something about how my years of training definitely gave me some expertise not held by my students—or what was she paying tuition for? I'm quite sure she was not persuaded, valuing her imagination over my stuffy insistence on parsing diction and syntax. As a theatre major with some thespian training in high school, she was admirably inclined to appreciate complexity of motive, but other skills would give her deeper insight into the world's most famous play about acting. The class as a whole would not have balked had I allowed them to evade direct engagement with Shakespeare's language and had instead used the play as a springboard; it can be more fun, and less scary, to jump than to dive deep. But, lacking a grounding in discipline, the insights thereby derived would be shallow. Even if our goal is not to provide a backstory for Ophelia (but especially if it is), it does matter, when we read *Hamlet*, what is denoted by Hamlet's bantering exchange with Ophelia in the first scene of Act 3 (ll. 90ff). Students understandably like to focus on "I did love you once," but, without the preceding assertion of a cynical principle—"the power of beauty will sooner transform honesty from what it is to a bawd than the force of honesty can translate beauty into his likeness"—the statement stands naked and uninflected. The intervening sentence—"This was sometime a paradox but now the time gives it proof"—elegantly redoubles its meaning in rhythm and form and works with the other sentences, one could argue, like the middle term of a syllogism. While, innocent of Hamlet's purposeful role-playing, Ophelia concludes he is mad, she nonetheless takes his meaning, and novice readers deserve to be in on the grim joke.

In considering the (unfortunate) sacrifice of style to "clarity" as a norm in expression, Richard Lanham invokes his early initiation into Sister Miriam Joseph's *Shakespeare's Use of the Arts of Language* (1947), "a complex nomenclature to describe how language works" illustrated with copious examples. "It is like a first-year biology class. Look and Describe." This is not drudgery but "fun because when you know the names of things you take greater pleasure in them" and also because style becomes essential to this pleasure and also a key to meaning. "You see that you can look at language in a different way, look *at* it rather than *through* it" (65). Throughout his book, Lanham unmasks the false opposition between "decoration" and "clarity," demonstrating how "saying things the hard way" can be eloquent or obfuscatory. Certainly the discipline of literature entails giving students the skills to distinguish between these uses of language. Noting with regret that this sort of education now seems quaintly antique, Lanham suggests the real reason for its loss is that it is "too hard, too much like chemistry or physics, full of incontrovertible assertions (a chiasmus really is a chiasmus 'til the end of time)" (67). Interestingly, as science education has moved to educate students in the nature of uncertainty, away from reductive dualistic habits, students of literature could use a bit more of the discipline's certainties as a way into understanding and appreciation. In both cases, however, mastery of criteria allows for evaluation: Not all inferences or assertions are equally "good" from the perspective of disciplinary understanding. I might have conveyed this more effectively had I been less surprised by a student's self-assurance in claiming otherwise.

Scene Four: A Class in the Literature of Adolescence

My frustration with the student who imposed upon Nabokov's essay the precise performance of reading against which it is the purpose of the essay to caution was not, I hope, palpable. In truth, the disappointment I felt was not really with her. A junior, she seemed to have suffered a kind of negligence, apparently not having been held accountable for the sort of growth that higher education is intended to provide and quite innocent of the concept of reading expository prose for any purpose beyond extraction of information. Nabokov asks, "Can we expect to glean information about places and times in a novel?" (571). I presumed that the student could easily answer this question from Nabokov's perspective because in the next sentence such an expectation is deemed "naïve." But the ease of adapting an argument to already firmly held beliefs enabled her to avoid noticing why Nabokov thinks the question is worth asking. I imagine she did not pause at his teasing parenthetical comment that "the boundary line between [a work of fiction and a work of science] is not as clear as generally believed" (573). While Nabokov's essay on novel-reading is not itself a novel, it does call for "an artistic harmonious balance between the reader's mind and the author's mind" (574). Here he is talking about joining the authorial audience, the imaginative role-playing familiar to good readers. Good readers of his essay will intuitively attend to the writer's own ingenious blend of artistry (mastery of linguistic evocation, sentence rhythms, the rhetoric of seduction) and science (the four correct answers to his little quiz, the two types of imagination, "major" authors vs. "minor" ones—an assertion of categorical differences in a sea of rhetorical flourish), so that the essay in itself proves the truth of the boundary-blurring casually pronounced.

Looking back on my study-question options, I can see the Tempter prowling here as in the ill-fated question on "Design." A question that specifies the inclusion of "your personal experience as a reader"—as opposed to, for example, a question that asks, How would you explain the "correct" answers to Nabokov's quiz? or Why, according to Nabokov, is identifying with a character in a book "the worst thing a reader can do?" and what alternative stance toward novels do good readers take?—is likely to seem appealing to students for whom reports of their own experience are evidence of the greatest authenticity and hence authority. That the first part of the selected question required a paraphrase of Nabokov's view of reading as rereading did not serve the intended purpose, since, like the consequence of an arithmetic error early in a mathematical solution, missing the central point of the author ensured a faulty sequence of logic. Unpracticed in reading as a rhetorical act, the student continued to work from the data-mining model, hobbled by the tendency toward assimilation discussed earlier: It is easier to rewrite a text to conform to one's ideas than to assume, even if temporarily, an unfamiliar perspective. To try to evade this tendency, I could eliminate the question that asks for personal experience—or I could do a better job of anticipating the pitfalls and clarifying them for students in hopes that such consciousness-raising will either encourage the choice of a different prompt or produce more adept responses to this one.

Together, these moments comprise many of the novice tendencies that confront teachers every day as students grapple with texts: isolation of words and sentences from contexts, resistance to meanings that do not fit neatly with deeply ingrained beliefs, shallow construals of genre and of disciplinary distinctions—all habits associated with weak rhetorical-reading skills. As one reflects on such experiences, it would be comforting to discern simple and natural ways to do better, but no such strategies can be easily defined. As always in dealing with emergent occasions, one must hope for sufficient self-awareness in real time to lead students forward without dampening their enthusiasm or discouraging their tentative efforts. In any case, taking into account the affective dimension of teaching is, we know, critical to our success. And, as William G. Perry argued half a century ago, understanding the connections between thinking and feeling is also an ethical and a civic imperative.

Rhetorical Reading and the "Destiny of Democracy"

Perry's landmark study, *Forms of Ethical and Intellectual Engagement in the College Years: A Scheme,* published in 1970, evolved from what was to have been simply a descriptive study of the self-reported progress of Harvard students through the curriculum and college environment of the 1950s and early 1960s. Often overlooked in summaries of the stages that became the memorable takeaway from Perry's book is the sense of the cultural revolution in which it was rooted. This revolution was a turn, in the words of Henry Adams, "from unity to multiplicity" both in philosophies of knowledge and in values, so that college students were being confronted with "pluralism" in coursework and in social interactions as never before (5). Such a shift, Perry observed, reflected pervasive changes in the American experience and demanded a more complex education for responsible citizenship:

> The increased mobility of the population at large, together with the new mass media, make the impact of pluralism part of experience in the society as a whole. The growing person's response to pluralism in thought and values, and indeed his capacity to generate pluralism himself, are therefore critical to the destiny of democracy. Whether he responds productively rather than destructively may be up to him in the end, but society may surely nourish the prospect of a productive outcome through an understanding of the learning and the courage the development entails. (7)

Of course, Perry's definition of diversity was much narrower than the current one: He cited the increasing number of schools as well as the states besides Massachusetts represented at Harvard by the (all-male) first-year classes between 1900 and 1960. But the same paragraph might have been written—indeed, is being written—today. While the population studied by Perry represented an elite group, the maturational patterns inferred from his lengthy longitudinal interviews with students at the Harvard Bureau of Study Counsel have continued to carry explanatory power; in fact, his exploration of the most profound and consequential aspects of education viewed developmentally seems, given the much more genuine diversity that higher education now aspires to, even more significant today than it was over a half century ago.

According to Perry's conceptual outline of ethical and intellectual development, the process of higher education brings psychological and emotional challenges as well as cognitive ones. In his interviews of Harvard students, he noticed forms of growth submerged beneath students' fledging performance of the disciplines they were struggling to internalize: Students typically move beyond seeing claims dualistically as simply right or wrong and beyond believing in the equal validity of claims in areas where incontrovertible truth is deemed indeterminable, i.e., the stage of "multiplicity," where "[a]nyone has a right to his own opinion" (Glossary). In considering Metzger's skill in addressing an essay topic from a class he had not taken, we can see a student at the stage Perry later called "relativism," which allows for a comparison and evaluation of possible positions without necessarily committing to the persuasiveness or worthiness of any particular one (Glossary). Successful students are generally the ones who learn to move to this position, where they understand how to apply disciplinary criteria but need have no personal investment in what is at stake in an argument or conclusion. Metzger, for example, knew that the professor expected an essay alert to the concept of cultural diversity and the dangers of ethnocentrism. He also "did not forget to be fair and balanced" in appraising the (unread) text.

Because *Forms* began as a descriptive study based on conversations with students, its data are largely qualitative, and the voices of the students that we hear, as transcribed from tapes, are deeply revelatory and compelling. The developmental "scheme" that is essentially the argument of the book is demonstrated throughout the narrative and also summarized in charts. However, also worthy of notice is the book's single graph, which shows the increasing tendency of faculty to move students beyond "just the facts" in assessing their understanding of humanities and social-science disciplines. In this graph (Figure 1, "Weight of Examination Requiring Considering of Two or More Frames of Reference. Courses Enrolling Most Freshmen in Government, History, English Literature, and Foreign Literatures 1900–1960"), all of the fields analyzed show significant increases, averaging a rise of 35 percent—from 10 percent in 1900 to 45 percent in 1960 (6). The most dramatic upturns are in government and history, with English literature, perhaps reflecting New Critical influence, leveling off more than the others. The increased expectation that students would need to deal with relativism and thus with uncertainty meant, Perry saw, that students needed to be offered not just static knowledge but intellectual and emotional tools for deciding among better and worse, more or less valid, alternatives. Thus the ethical was necessarily implied in the cognitive. It was with this assumption that Perry sought to describe over time how students coped not only with "fragmentation and integration" but also "alienation and involvement" (7). The challenge for educators was then, as it is now, to honor uncertainty while fostering expert ways of analyzing and evaluating claims.

Perry was aware that the pedagogic art of achieving this subtle balance was as pertinent in science as in humanities areas. Students he interviewed discussed the difficulty of exchanging closely held and largely unquestioned ideas for "tentative answers," a process that meant redefining the meaning of "authority" as resting not on absolute knowledge but "rather on an experience and expertise in groping which are only more advanced than the students' own" (135). He noted that students who arrive at this understanding early may find the college environment immediately liberating rather than threatening. Such was the case of a first-year student who, having been trained in a high school chemistry class to think in terms of absolutes but privately subscribing to a more nuanced idea of science, wrote a paper for his first college science course in which he decided to "stick in the word 'absolute' once, just to make [the instructor] happy." Receiving the paper back with no marks except a B+ and "a big question mark over that one 'absolute' [he had] put in," the student was thrilled by the new way of thinking: "And from then, I said, well *that's wonderful!*" (137).

However, such first-year students were—and are—the exception. Building on Perry's work, Craig Nelson has spent a large part of his career not only refuting the alleged incompatibility between covering sufficient content and fostering critical thinking but also demonstrating effective methods for helping students relinquish unhelpful preconceptions about the nature of science and its methods, the ways in which its truths are and are not relative, and contested definitions of "proof." Nelson draws upon the history of science and uses exercises that engage expert practices in evaluating hypotheses and theories to show students how to determine, from a scientific perspective, which accounts of natural phenomena are better: "The basic task here is to explicitly delineate, and to help students learn to use, the forms of argumentation and the criteria used by our disciplines in deciding which ideas to accept tentatively" ("On the Persistence" 172). This process might be seen as analogous to rhetorical reading: In the kinds of role-playing I have described, students are inevitably comparing one position against another, trying on sometimes incommensurate perspectives.

Many students like to begin and end with an acceptance of relativism without a commitment to values that have been deeply considered; however, "essentially unlimited toleration for different frameworks is not enough," as it does not in itself entail the responsibility of shaping values defensible to oneself and others and making considered judgments, as adult life requires. Nelson has summarized students' view of demonstrating disciplinary competence at this stage as playing "teachers' games," since they can achieve good grades by using the expected methods and frameworks to "make sense of the chaos of uncertainty" to their teachers, if not to themselves "and may cynically regard the justified answers teachers require as 'bullshit'" ("On the Persistence" 173). This is in fact the stage at which studies have found many adults, including college graduates, to have plateaued. However, education for a satisfying life and for productive citizenship makes additional demands and offers the potential for more meaningful rewards: "We see decisions as contextual, as based inevitably on approximations, as involving trade-offs among conflicting values, and as requiring that we take stands and try to make the world a better place" (176–77).

Universities do not always do an outstanding job of distinguishing among multiplicity, relativism, and commitment. In discussing the complex aims of education, Kegan offers us the productive distinction between "wondering at" ("watching and reverencing") and "wondering about" (a means to some sort of action), cautioning about the dangers of privileging one over the other:

> An educating intention that is too exclusively wondering about inspires a measuring mentality in which teaching standards, national examinations, and a canonical approach to curriculum predominates. But a way of teaching that is imbalanced toward wondering at replaces awe with zeal, and is reminiscent of the passion of Miss Jean Brodie celebrating the courage of her students—which courage is then as easily offered up to the cause of the Loyalists as to that of the Republicans in the Spanish Civil War regardless of their respective allegiances to fascism and democracy. (8)

Well-intentioned efforts to create a hospitable climate for diverse viewpoints can too easily be deflected from the challenge of fostering habits that usefully combine skepticism and passion.

Humanistic qualities have been usefully exploited by demagogues: "[E]very tyrant and tyrannical movement in human history draws energy not from fear alone but from the courage and caring of its adherents" (Kegan 9). Here I am reminded that as a young assistant professor I was asked to review a new "Respect for Others" statement that would become part of the university's public philosophy. While I do not have the exact language of that draft, I recall being troubled by its underlying assumption that all views are worthy of respect. Would that mean that, were I a student, I would have to acknowledge the worthiness of a roommate's promotion of ideas such as fascism, homophobia, white supremacy? I suggested amendments to the statement, not to repress the free expression of ideas with which one might disagree but rather to avoid the false impression that multiplicity is the essential value rather than an ongoing search for understanding made possible by both empathy and intellectual rigor.

Nelson reminds us that all disciplines, not only the humanities, are built on values and assumptions that determine the prevailing truths at a given time and that even ideas proven or widely accepted as wrong (such as the notion of a flat Earth and the big bang theory) can serve useful purposes ("On the Persistence" 173). The domain of ethics, therefore, is not something we must "apply" to science so much as see as a dynamic that, for better or worse, drives its pursuit and the perpetuation of its norms. Consider, for example, some contemporary questions: How do we decide what counts as compelling evidence of the role of human activity in climate changes that are reshaping the conditions of and the possibilities for the diversity of life on Earth? What role does understanding of the human body under stress play in determining the criteria by which we agree, as a society, to define some treatment of enemy combatants as appropriately "harsh interrogation" (and therefore acceptable) and some as "torture" (and therefore not)? How do we assess the risks and benefits of GMOs? How does the equation change when we apply such engineering to human beings? How will we decide when the fruits of artificial-intelligence technology promise more harm to humanity than benefit? Is democracy a desirable form of government?

Lest this last question seem merely rhetorical, we need to consider the disturbing findings of two political scientists (currently at Cambridge University and Johns Hopkins University, respectively) that liberal democracy has been "deconsolidating" and is in danger of dissolution. Most striking is the rise in the number of young people who see democracy as expendable and are open to the idea of rule by the military. In the United States, only a third of millennials are committed to the idea of individual human rights, and a quarter are not convinced that free elections are critical aspects of a desirable society. These numbers indicate a marked shift over the past couple of decades. And, while such trends might invoke the warnings sounded by Kegan about the fungibility of passions and ideologies, the researchers found that they indicate what seems to be a growing apathy about civic life and the responsibility of individuals to shape it. Perhaps because they don't think they can make a difference, the percentage of young people interested in politics declined significantly from 1990 to 2011 (Foa and Mounk 10). The researchers come to a rather chilling conclusion: "Even as democracy has come to be the only form of government widely viewed as legitimate, it has lost the trust of many citizens who no longer believe that democracy can deliver on their most pressing needs and preferences" (Foa and Mounk 16). Further, while the rich used to be the group most supportive of democratic processes and structures, they have come to constitute the majority of those willing to entertain the idea of military rule (13).

If informed deliberation on such matters is deemed worthy of only a select few, our slide toward oligarchy or worse will be accelerated. In our current climate of "fake news," "alternative facts," increasingly pervasive propaganda, and all of the other threats posed by the ubiquity of social media, we feel more than ever our obligation to educate our students for information literacy in its most capacious sense. The challenge of "multiplicity" and "pluralism" that prompted Perry's research in the decades following World War II has become a crisis of truth. While Perry's schema might be vulnerable to the charge of elitism because of the privileged and rather homogeneous population he studied, it has actually offered a framework for thinking about how best to address the needs of all students. In this way the developmental theory is both democratic and persistently relevant to curricular design, especially as the connection between education and freedom is brought more clearly into focus by historical trends. Toward the close of the last century, philosopher and legal scholar Martha Nussbaum summed up her recommendations for a "new" liberal education that embraces both tradition and reform by proposing that the then-hot culture wars in the academy were a mirror of the dual meanings of *liberalis*—"fitted for freedom"—as applied to education in Seneca's time. Prevailing norms restricted such freedom to the few born to wealth and status; Seneca, however, proposed that a liberal education should enable the *cultivation* of free citizens by offering them the opportunity to achieve independence of thought (293). Nussbaum observed that in attempting to normalize for all such an education—"a general preparation for citizenship, not just a specialized preparation for a career" (294)—the United States has undertaken a huge experiment, one we have in some ways been fumbling but cannot afford to flub.

It is encouraging to note that dovetailing with the practical considerations of campus solvency, employer satisfaction, and career prospects for diploma-holders are the ethical concerns that have driven the discussions of equity and excellence. Graff has long been concerned with ameliorating the purposeful obfuscation and mystification noticeable among the professoriate, practices that emphasize the line between insiders and outsiders and, whether deliberately or not, give many students the impression that they are indeed "clueless," that they do not belong in college and cannot succeed there (*Clueless*). Arum and Roksa conclude *Academically Adrift* by calling academics to consider anew their traditional role in promoting the foundational moral missions of higher education—"instilling in the next generation of young adults a lifelong love of learning, an ability to think critically and communicate effectively, and a willingness to embrace and assume adult responsibilities" (144). Arum and his coauthors, in the introduction to their report on a multi-institutional effort to define essential discipline-based concepts and develop assessable learning goals, insist that short-sighted utilitarian outcomes, while appealing to certain stakeholders in the near term, will not serve the needs of students or of the larger society over time. By focusing on faculty perspectives and on the rich complexity of cognitive development, they hope to raise our consciousness of what students derive from our classrooms—to "illuminate the characteristics of assessments needed to capture the complex knowledge and skills that are at the heart of learning in higher education" (20–21).

As institutional accountability based largely on systematic assessment of student learning has become nonnegotiable, many institutions are taking guidance from organizations such as the Association of American Colleges and Universities and the Lumina Foundation, which, in conjunction with the Tuning Project, have defined learning goals for undergraduate and graduate students as well as structures and methods for effective design of curriculum, assignments, and assessments. According to the Lumina Foundation, "American higher education is at a critical junction with regard to equity and excellence" and is "in need of major redesign" to address disparities in access and in success based on race, ethnicity, and socioeconomic levels ("Lumina"). Similarly, a core goal of the AAC&U is building equity through "inclusive excellence," which requires "the creation of opportunities for historically underrepresented populations to have equal access to and participate in educational programs that are capable of closing the achievement gaps in student success and completion" as well as curricula that recognize diversity among individuals and across curricular fields ("Making").

The AAC&U specifies that the desirable practices be both "high quality" and "practical." Too often, because of marketplace exigencies that naturally create pressures on higher education, the former attribute is defined in terms of the latter: Immediate applicability of skills to narrowly construed workplace demands becomes the criterion for excellence. Lumina calls for "[a]ssurance of high-quality learning that aligns with twenty-first century workforce and industry needs." However, as Kegan has argued, the complex conditions of modern life present a "hidden curriculum"—including not only knowledge of cultural structures and artifacts but ways of understanding them that are increasingly demanding. What Graff has said about the disconnectedness of the school curriculum Kegan extends to other key aspects of life—professional relationships, intimate relationships, parenting—arguing for what is sometimes called connected learning, but in its deepest sense. Using the metaphor of life as a kind of university, Kegan notes that the demands made upon adults in the various realms of interpersonal experience constitute "a school in which each of the departments [specialists in marriage, management, and adult education respectively] is passionately engaged in its demands upon students, but no one is considering the students' overall experience, their actual course of study and the meaning for them of the curriculum as a whole" (5–6). In the quarter century since this argument was made, the demands on students to make sense of disparate and seeming incoherent data and messaging have dramatically increased.

Faculty have an obligation to ensure that school itself purposefully addresses this discontinuity by fostering complex habits of mind, intellectual versatility, and an empathetic imagination. The need, it bears emphasizing, is both ethical and pragmatic. Narrowing education to specialized training per se, no matter how esoteric the skills and content, will not serve the interests of students because the future will inevitably bring unanticipated cognitive and emotional demands (Arum et al.19). Beyond the privileging of allegedly exclusive or robotic reading in the pedagogies of the CCSS or other such directives, the need to attend to the persistent inequities in a sustained, holistic, and assessable way is the real social-justice issue facing postsecondary education. The intersection of this ethical challenge with increasing demands for external accountability predicated on marketplace pressures offers hope for a real culture change. In a climate of existential pressure, the survivors will be campuses where administrators, understanding the deep issues, offer support and leadership for faculty excellence in teaching and learning. Certainly a key focal point of such excellence will be the habit of rhetorical reading in all of its many facets.

Appendix 1

Facts and Fiction: Are Literary Texts a Special Case?

Narrative and "Reading Well"

A key element of the Common Core State Standards is their emphasis on informative or argumentative nonfiction over narrative. Thus, "the standards emphasize arguments (such as those in the foundational US documents) and other literary nonfiction that is based on informational text structures rather than fiction that is structured as stories (such as memoirs or biographies)" (Coleman and Pimentel 5). The standards also caution against "the traditional focus in ELA classrooms on the narrative aspects of literary nonfiction (the characters and story)," so that students can attend to "more in-depth engagement with the informational and argumentative aspects of these texts" (8). The thinking behind this shift is connected to the shortcomings of the "springboard" assignments discussed earlier, which tend to elicit reactions rather than analysis. Because stories tend to be inherently engaging and, even when not, resist translation into a set of precepts or chain of logical argument, students, it is assumed, will not be able to apply to them the necessary comprehension exercises. Since "reading well means gaining the maximum insight or knowledge possible from each source" (Coleman and Pimentel 1), stories, which seem less like buckets of information that can be mined than opportunities for an emotional or psychological experience, are demoted to a less prominent position in the language arts curriculum.

Traditional strategies for teaching literary texts have tended to reinforce the notion that reading narrative is relatively undemanding and largely useful for engaging emotions based on instinctive identification with characters. Even among some college instructors, one can discern the idea that reading literature, even in a sophisticated way, is less demanding than the literacy skills expected across the curriculum. Justin Young and Charlie Potter, in their advocacy for translating elements of the standards curriculum to the college level, contend that "the reading of literary texts requires only a knowledge of literary discourse, while the reading of, for example, a newspaper article on American economic woes requires some knowledge of terms and ideas from a variety of disciplines." Aside from the dubious nature of the claim that reading newspaper articles will help "student facility with cross-disciplinary discourse," this assertion suggests a naïve view of the nature of literary discourse and what it means to "know" it. Possibly because the experiential aspect of reading a story or novel is so evident, students in English classes can be readily engaged in a familiar topic—or a pseudotopic—embodied in a single word such as *family* or *rebellion* or *prejudice,* prompted by a text whose own implicit arguments or themes are left unexplored and undigested. In a 1994 study by Judith Langer of high school teaching in four disciplines (biology, history, physics, and English), only in English classes did readers' personal responses (rather than disciplinary practices) drive the discussion of the material being studied: "The literature teachers in the present study invited their students to become literary thinkers by orienting them toward examining, sharing, and expanding their personal interpretations. This was often accomplished by asking open-ended questions that tapped the students' responses" (33). To the extent that such practices have persisted, we can understand why the standards have pushed back against so much fiction in the curriculum.

Alternatively, as Sheridan Blau has argued, students in literature classes may find that textual interpretations are delivered by instructors so that the practices of disciplinary expertise (nicely articulated in the "postulates" and "theorems" outlined by Peter Rabinowitz and Corinne Bancroft) remain tacit or are, perhaps, altogether absent. Blau posits that while a focus on process has increasingly dominated the teaching of writing, the teaching of reading (particularly of literary texts) has remained relatively static. His research suggests, that is, the persistence of pedagogic practices that supply interpretations to students, who thereby emerge with the ability to parrot words and ideas but with limited skill in autonomous critical reading and an inability to "sustain any serious challenge or interrogation by any other reader who is having trouble trying to achieve the same reading" (271). This is why English majors may graduate with illusory expertise and a superficial knowledge that only thinly masks a dearth of confidence in approaching texts not already "taught" by an instructor. The difficulty of nurturing students' development of sophisticated engagement with literary texts may help to account for the marginalization of such texts in first-year writing courses. As a result of the two equally problematic approaches to teaching literature noted here—on one hand, eliciting superficial personal responses; on the other, sharing a packaged "expert" interpretation—one answer that has been offered to the question posed in this chapter's title is "Yes: reading fictional narratives will not substantially address the identified inadequacies in our students' reading."

The insufficiency of this answer reveals itself in two ways. First, as noted in Chapters 2 and 3, not all texts fall neatly along the literary/informative divide, a blurring of boundaries that in a way diminishes the inherent specialness of fiction. Louise Rosenblatt's distinction between aesthetic and efferent readings is pertinent here, since it at once rejects the necessity of regarding the "literary" as an inherent aspect of a text—*Julius Caesar,* e.g., "can be read either as a work of art or as an example of Elizabethan syntax [while] a weather report can be read as a poem"—and recognizes that different kinds of texts will invite different approaches by readers ("Transactional" 382). "Aesthetic" and "efferent" define different purposes for reading—lived-through experience versus takeaway message—but the text itself must ultimately be assessed according to agreed-upon criteria, "a fulcrum or outside point of view from which to judge the adequacy to the text of the work that the reader organizes in response to it" (*Reader* 124). With any text, readers assume a "stance," deciding "what to pay attention to, what to select out and synthesize, from among the elements stirred up in the stream of consciousness during the transaction with the text" ("Transactional" 383).

While validating this rigorous experiential standard, Blau suggests that we broaden the traditional definition of literature to include a variety of well-written and culturally important nonfiction texts (he mentions, e.g., works by Niccolò Machiavelli, Max Weber, Sigmund Freud, Paulo Freire, Steven Pinker, Oliver Sacks, and Stephen Greenblatt)—books that transcend a particular discipline and have resonance for a public that aspires to be well educated. This focus on the centrality of content may seem old-fashioned, yet the case for it—the reciprocity of reading and writing—is a timely idea indeed, as I have tried to illustrate in Chapters 4 and 5. As Blau argues, texts that we call literary in the broadest sense can serve as models for good writing and "are also the works most likely to reward deep and careful, and repeated, reading [thereby offering] the most rewarding and fruitful opportunities to develop the dispositions and habits of mind" characteristic of effective college reading (277).

Also of note is his observation that a particular text may itself comprise various types of discourse and disciplinary emphases. As a reciprocal of his point that many important works of fiction such as *Moby Dick, The Naked and the Dead, The Brothers Karamazov, The Plot against America,* and *To Kill a Mockingbird* contain scenes that explicitly engage moral, philosophical, scientific, and historiographical issues (280), he urges us to consider that many worthy nonfictional works rely on compelling narrative strategies and stylistic tropes usually classified as literary. I would agree. In this regard, I think not only of classics but also of such contemporary books as Bryan Stevenson's *Just Mercy: A Story of Justice and Redemption,* Martha Nussbaum's *Poetic Justice: The Literary Imagination and Public Life,* Atul Gawande's *Being Mortal: Medicine and What Matters in the End,* Michael Lewis's *The Undoing Project: A Friendship That Changed Our Minds,* Helen Macdonald's *H Is for Hawk,* Michael Pollan's *The Botany of Desire: A Plant's-Eye View of the World*, and Paul Woodruff's *The Ajax Dilemma: Justice, Fairness, and Rewards,* as well as the wide array of creative nonfiction essays by prose masters. Selecting for close study any chapter of Adam Gopnik's *Angels and Ages: A Short Book about Darwin, Lincoln, and Modern Life* (on Darwin and Lincoln as thinkers, writers, husbands, and fathers), for example, would be illuminating in any writing class. In such texts the efferent, aesthetic, and emotional effects constitute a tapestry of inseparable threads. Thinking about literature in this way certainly adds weight to David Jolliffe's judgment that the distinction between narrative and informational texts is "naively treated in the [Common Core] standards" ("Common Core Standards" 147). It also coincides, as explained in Chapter 4, with my experience of sharing challenging classic and contemporary texts with students at all levels of preparation.

Yet (and this is the second way that devaluing the potential impact of imaginative literature is mistaken), fictional texts do, in fact, require special kinds of meta-reading for the very reason that they are fictions; unlike texts that invite mainly efferent readings, they depend not only on analysis and abstraction but also on a consciousness of the difference between art and reality, of the role of "verbal mediation" (Rosenblatt, *Reader* 31). Because of the nuances created by an author's use of narrative point of view, novels, even more than nonfictional texts, require rhetorical reading. In earlier chapters, I argued for the value of role-playing assignments; reading fiction is quintessentially an act of role-playing. What fiction demands in particular is that readers be able to shape-shift—to become both the authorial audience (what the author hopes or expects their readers to be like) and the narrative audience (what readers become as they experience the world of text as participants) (Rabinowitz and Smith 24). "To read a work responsibly involves taking on this double role without, at the same time, abandoning our actual selves" (28). Novels present additional challenges because they must normally be read in pieces, meaning that any coherence does not emerge until at least the first reading is complete.

The payoff in engagement and pleasure may be what keeps us reading, but there are social and intellectual benefits that result. The assignments designed by my colleague Terra Joseph, as summarized in Chapter 5, exemplify how literature professors can support the desirable combination of emotion and intellect. Readers of literary fiction may even be developing skills that enable higher achievement across the curriculum, as is argued by Lisa Zunshine, who has theorized the field of cognitive narratology, a combination of literary theory and cognitive science. Because understanding fiction requires metacognitively complex processes—the ability to infer thoughts and feelings from indirect evidence, often through multiple sets of lenses that are "nested" within each other—practice in this sort of reading helps to develop theory-of-mind comprehension, an awareness of self and other that underlies complex reasoning. Showing how studies in developmental psychology support her analysis of the distinctive effects of fiction reading, Zunshine roundly condemns the idea that reducing fiction in the reading diets of children, per the CCSS directives, and thus minimizing the habit of thinking about thinking—one's own and others'—will be beneficial; this decision, she says, "will affect the future of higher education as severely as drastic budget cuts, yet more insidiously," inhibiting achievement in the more technical and more applied fields so highly valued in our culture and economy ("What" 91).

Psychologist Keith Oatley's analyses of the way fiction reading enhances empathy offer insight into why this would be so: "Fiction is not well thought of as an imitation of life. . . . [I]t is better thought of as a kind of simulation that enables exploration of minds and their interactions in the social world. The social world is complex and, although we humans are good at understanding others, we are not always that good; literary simulations help us to improve" (626). Because implicit in fiction reading is the need to imagine others (the author, the authorial audience, the narrator, the narrative audience, the characters as they change over time, ourselves as we change over time), it offers distinct ways to help us understand others more profoundly than we might otherwise do. Literary theorists and cognitive scientists concur that, contrary to conventional assumptions that reading for "pleasure" (usually a reference to reading novels) does not stretch the capacity of readers, in fact the ability to "read minds" (and thus to think inferentially), a skill invited by fiction (Zunshine, "Theory of Mind" 92; Rabinowitz and Bancroft 8ff.; Oatley 619), would confer a practical advantage in any educational program or profession—and indeed in life's interactions overall. So, yes, in this way literary texts (especially extended prose fiction) are, after all, a special case—or at least can be said to amplify effects that may be discernible but are not often as salient in nonfiction, which typically does not impose the sociocognitive challenges of stories that are worth rereading.

"The Text Itself"—Reading Metatextually

The kinds of challenges facing students as they make the transition to literary interpretation in college classrooms is illuminated by the alternating chapters in Rabinowitz and Michael Smith's compelling 1998 volume, *Authorizing Readers*. The juxtaposition of Smith's reflections on teaching literature to high school students with Rabinowitz's more theory-driven expositions as a university professor of comparative literature illuminates Smith's description of how he grappled with teaching *To Kill a Mockingbird* and reveals the trickiness of helping adolescents to read literature with disciplinary expertise. I want to spend a bit of time on this discussion because it dramatizes the complexity of the issues I have noted so far—in general terms, the difficult art of using one's own authority to help students engage with reading rhetorically, especially when narrative point of view is a critical aspect of the text. While high school teachers must invent ways to interest and encourage reluctant readers, college English professors (while also concerned with engagement and motivation) will have been trained to initiate students into disciplinary methods that tend not to play as large a role in high school lesson plans. Complex narratives, because they demand a range of readerly roles, present the greatest challenges for English instructors who want to avoid the pitfalls noted by the developers of the CCSS. As Harper Lee's narrative audience, we need not only enter happily the protagonist's affectionate retrospective re-creation of her small-town Southern childhood, enjoying her nostalgia-infused meditations on the pleasures of innocence, but also appreciate the nuances of irony and satire that Lee expects adult readers to understand. And then we need to step back further and consider the implication of the author's moral and artistic choices, the significance of what we take to be the text's meaning, in its own time and in our own.

Because many of his students were not habitual readers, Smith tried to help them become better at reading novels by encouraging not just decoding but metacognition: "I theorized that reading a novel required readers to be able to identify the salient themes and then to integrate those themes in a coherent statement of the whole" (Rabinowitz and Smith 105). However, the evolution of his strategies for accomplishing this goal reveals how difficult it is to deploy one's own expertise as a teacher in order to cultivate expertise in others. In this case, the selected strategies—e.g., defining for students, prior to their reading, particular themes and creating supplementary assignments such as drawing a map of the Finches' street, writing an issue of the local newspaper, and re-writing and performing the trial scene as a play—while interesting and potentially engaging, seem to be the sort of "external" interventions that the standards were crafted to discourage, as they deflect attention from the text per se. The interpretive conclusion emerging from these strategies—"when [the instructor] helped students put everything we had been doing together"—did leave students with a sense of how parts relate to whole but encouraged a reading of *Mockingbird* that ignored its disruptive moves: Lee wants us to understand that families play a key role in whether children will grow up with prejudice, and she is "optimistic" (106). Later, Smith felt the limitations of his approach; he explains that while he modeled how a trained reader decides what to notice and looks for ways to integrate pieces into a coherent vision, his instruction was still too dependent on his own prior understanding and thus did not do enough to help students practice the process on their own.

Subsequent classroom activities essayed by Smith, such as having students role-play characters and discuss the different "positions" taken by paired texts as a ground for debate, remain evident in more-recent lesson plans, along with rigorous efforts to give students background on historical contexts and events such as the meaning and prevalence of lynching, the Great Depression, and the trial of the Scottsboro boys. Such approaches have value, but the challenge is to make sure that historical materials do not merely frame but penetrate the literary experience and that attempts to enhance the experience do not become springboard assignments that take students outside the world of the text or ask them to impose their own values on it—e.g., recount personal experiences related to those experienced by the characters (Gibbons), or explain and justify how you would have voted as a member of Tom Robinson's jury (Elish-Piper et al.). As is the case with the optional CCSS assignment, described earlier, on the Gettysburg Address, asking students to debate positions before they have developed rich contexts for shaping their thinking defeats the purposes of close reading and fosters either/or categories. On the other hand, Smith's idea to have students reflect on and document, as they read, their understanding of various characters' moral choices (112) seems to me an excellent way to help students develop habits of "sociocognitive complexity" (Zunshine, "What" 89).

A high school teacher's struggle to achieve a balance between imposing a reading and respecting his students' responses to the book—"between honoring a student's experience and educating it" (Rabinowitz and Smith 111)—is a challenge that college English instructors can well appreciate. Consider, for example, the concept of theme, a staple of literature classes. By guiding students in eliciting themes from literary texts, instructors can help them arrive at coherent readings by connecting concrete elements to broader ideas that emerge from a work as a whole. However, deriving a theme from a complex text is a subtle, recursive, and ill-structured task, one that can easily slide into cliché seeking, a reduction of contingency and complexity into morals and lessons. Moreover, the word *theme* has often been used interchangeably with *topic*, a slippage that inhibits rhetorical reading. A 1999 guidebook for teaching Lee's novel, apparently directed at middle school teachers, identifies as themes such topics as what a hero is, what a family is, ways of dealing with violence, and children as "bridges" between races and classes (Robbins). Smith tells us he originally designated for discussion "four themes: the Southern mind, the family, growing up, and the outsider" (105) and then planned lessons that would help his students unify discussion of these topics in support of a central idea—"Lee wants her audience to believe that children are naturally good" (109). In a later volume on teaching literature in middle and high school, a guidebook admirable in its translation of theory to practice, Smith and coauthor Jeffrey D. Wilhelm took pains to differentiate "topic" from "theme," emphasizing that the latter is a "rich understanding" rooted in an "ongoing cultural conversation" akin to what Kenneth Burke describes in his "parlor" (Smith and Wilhelm 155). This distinction, while apt and helpful, does not necessarily encourage nuanced reading; in this case it enables the conclusion that Lee, like the adult narrator with whom she seems "closely aligned" (120), wants readers to emerge with the belief that "change [in the direction of equality] must be gradual," a claim based in a debatable interpretation of point of view and in any case more like a main idea or moral—terms, the authors say, that do not capture the complexity of themes (155).

Needless to say, attempts to help students learn how to derive themes that go beyond commonplaces are further hobbled by students' reliance on formulaic study guides that reinforce patterns of thought not helpful in high school or college. From *SparkNotes* we learn that "[t]he most important theme of *To Kill a Mockingbird* is the book's exploration of the moral nature of human beings—that is, whether people are essentially good or essentially evil," an inference that both shrinks the experience of the novel and imposes upon it an unwarranted definitional burden. To be sure, some critics have themselves argued that the novel eschews nuance, enabling easy sentiment and interpretation as "a story whose morality is defined in black and white terms [so that] right and wrong, virtue and vice do not blend into each other and are not relative" (Heims 56). But such a judgment of the book reduces it to a parable, a story in which every choice is easily categorized. And even if such a characterization were true, we would have to admit that the moral categories are historically, culturally, and racially contingent: In a review of Tom Santopietro's *Why "To Kill a Mockingbird" Matters* (2018), professor and critic Roxane Gay writes, in a move that takes her beyond both authorial and narrative roles, "The book is a 'product of its time,' sure, so let me just say that said time and the people who lived in it were plain terrible." The nostalgia that lies behind the book's endurance, Gay observes, is "a uniquely white yearning, because it is white people to whom history has been kindest." The point seems inarguable, as is her assertion that Lee's shallow portrayal of Black lives, her use of them as "narrative devices, not fully realized human beings," sharply delimits the novel's vision.

Yet to attribute the book's lasting appeal only to its success in making white people feel good is to overlook the demands that the narrator makes of the attentive reader. Gay herself acknowledges Lee's "dry wit and intelligence" and "moments throughout the narrative that are exquisitely drawn." And even an instructor who wants to see Lee as "optimistic" can guide students in noticing how a fictional narrative that on one level invites hope and a sense of resolution simultaneously provokes discomfort in readers who are prepared to grapple with it. Students could be asked to consider how "social-issue" novels like *To Kill a Mockingbird* tell stories not only about their immediate subjects and not only about the time in which they were written but also about the often ambivalent position of the author vis-à-vis those subjects. The Dolphus Raymond scene (Chapter 20) is among many in the book that ask readers to move beyond simple binaries of good and evil, but, because it so effortlessly lends itself to a conventional "theme," its challenges can easily be evaded. Perhaps it is no coincidence that this scene in particular became a focus of Smith's rereading.

Readers are likely to recall the striking incident when Jem, Scout, and Dill, upset by the treatment of Tom during the trial, are comforted outside the courtroom by Dolphus Raymond, the "town drunk," who reveals to them that he only pretends to be an alcoholic because the pretense allows him to build a family as he chooses and live with whom he wishes. Dolph explains that the white inhabitants of Maycomb leave him alone because they attribute his domestic arrangements to his alcoholism, something beyond his control—"It helps folks if they latch onto a reason." The children's shock at this deception recalls Huck Finn's pangs of conscience in defying the law by protecting Jim, the effects of the moral inversion perpetrated by a racist culture. This scene fits neatly into the theme of the innocence of children and hence their moral superiority, as Dolph, responding to Scout's query as to why he had "entrusted [them] with his deepest secret," replies, "Because you're children and you can understand it." From a contemporary perspective, we may be, as Smith was, inclined to "wonder why Dolphus Raymond was content to do so little [since] [h]e was from a prominent family" and to speculate that "Tom Robinson wouldn't have been convicted if more people had spoken out" (Rabinowitz and Smith 109). But the sin we are meant to confront is not that Dolph does so little—would the town have responded to the moral concerns of the town "drunk" who has already violated their most closely held racial rules?—but that he must do so much in defense of his family life. Whereas Scout is puzzled as to why an adult would pretend to a vice, it is quite clear that the mature narrator invites readers not to judge Dolph's survival strategies as morally deficient but to see them as an ironic counterpoint to the town's pretense of moral virtue. Lee, no doubt, appreciated Dolph's invention of strategies for living a satisfactory life outside the rigid boundaries of a twisted moral code and hoped that many of her readers would recognize or at least experience the combination of pathos, satire, and comedy in this scene. Asking high school students to attend to these issues is helping them to join the authorial audience in ways that will better prepare them for college reading than will premature debating about moral choices ill-understood and considered as largely independent of historical contexts.

The richness of a book may be measured in the ways it rewards attention to what Wolfgang Iser has called the "blanks and gaps" (*How to Do Theory* 64)—its invitation to readers not to fit each moment into a neat frame but to enter the world created by the author, whose artistry imposes a kind of order on the "chaos" of experience, allowing it to "flicker and to fuse" (Nabokov 572). Where, for example, does the perspective of the adult narrator collide with the child's innocence to create irony? To address this question, students could consider such deadpan statements as the following: "Aunt Alexandra owned a bright green square Buick and a black chauffeur, both kept in an unhealthy state of tidiness" (129; ch. 13); "'They c'n go loose and rape up the countryside for all of 'em who run this county care,' was one obscure observation we heard from a skinny gentleman when he passed us" (137; ch. 14); "As Dolph Raymond was an evil man I accepted his invitation reluctantly but I followed Dill" (202; ch. 20). Where does the narrator expect the reader to see beyond the innocent reportage of the child?

Students could analyze the double point of view in observations such as, "The court appointed Atticus to defend [Tom]. Atticus aimed to defend him. That's what they [the Idlers' Club members] didn't like about it. It was confusing" (166, ch. 16); "[Mayella] couldn't live like Mr. Dolphus Raymond, who preferred the company of Negroes, because she didn't own a riverbank and she wasn't from a fine old family" (194; ch. 19). At what points might readers be unsure how the authorial audience is supposed to respond to the narrative point of view? What to make, for example, of the narrator's apparent agreement with Atticus that women don't belong on juries (224; ch. 23)? Is this the adult's amused perspective at the thought of certain "ladies" sitting in judgment or only a report of the child's embrace of her father's patriarchal viewpoint? And what of the indications that the language of the sophisticated adult narrator retains the imprint of the racist society in which she was molded—passages in which contemporary readers seek but do not find irony, e.g., cringe-inducing descriptors such as the "smell of clean Negro" (121; ch. 12)?

As Jennifer Murray has argued, the subtler frictions in the novel tend to be smoothed out by critics whose repression of the adult aspect of the narrative voice casts over the story a glow even rosier than that diffused by the whip-smart child narrator. Such repression accounts for Sarah Churchwell's overstated claim, in her otherwise incisive *Guardian* review of *Go Set a Watchman,* that *Mockingbird* settles for the "complete but limited" feat of "entirely mastering a child's perspective," and might be classified among our "consoling, whitewashed, childish fables." From this perspective, Lee would fit Nabokov's definition of the minor author whose effect is "ornamentation of the commonplace" (572). But such a judgment presumes a reader who has not sufficiently balanced the roles of narrative and authorial readers or, in other words, has not achieved the combination of "passion" and "aloofness" that the text enables and rewards.

In fact, the fable-like aspects of the book are the ones selected for the now-classic 1962 film version starring an irresistibly avuncular Gregory Peck; in the book they are interrogated not only by the shifting demands of the layered narrative voice but also by the text's contradiction of its own "lessons." Consider, for example, the following:

Atticus's failure to recognize the potential for evil in others is endearing but has grave consequences. "Only children weep" at injustice (215; ch. 22), but Atticus's own childlike faith in the basic goodness of people despite their heinous behavior and his overconfidence in his understanding of motive—traits that young Jem finds unsettling—nearly result in the revenge murder of his own children. The child Scout may be comforted by Atticus's assurance that "'[t]he Ku Klux's gone'" and that "'[i]t'll never come back,'" but the grown-up Jean Louise knows that this claim is a "polite fiction" as dangerous as the myth of "Southern womanhood" that, in the next breath, Atticus admits he must dismantle in his defense of Tom (149; ch. 15).

Atticus sees the law "as the great leveler" but is willing to compromise its rigor when the blindness of justice to the uneven field upon which people play out their lives violates his sense of fairness and decorum. Thus he chooses to use discretion in his selective enforcement of the laws against truancy and poaching and, encouraged by his precocious daughter, agrees to protect Boo from accountability in the killing of Bob Ewell. Despite his good intentions, the implied lesson of Atticus's virtuous evasions of the law—that the righteous man is somehow above the law and must address in his decisions the insufficiencies of the legal code—carries, as Tim Dare has argued, its own moral dangers.

Atticus is praised repeatedly for his authenticity and unwaveringly principled behavior, whether as family man or public servant. But the events of the novel reveal that the freedom to be consistent in this admirable way is contingent on a position of privilege defined by race, class, and gender. The opposite of Atticus's defining trait might be pretense and hypocrisy, but it might also be performance—ingenious, desperate, or both—necessitated by oppression. In addition to the performance enacted by Dolph Raymond, students should be prompted to consider several others: the nature of Calpurnia's bilingualism and the quality of its exceptionalism, which alarms and mystifies the children; the contrast between Boo Radley's imagined life first as a delinquent and then as a gothic ghoul who can't or won't "come out" and, later, his coming out as a man of physical courage and moral gravity; the tragic charade Mayella Ewell is forced to play as both victim and victimizer; and the impossible role foisted upon Tom Robinson, whose genuine kindness is cast as an act of violation because the beneficiary is a white woman. While Atticus's public and private lives seem seamlessly integrated, others do not have the luxury of such wholeness, consistency, or transparency.

Atticus insists on the importance in civil society of the right to privacy, a principle that seems unexceptionable on its face. But the book as a whole suggests that his willful evasion of certain evils in the community is a moral failing. Connected to the novel's interrogation of privilege is the unsettled question of mutual responsibility: How much ought we to consider what goes on behind closed doors; in other words, when is it right to mind other people's business? A fable-like reading will foreground Atticus's perfect balance of concern for neighbors and respect for privacy in his treatment of the dying and morphine-addicted Mrs. Dubose, whom Jem must help usher out of the world through the comfort of his story-reading voice. But other features of the narrative disrupt the balance. Why, for example, is the children's curiosity about the life lived by Arthur Radley—a house prisoner since adolescence for reasons known by the community to be dubious—so rigidly repressed? Their attempt to imagine it is seen not at all as an anxious move toward empathy, which in part it surely is, but only as disrespectful of the family's privacy. Dramatic irony complicates the child Scout's report of how the town chooses to view old Mr. Radley's aura of respectability: "Miss Stephanie Crawford said he was so upright he took the word of God as his only law, and we believed her, because Mr. Radley's posture was ramrod straight" (16; ch. 1).

Atticus assures the children that Arthur is not chained to his bed at night, that "there were other ways of making people into ghosts," revealing his recognition of the disturbing family dynamic that has turned a misbehaving adolescent into what the children fear must be a "malevolent phantom" (16). Yet Atticus insists that the curious Jem "mind his own business and let the Radleys mind theirs; they had a right to" (15). The children—especially Dill and Scout—are interested in the truth, but only Calpurnia dares to speak it in their hearing. She breaks her custom of keeping silent on the ways of white people when old Mr. Radley's coffin is carried past the Finch house: "'There goes the meanest man ever God blew breath into,' murmured Calpurnia, and she spat meditatively into the yard" (16–17; ch. 1). Scout senses the unfairness and no doubt the horror of being kept prisoner, asking Dill why he thinks Boo never ran off, and Dill, who knows the misery of feeling unwanted by one's own family, is precocious enough to imagine a plausible answer: "Maybe he doesn't have anywhere to run off to. . . ." (146; ch. 14). Such matters, it seems, trouble only servants and children.

During Tom's trial, Scout also wonders, as others apparently do not, about the life lived by Mayella Ewell. Mayella blurts out on the stand what the adults in town no doubt already know—that she is a victim of incest, grinding poverty, emotional neglect, and social isolation. With Mayella on the stand, Atticus slowly paints a picture of her brutal existence, a portrait normally repressed and drawn now only because exposing her as desperate, powerless, and victimized is necessary to defending Tom. Otherwise, like Boo, she would remain invisible, receiving from the town an occasional handout "and the back of its hand" (194; ch. 19). A girl barely emerging from adolescence, Mayella Ewell seems to Scout to be "the loneliest person in the world" (194). That, and the fact that she is assaulted by her father, has been—and will continue to be—nobody's business. Scout understands the position of a child seen as white trash: as "sad" as a "mixed child," acceptable in no part of society.

Growing up as a child who resisted being molded to the stereotypes of her time and place, Lee might well have felt "mixed" herself, just as a child like Dill, who felt unwanted, could understand Boo's loneliness. Mayella lacks the protection and autonomy afforded Dolphus Raymond, an independent man of property and proper ancestry. Even Dolphus, however, enters town only rarely and then must pretend to be under the influence, whereas the upright Radleys, we may recall, "are welcome anywhere." Such details build a complex social portrait whose nuances, while unavailable to the child-persona aspect of the narrative voice, invite reflection by adults. From this perspective, even Atticus is revealed as a man whose compromises reflect not so much the definition he teaches to Scout—"an agreement reached by mutual concession" (36; ch. 3)—as an accommodation of the existing "ethical culture" (40; ch. 4). Several months after the trial, "Mr. Ewell was as forgotten as Tom Robinson" and "Tom Robinson was as forgotten as Boo Radley" (251; ch. 27). Not much optimism there.

To reinforce the insights enabled by metatextual reading, teachers might direct students to passages where Lee pointedly uses comedy and satire, cutting the sentimental sweetness with an acid infusion of irony and implicating the reader along with the targeted characters. Underlying the witty portrayals of small-town gossip—the sin of improperly intruding into the affairs of others—are tragic themes of negligence masquerading as respect for the rights of all to live as they please. It is a hypocrisy hovering above the surface of propriety and Christian charity. In a particularly brilliant scene (Chapter 24), the comedy and tragedy collide, as the town's most upstanding ladies meet to congratulate themselves and each other on saving the souls of the African pagans even as news of Tom Robinson's murder is delivered to Atticus and paternalistically withheld from the tea-sipping do-gooders. The ladies as portrayed by Scout are satiric objects perfectly calibrated to make the narrative audience feel superior; they are terribly dedicated to the welfare of the poor savages in Africa even as they complain that the outcome of the trial in their town has made their Negro servants "dissatisfied" and "sulky" (234) and claim that "there's no lady safe in her bed these nights" (233ff). Yet, if we have followed the motifs of insider versus outsider and private versus public as framed by the incidents noted above, we too are indicted, along with the novel's touchstone moral character, as we wonder what moral price we are willing to pay so that we can simply go on minding our own business. To the extent that the narrative perspective lets Atticus (and readers) off the hook, we might say, along with Howell Raines, a former executive editor of the *New York Times* (and an Alabamian), that *To Kill a Mockingbird* "wobbles morally," and thus so do we.

Why are the comforting, transcendent aspects of this beloved book—the sentiment, hopefulness, feeling of growth and development—more often emphasized than the provocations and limitations? An answer is suggested by Bryan Stevenson, the black lawyer who chronicled in *Just Mercy* (2014) his often heartbreaking fight on behalf of poor and underprivileged defendants in the South. Stevenson has observed that "sentimentality about Lee's story grew as the harder truths of the book took no root" (23), and he has responded to comparisons of himself with Atticus Finch by noting that Atticus lost his case, while justice depends on winning. Yes, the story arc favors a sense of moral maturation in the narrator and foregrounds the sentiment, thus producing what can easily be seen as an uplifting memoir, especially for white readers. Yet the disruptive qualities, while less part of the popular conversation and erased completely by the film version, can perhaps account for the book's enduring power; eliding these qualities does a disservice to students, who, when given permission to feel the unresolved anxieties of the narrative, will also deepen their understanding.

An analysis of the Dolph Raymond scene from a theory-of-mind perspective illustrates the power of narrative complexity to illuminate dark corners. Drawing on Zunshine's strategies, we can see that in this episode the reader is asked to consider the adult narrator's recollection of her childhood reaction to learning that a notorious and marginalized town character has been faking his chronic drunkenness because the sin of alcoholism is, to the community, more acceptable than the sin of crossing the color line as he did. The reader simultaneously joins the authorial perspective in appreciating the tragic irony of Dolph's options and shares the pathos of the child's moral judgment of Dolph, whose behavior she is too young to understand, as a distressing fraud who nonetheless seems to echo her father's most noble moral sentiments. At this moment, the reader is as likely as the child Scout to be torn between a desire to hear more from and about Dolph and a need to return to the drama playing out in the courthouse, a choice between "two fires" to which we are, in dread, drawn. Directed by the narrator, we head with Scout to the courtroom, where the children attend to the legal proceedings as best they can. Yet the scene lingers with us, as it apparently somehow did with the child who, decades later, recalls it sufficiently to bring it to life, now as an emblem of the journey from innocence to disturbing experience. For Lee's contemporary audience, as for more recent ones, the mind-reading demands of the interlaced narrative layers must have done what fictions in particular can, remarkably, do. The novel must have offered readers an "understanding [of] people from the inside as well as from the outside, in a manner that is not always easy to approach in other ways" (Oatley 626).

Of course, metacognitive complexity is not necessarily sought by readers, and skilled writers can choose to make comfortable responses possible even as provocation lies in wait. We know now that the invitation to disturbance and critical insight that is perhaps too easily unheeded in *Mockingbird* was far less restrained in the first draft of the novel, submitted by Lee in 1957. In *Go Set a Watchman* (2015), believed to be an early version of *Mockingbird* that was reconceived upon the advice of Lee's then-editor and published in its original form as a kind of sequel fifty-five years later, Jean Louise's sudden awareness of her father's temporizing with regard to racial equality leaves her feeling like a pariah, a young woman bereft of community—"in a no-man's-land but good." As a result she feels "cheated" (248) and calls her father a "double-dealing, ring-tailed, old son-of-a-bitch" (253), a judgment that has agitated readers who prefer the idealized version of Atticus and a gauzy reading of *Mockingbird.* However, given the deep ambivalence and conflicts of the woman torn between tribal loyalties and cosmopolitan consciousness, it is no wonder that even in the much-softened revision of her first cathartic effort—the novel that became *To Kill a Mockingbird*—Lee could make her readers feel with intensity, using quick but incisive strokes, the inner lives of Boo, Dolph, Calpurnia, and Mayella.

One might even speculate that she deployed in her artistic choices the clever realpolitik with which she endows one of these outsider characters. That is, what the "evil" Dolph says of his attitude toward the residents of Maycomb who despise his lifestyle is pretty much what the implied author of *To Kill a Mockingbird* is willing to say, in effect, of the destabilizing aspects of her text and their potential for alienating her audience: "'Now I could say the hell with 'em, I don't care if they don't like it, right enough. I do say I don't care if they don't like it, right enough—but I don't say the hell with 'em, see?'" (203; ch. 20). This dialogic aspect of the text occasions what Patrick Chura has called "a lingering uncertainty about whether Lee's text is subversive or orthodox in its insights" (16). As I have been suggesting, teaching students to understand and accept the nature of this uncertainty is the challenge and opportunity provided by good fiction. This is the alternative to a reading that guides students toward "coherence" based on preset themes or messages, privileges untutored reaction, or tolerates incoherence as the price of superficial engagement in topical issues. Ironically, it is these most demanding texts that, although they require the most sophisticated reading habits, are often taught mainly as occasions for students to merely connect and respond.

Text and Context: Reading Metacontextually

If, as Iser claims, literature both contains the dominant systems of the culture from which it arises and allows us to "construct whatever was concealed or ignored" by these systems, familiarity with the relevant cultural norms will facilitate the reader's ability to play the roles of authorial and narrative audience as well as to assess the implications of the questions and conclusions developed by the reading experience. Thus a reader familiar with prevailing theories of human understanding in the eighteenth century, especially the dominance of Lockean epistemology, will be able to assume the readerly stances summoned by *Tristram Shandy,* and awareness of common portrayals of heroic revenge in Shakespeare's time will enable greater insight into the complexity and originality of *Hamlet* (*How to Do Theory* 61–66). Some texts, it might be argued, invite the application of methods less explicitly cognizant of social conversations—e.g., a lyric poem might well repay a traditional "close" reading, and a novel by Franz Kafka a psychoanalytic one. Yet interpreting such texts does require contextual knowledge, if only the understanding of which approaches seem likeliest to enhance the literary experience. Even a worthy New Critical reading, as discussed in Chapter 2, is grounded in a cultural awareness that is broad and deep.

Accepting that it is "futile" to read without sensitivity to the "presuppositions [that] are expected, even demanded, by authors" (Rabinowitz and Bancroft 18), one would wish to emphasize that some of our culture's best-known texts exert such a demand with special force. *To Kill a Mockingbird* owes its classic status largely to its role in pricking the conscience of a nation that continues to be roiled by the effect of its original sin. Such a book cannot be appreciated by relying exclusively on aesthetic, mythological, or psychological categories of analysis. To the extent that *Mockingbird* is a particularized social critique enabled by a multilayered narrative persona, effective reading of the novel requires an explicitly metacontextual strategy—the deployment of background knowledge that illuminates the issues at stake and the terms of their engagement in the culture at large. The CCSS's insistence on "the text itself" and in isolation will no more suffice here than it does for "A Modest Proposal," the Gettysburg Address, or King's letter.

In a 2012 public-television celebration of Lee's achievement (Murphy), novelists, historians, and public figures—both black and white—noted the courage it must have taken for a white Southerner to write this novel in the 1950s, calling it "pretty damn brave" (Oprah Winfrey), an "act of protest" (Diane McWhorter), and "a very brave book when Harper Lee wrote it" (Scott Turow). In a classroom, the boldness of the narrative stance and the way in which fiction as protest might be a kind of action will be better understood, appreciated, and subjected to critique only if the historical contexts for Lee's choices are brought into the conversation. While Lee was writing in the 1950s, a confluence of events was exposing the fault lines of a long-standing system that many preferred to leave concealed or ignored. In the lead-up to the full-fledged Civil Rights Movement, the country grappled with culture-shifting events such as the decision in *Brown v. Board of Education* (1954), the savage mutilation and murder of fourteen-year-old Emmett Till (1955), and the Montgomery Bus Boycott (1955–56); only a few years later, in 1964, the nation would be confronting the horrific murder of three young civil-rights workers in Mississippi. Underlying resistance to integration was, above all, fear of "miscegenation," which would erase the essential differences on which the structures of white supremacy depended. This is why Till, who allegedly made a pass at the wife of a white storekeeper, had to be made an example of, and why "Tom was a dead man the minute Mayella opened her mouth and screamed" (244; ch. 25). It is also why "mixed children" like Dolph Raymond's, and their parents, had to be shunned. In his insightful study of how Lee merged her memory of the 1930s South with the culture and zeitgeist of the 1950s (when she was composing the text), Chura notes that white anxiety about racial mixing became more urgent as the Civil Rights era began: "Foremost among all latent and overtly expressed fears that were directly intensified by the Brown decision was that surrounding interracial sex" (3).

Stevenson's central client in *Just Mercy,* Walter McMillian, was wrongly convicted of a murder in 1987 partly, we come to learn, because he had a romantic involvement with a white woman. "Walter didn't know the legal history [of "anti-miscegenation" laws] but like every black man in Alabama he knew deep in his bones the perils of interracial romance" and was aware that even a minor "interracial social misstep . . . could trigger a gruesome and lethal response" (30). Southerners who considered themselves enlightened held that the decision in *Brown* had to be resisted not because integration was wrong in principle but because, as Atticus, a self-proclaimed "Jeffersonian Democrat," says in *Go Set a Watchman,* equality must be earned, must come gradually to a race "still in their childhood as a people," and because the federal government's overreach on states' rights must be restrained (246–47). On the latter grounds, even Jean Louise, whose Southern roots inform her dedication to the Tenth Amendment, is made "furious" by the *Brown* decision (238). Yet even as Jean Louise embraces the states'-rights argument, Atticus reveals his deepest fear—that racial mixing will blur essential differences that must be preserved. He sees the NAACP activists as outside agitators dedicated to this goal: "Can you blame the South for wanting to resist invasion by people who are apparently so ashamed of their race they want to get rid of it?" (247). It is no wonder that *Go Set a Watchman,* Lee's first draft of her novel, with its raw confrontation of racial politics, had to be fully re-envisioned as a childhood memoir if it was to be published in 1960 as *To Kill a Mockingbird.* The metamorphosis, with its achievement of both reassurance and provocation, is an ideal medium for helping students see a text in conflict with itself and in dialogue with history.

Historian Jon Meacham has said that the novel "is a tale of good and evil that ends on a note of gray" (qtd. in Murphy), but, as with the metatextual anxieties noted above, students can be helped to see the gray throughout. How, they might be asked, do historical contexts shape one's definition of moral choices and the power one has to enact them? The characters of Atticus, Dolph, and Calpurnia seem to fill discrete social and moral categories, but all of them feel acutely the pressure of having to compromise principle for social survival; each resists the urge to tell ignorant, bigoted, and even dangerous people to go to hell, in order that life in a community be possible. Calpurnia, whose "command of two languages" and whose code-switching in her church are witnessed by Scout and Jem, patiently educates the alarmed Scout ("But Cal, you know better") in the practical virtue of decorum and the pragmatics of versatility: "It's not necessary to tell all you know. It's not ladylike—in the second place, folks don't like to have somebody around knowin' more than they do. It aggravates 'em. You're not gonna change any of them by talkin' right, they've got to want to learn themselves, and when they don't want to learn there's nothing you can do but keep your mouth shut or talk their language" (128). Learning a second language can be a means of survival in a harsh and unjust world, and knowing when to shut up or speak one language or another requires judgment both practical and moral.

In *Watchman,* Jean Louise's suitor, the attorney Henry Clinton, who lacks family "background" but has been apprenticed to Atticus Finch, offers a similar explanation as to why he belongs to the White Citizens' Council, but he takes the rationale a step further by contending that the virtue embedded in conforming is exactly what enables service *to* the community; moreover, such acceptance of conventional mores is especially demanded of men, who lead public as well as private lives (230). However, while Calpurnia's versatility has an admirably subversive edge (choosing to bring Atticus's children to her church is itself transgressive), Henry's role-playing is driven by fear. Voicing his objections to the council or even refusing to participate in their meetings will provoke accusations from respected town members that his "white trash" traits are in evidence and increase the likelihood that he will thereby ruin his budding legal career. Readers are inclined to agree with Jean Louise's assessment that Henry is "a scared little man" (232).

However, from an authorial perspective, Henry's qualms may deserve deeper consideration. In discussing what he calls Lincoln's "least defensible speech," delivered in Charleston, Illinois, in a debate with Stephen Douglas, Garry Wills has said, "Lincoln's accommodation of the prejudice of his time did not imply any agreement with the points he found it useless to dispute" (96). Might the same be said of Henry—and of Atticus? Even without having read *Watchman,* students who have been asked to consider historical contexts can be asked to ponder a question that naturally arises from a metacontextual reading of *Mockingbird:* Under what conditions is fitting in too much of a compromise, standing out too dangerous—or just foolishly reckless? What sorts of circumstances might make it wise to "sneak around the frontal defenses of prejudice and find a back way into agreement with bigots"—i.e., to assert common ground as a means of moving forward (as Wills says Lincoln and Mark Twain knew how to do [99])? One's sense of how to answer this question will necessarily be inflected by the reader's experience of the narrative, which will depend on recognition of how the text in question achieves its effects. Pondering that is necessarily an exercise in sophisticated rhetorical reading.

Reconsidering the Binary of "Fiction vs. Information"

Needless to say, to emphasize the complexity of helping students read literature in the particular ways demanded by notable fiction in no way diminishes the versatility in readers that expository and argumentative texts also require. While the difference between authors and narrators may not be foregrounded in such texts, skills entailed in both close and distant reading are nonetheless essential to comprehension. In broadening her comments to include texts not considered literary, Rosenblatt acknowledges that students must develop a repertoire of approaches flexible enough to be invoked as appropriate as the purposes for reading and rereading vary. Her recommendations continue to resonate with the current challenges of improving literacy skills and could offer curriculum designers a helpful perspective on close reading as an endeavor of metaconsciousness:

> We increasingly hear arguments for the reading of a wide range of genres in both writing and criticism courses. All the more reason why, in writing or reading, students need to develop a guiding principle for choice at a point on the [aesthetic-efferent] continuum appropriate to their situation and their purpose. . . . For an historical work or political speech that uses many so-called literary devices, it will be especially important to decide what major stance to adopt. ("Transactional" 383)

Rosenblatt's conception of texts as occupying not discrete prior categories but rather a continuum of motives and traits that call forth different types of reader responses, a theory adumbrated in *Literature as Exploration* (1938) and elaborated in *The Reader, the Text, the Poem* (1978), has informed other thoughtful meditations on the pedagogy of reading (and writing). It underlies, as mentioned earlier, Rabinowitz's definition of genre in terms not of attributes per se but of the interpretive strategies summoned (Rabinowitz and Smith 60). And Richard Lanham probes the same categorical thinking in his revision of the traditional tripartite view of style ("high," "medium," "low") from a vertical to a horizontal plane, one inviting unbounded responses along a "spectrum" determined by "our stylistic self-consciousness"—our sense of the writer's invitation to notice the text's "style *as a* style" and thus to read it for more than information. From this perspective the fiction/nonfiction divide blurs. "What difference," Lanham asks, "does it make that Moll Flanders never lived? Diarists who have lived inhabit the same stylistic universe" (94). Here we may recall the judgment of Charles Lamb on Daniel Defoe and that of William Hazlitt on Samuel Richardson, that reading their novels is like examining evidence as reported by an eyewitness in a court of law (Watt 34).

Conversely, Lanham observes, the rhetoric of logic usually associated with nonfictional texts can also be used to invite an "aesthetic" response. He demonstrates (84–88) by unpacking the artful syllogistic strategies of John Lily's *Euphues: An Anatomy of Wit* (1574), but we could also see the effects operating in the Declaration of Independence, a Common Core text. Rosenblatt's labels for the two ends of the spectrum (aesthetic and efferent) are for Lanham "opaque" and "scientific," but these mean much the same thing and, as such, similarly constitute a continuum rather than a dichotomy: "Fictional prose is simply prose where the play attitude, the formal expectation, figures as strongly as the scientific explanation, sometimes more so" (139). Also common to these theorists is the sense that style, hardly equatable with mere decoration, entails principles of belief and of behavior. Lanham, like Rosenblatt, Wayne Booth, and Rabinowitz, shows us how style is inflected by a moral attitude, since "the feeling for right behavior is as much aesthetic as moral judgment" (179). A sharp division between "informational" and "literary" texts thus seems to emerge from an underdeveloped appreciation of the complex reading lessons afforded by well-crafted narrative, of the aesthetic aspects of influential texts generally read as efferent (i.e., mined for takeaways), and of the inseparability of even the most seemingly universal or transcendent message from its cultural contexts.

Texts such as the Gettysburg Address and the "Letter from Birmingham Jail" appear to fall about midway on the aesthetic-efferent continuum, and it is likely that they are selected for this reason. Certainly, one might question whether the Gettysburg Address or King's letter is best described as "built on informational text structures" (Coleman and Pimentel 5). Perhaps the arguments about how to teach such texts derive largely from what might be considered their hybrid nature. The enduring qualities of their arguments, the reasons for their canonicity, are bound up with and determined by their artistry. While they do not foster the identification with fictive characters that composers of the CCSS fear discourages critical reading of novels, poems, and plays, their artful and impassioned rhetorical turns invite aesthetic responses that inform their persuasive impact. The type of close reading reflected in the CCSS is a necessary but insufficient condition for achieving a felt understanding of the text. For that, one would need to nurture the sort of transactional reading argued by Rosenblatt. As she observes, while persuasive texts invite efferent readings, they are not therefore devoid of emotional appeal: "Emotions are to be aroused, but in order to affect judgments and decisions" (*Reader* 89n). Thus the isolation of the text from its rhetorical and cultural contexts further handicaps novice readers who need to develop more fully engaged ways of reading by gaining practice in playing the authorial audience.

David Coleman's instructions for directing students in a close reading of King's letter are somewhat modulated by his sense that the text is more than the sum of the points made in its discrete parts, that students must "dare to read the mystery of what's on King's mind" ("Bringing" 17). Indeed, among the "techniques" recommended, "The first and most important is to let the mysteries that the letter provokes be the source of student motivation" (22). However, the inspiring sense of the ineffable will reside more in the mind of the reader prepared and predisposed to entertain it rather than in the structure of the close-reading lesson. As another example, the exemplar lesson for the Gettysburg Address builds to an assignment asking students to "reflect on the particular genius of Lincoln's brief speech" ("Common Core Unit"). While well-intentioned, such an assignment is not likely to produce the desired results. Indeed, it is asking for trouble. How can students appreciate "genius," let alone the "particular genius" of Lincoln's rhetoric, without understanding the complexity of his task in its moment and with no bases for comparison? In his study of the address—the text in its political, cultural, and rhetorical contexts—Wills demonstrates irrefutably that "Lincoln was an artist, not just a scholar" (52), who effected his own mysterious transformation of the speech rhythms of his time into a "plain style" grounded in architecture that only seems simple because of the depth and discipline that underlie its construction: "'Plain speech' was never *less* artless" (174). Unfortunately, the recommended pedagogy of the standards is so fearful of undisciplined and idiosyncratic reading—what Rosenblatt has called "self-exploiting narcissistic impressionism or subjectivism" (*Reader* 174)—that it ends up paying only lip service to the aesthetic end of the reader-response continuum. The over-objectification of the text represses whatever prior understanding the reader may bring to it—"a whole body of cultural assumptions, practical knowledge, awareness of literary conventions, readinesses to think and feel" (*Reader* 88)—and conveys that such resources are irrelevant to reading.

To illustrate: One aim of the exemplar lesson is to show students "that a careful study of a crucial word [in this case *dedicate,* a form of which is used six times] as it develops across a piece is a way into understanding the entire piece" and to have them "reflect on how lingering on a key word can help to unlock the meaning of a piece." However, tracing the uses of the targeted word through the text, while it may help students see that words are not mere representations of specified things and that repetition can be strategic rather than redundant, will likely do little to engage their sense of Lincoln's rhetorical and emotional accomplishment. Rather, it may encourage the idea that focusing on one word is the way to expose an apparently hidden meaning. Moreover, the choice of a particular word is itself an act of interpretation delivered to students, who, in using this "key," will necessarily overlook other patterns such as the overarching "hook-and-eye method" (Wills 172) of Lincoln's sentence rhythms and word choices, including, e.g., the strategic repetition of common words like *here* that acquire special resonance on the bloody battlefield. The effect is to portray the text as a static and lifeless document, an approach that resembles the presentation of arguments in some composition textbooks as critiqued by Patricia Harkin and James Sosnoski: "textualized artifacts open to investigation rather than as cultural practices fraught with struggle and pain" (119). Empirical studies of how reading texts of various kinds affects empathy and cognition have focused not only on the cultivation of inferential thinking that develops the reader's theory-of-mind capacities, but also on the role of transportation into a text—the emotional engagement with a story that may allow us to feel "lost" in it and perhaps be transformed by it (Oatley; Green and Brock; Mar and Oatley). While fiction, by its very nature, depends on emotional transportation, nonfictional texts marked by rhetorical sophistication may also invite emotional engagement, provided that readers far from the occasion of their composition are helped to join the authorial audience, a key "starting point" (per Rabinowitz, *Before*) for interpretation.

In his reading of the Gettysburg Address, Wills's reminder that Lincoln was an artist as well as a scholar (52) suggests that the speech was as much a performance as a closely reasoned argument: "What should not be forgotten is that Lincoln was himself an actor, an expert raconteur and mimic" who enjoyed reading Shakespeare out loud to any who would listen (36). In a similar vein, Adam Gopnik observes that by deploying the rhythms of the King James Bible, Lincoln could "mak[e] the proposition that Texas and New Hampshire should be forever bound by a single post office sound like something right out of Genesis" (33). Since Lincoln's task was transformation—ensuring that the interpretation of the war's meaning would reflect his vision—his audience was also called upon to be transported by his words. During the three or so minutes that it took him to deliver the speech, his words elicited applause five times (Wills 36). We cannot, of course, expect our students to spontaneously erupt as did the crowds of citizens gathered in Gettysburg that day. But how might students approach the address if they knew that tens of thousands of soldiers died at Gettysburg in a war that was shocking in the vastness of its bloodshed, "that the killing was horrifying in its suddenness[, that] eighteen-year-olds were ripped apart at close quarters by minié balls [a type of bullet prominent in the Civil War], or shot down in the middle of normal drill by tree-infesting snipers" (Gopnik 116)? And that Lincoln had to accept his responsibility for the appalling loss of so many young men on both sides even as he dealt with the grief of losing his eleven-year-old son to an infectious illness? And, more broadly, that in Lincoln's time the notion of sacrifice was being recentered from the prospect of the soul in an eternal heaven to a focus on the achievements that might outlive us (Gopnik 121)? The picture will not come into focus without a frame. Dissection, no matter how expertly done, tends to atomize; equal attention must be paid to how overall effects are achieved. For such understanding—whether texts are narrative, expository, or argumentative, whether they call up readings that are aesthetic/opaque or efferent/scientific—both metatextual and metacontextual reading must be nurtured.

The argument, however, cannot rest there. Having made this case, I want to conclude by affirming nonetheless that we should indeed consider fiction a special case, though not in the way that the standards assume. Curriculum designers who draw a bright line between fiction and nonfiction have gone astray not because no such distinction can be made but because they have mistaken the nature of its import; that is, they have ignored or undervalued the complex interactions that stories in particular prompt in readers, offering a "laboratory" for rehearsing behaviors that might be impossible or unwise to enact in real life (Mar and Oatley 183). Since the effects of such role-playing and the inferential thinking it entails can potentially transform feeling, thinking, and acting, we who are involved in the high-school-to-college transition are positioned to teach literature in ways that are rigorous, relevant, and empowering. Guided by the theorized and experience-based arguments of notable teacher-scholars such as Rosenblatt, Booth, Rabinowitz, Blau, and Zunshine, along with the compelling body of empirical research into the transformative impact of well-crafted fiction, we can shape our teaching strategies to stretch our students as we illuminate the disciplined practices of interpretation and critique. The singular ways that reading narrative fictions, especially those of literary distinction, can enlarge our minds and spirits by taking us out of ourselves, only to let us return with deeper understanding of ourselves and others, yield extraordinary opportunities to deepen in our students the dispositions and behavior that are valued in classrooms across the curriculum, in the workplace, and in the complex webs of social and personal life.

Appendix 2

Reading Support for History Majors

Professor Anne Osborne, Department of History, Rider University
HIS 160 Seminar in History
Schecter, "Bastions of Authority"
Reading and Summary Assignment

1. Read Chapter 1, "Bastions of Authority," from Barnet Schecter, *The Battle for New York: The City at the Heart of the American Revolution*, Walker, 2002.
As noted in class, it is a good idea to perform a preliminary reconnaissance of a text before plunging ahead into unfamiliar territory: it will be much easier not to get lost. Read the first and last paragraph or two, whether or not they are formally labeled as introduction and conclusion. Note also the structure of the article or chapter: are there subheadings or blank spaces indicating separate sections? Is there a brief summary or concluding statement at the end of each section? See if you can tell what main topics will be addressed and what the main conclusions may be. Now that you have a map indicating where the author is trying to take you, go back and read the article carefully, paying attention to the evidence offered to support the author's historical account and prove his point. Also be alert to the claims the author may make about how this study fits into the broader conversation on this topic.

Obviously you cannot effectively engage a text if you do not understand the vocabulary. Look up unfamiliar words. For example, do you know what a *bastion* is? What might Schecter mean by "bastions of authority"? Once you have identified the argument of the chapter, consider why he uses this phrase as the title of his first chapter. What idea does its use reinforce?

Your goal in this process is both to master the key points in the narrative, and, equally important, to identify the argument the author is making and the evidence he presents to support it.

2. Prepare a summary of Schecter's "Bastions of Authority."
A summary condenses the main ideas of a text in one's own words. It should include the author's main idea or thesis, the main topics addressed, and the main evidence used to support the thesis. It should preserve the structure of the author's argument. It does not include your

reaction or evaluation of the author's argument. (You'll get a chance to share those ideas in class.)

Your summary of Schecter's Chapter 1 should fulfill the requirements noted above in approximately one typed page, single-spaced.

HIS 260: The Craft of History

Class Preparation:

The materials you will be reading are challenging. They are significantly different from simply reading textbooks. Such books are distillations of information, presented in a simplified way. Section and chapter introductions sketch out main themes; subheadings articulate the structure of the chapter; definitions are given for unfamiliar terms; a conclusion summarizes the main ideas. Key terms signal the most important details. A textbook is thus a vehicle for the quick and easy transmission of factual information, and a useful reference to supplement information gained in other ways. It does not usually ask the reader to evaluate an argument or the evidence for a particular claim.

Unlike textbooks, historical scholarship generally attempts to make an argument. It marshals evidence to prove a point: it is interpretive rather than merely descriptive. The most important things to be aware of when reading historical scholarship are the historical question the author is asking; the author's thesis (that is, the argument they are making) and the evidence that supports that thesis, including primary sources. In reading historical scholarship, you need to be alert to the author's thesis and analytical in evaluating their argument. Ask such questions as: Does the evidence offered prove the author's thesis? Could it be interpreted in a different way? Is there evidence that would refute the author's argument? Generally, when reading such scholarship, it is at least as important to evaluate the interpretation of why things happened and how the author makes the argument as to master what the facts are.

Give yourself time first to skim each work to get a general sense of the main points each author is making. It is often useful first to read the beginning and end (whether formally labeled *introduction* and *conclusion* or not). As you do this, pay attention to the structure of the piece, as this can help you understand which are the main points and which are subsidiary or illustrative details. Consider the purpose of the selection: for example, an introduction will probably describe points that will be elaborated further in the rest of the work: it will not necessarily make or prove an argument. An article, however, normally makes a specific argument about the past (rather than simply describing some aspect of it) and offers evidence to support that argument. Then reread the work carefully so that you can follow and evaluate the author's argument. Look up vocabulary you are not familiar with.

You will complete a written article review sheet for some readings, but you should be able to describe key aspects of all the works we read. Pay particular attention to the thesis of the article, its scope, and the sources and methods used. (The thesis is the main point the author is making; the scope is the subject of the article. Thus for example, "an attempt to explain the causes of afflictions attributed to witchcraft in Salem in 1692" might be the scope of an article; its thesis might be, "The symptoms interpreted as signs of possession were in fact caused by hallucinogens produced by spoiled grain.") Also note how the given work fits in with other scholarship we have read on that topic. Without this information, you will be able to sit in on the class, so that you do not fall even farther behind, but you will not be able to participate effectively, and your class participation grade for the day will reflect that.

If despite a genuine attempt to grapple with the piece, including reading it at least twice, you do not understand it, bring in as much of the required information as possible together with specific questions on the aspects you do not understand. Be prepared to show what you understand and precisely what points are still unclear to you, and show how you have grappled with possible meanings.

Appendix 3

Examples of Answers to Preworkshop Exercise for Diving Deep in the Disciplines

Example 1: Literature

Epistemological and conceptual assumptions:

1. Fictional texts can embody important truths about the nature of the human condition.
2. Form and content are always implied in each other and always mutually determinative.
3. Texts have value as both aesthetic constructs and as indices to social and political dynamics in historical context.
4. Different theoretical approaches will yield different emphases and even entirely different meanings and implications; such choices are therefore not neutral (free of ideological perspective).

Methodological assumptions:

1. Assertions about a text must be located in conversations with other critiques or analyses. Often literary arguments take the form of "they say/I say."
2. Interpretations of texts must account for the various aspects of the text as a whole. This does not mean, however, that each text must present an answer to a question or a single coherent vision. Rather, the conflicts and tensions within texts are often the subject of argument and can illuminate the text's complexity and therefore its deep relationship to real human experience.
3. All approaches to the text, regardless of theoretical stance, should begin with multiple close readings.

Fundamental questions:

1. How should the value of a text be determined?
2. What kinds of texts are worth studying? How are the criteria for making these judgments derived, and how have they changed over time?

3. What are the implications of using one set of value criteria over another?

4. How have genres been defined? How and why have these definitions shifted historically?

Tacit habits of mind:

1. One reads in various roles, per Wayne Booth's analysis of the various forms of the "implied reader."

2. In reading narrative fiction, one is always sensitive to point of view.

3. One is alert to patterns (of image, syntax, allusion, etc.) as a way into the text's theme and effects.

4. One is conscious of the effects of the text as a temporal experience and to one's own shifting responses upon rereading.

5. One reads for the pleasure of the aesthetic experience (which inevitably has other dimensions—moral, spiritual, intellectual) while also recognizing the material circumstances that generated the text.

Common misconceptions/novice habits:

1. Since literature is "open to interpretation," all opinions about its meaning should be considered equally valid.

2. If one probes the text deeply, one runs the danger of "reading things into" it.

3. Only the author can know what the text "really" means.

4. The best literature enables easy identification of the reader with the protagonist.

5. Literature should not be disturbing; the best literature affirms one's closely held values, beliefs, and ways of understanding oneself and the world.

6. Reading literature through a theoretical lens is just a "teacher's game" (cf. Craig Nelson on the Perry Scheme ["On the Persistence"]).

Example 2: Chemistry (composed by Danielle Jacobs Duda, Department of Chemistry, Rider University)

Epistemological and conceptual assumptions for practitioners of your discipline:

1. We live and think in two worlds: the macroscopic world, where we make observations, and the microscopic (or "real" world of atoms, molecules, cells), where we exist.

2. We represent and explain these two worlds using chemical and/or mathematical symbols and conventions.

3. Everything a person does or uses involves a chemical and/or physical process (e.g., driving a car is a chemical process and the motion of the car can be modeled by physics; clothing is made of chemicals; water is a chemical; food undergoes chemical changes when it enters our bodies).

Methodological assumptions for practitioners of your discipline:

1. To understand that microscopic world, we create representations of it and equations that describe those representations.

2. To understand how the microscopic world affects the macroscopic world, we use models that are based on current knowledge, and establish rules about how those models work that explain physical observations.

3. We use observations in the macroscopic world to verify that our representations of the microscopic world are valid.

Fundamental questions for practitioners of your discipline:

1. How do we synthesize our research findings to design a model or models that best represent the chemical and physical phenomena we observe?

2. Can we use those models to help predict the behavior of other chemical and physical systems, both previously known and currently unknown?

3. How can we use the information garnered from these models to improve the quality of life for current (and future—sustainability is a relatively new question) generations?

Tacit habits of mind for practitioners of your discipline:

1. Our understanding of the microscopic world is controlled by our ability to make an observation and develop a model to explain that observation.

2. Chemists readily jump from one representative framework to another. See A. H. Johnstone, "You Can't Get There from Here," *Journal of Chemical Education,* vol. 22, no. 29, 2010, pp. 22–29. doi:10.1021/ed800026d.

APPENDIX 3

The scientific method permeates the questions we (chemists, biochemists, physicists) pose in our disciplines. The method starts with a hypothesis or educated guess about the outcome of an experiment. This hypothesis would likely be based on an existing model or an extension of an existing model. Once an experiment is done, we then make sure that the results either fit the existing model or require development of a new understanding/model/rule for model.

Responses to common misconceptions/novice habits of mind:

1. The practice of science is a rational process of developing models to explain how the universe works and *not just a body of facts.*
2. All scientific phenomena follow a reasonable pattern with a rational explanation, following a model that can explain more than one scientific observation; *scientific realities are not isolated phenomena, and can help predict other phenomena.*
3. Our knowledge of the world is fluid, not stagnant. *Our understanding of that world can change* as new experiments provide other evidence that may require modification of our representation of the microscopic world.
4. The real world can be understood by more than one model, and *all models do not work for all circumstances,* so an appropriate model must be carefully chosen to match the circumstances.
5. A competent person should be able to distinguish between *evidence-based science and pseudoscience* or at least recognize when further information is needed to make that distinction.
6. Not every source of information is valid; *novices must learn how to distinguish between statements/conclusions based on evidence and sources that do not use evidence or use it incorrectly or unethically.*

APPENDIX 4

SAMPLE ASSIGNMENTS FOR A FIRST-YEAR COURSE SEQUENCE IN RHETORICAL READING

Texts and Assignments

The assignment sequences below are intended to illustrate the pedagogic approach advocated in this book: assignments are crafted to help students practice rhetorical reading across disciplines and genres and writing that is based on understanding of enduring conversations that emerge from significant texts.

Ideally, all sections of each course would share a few significant "anchor" texts, as indicated. This consistency offers students a common intellectual experience, enhances faculty development, and provides a base for vertical integration of content and skills. It can also aid in meaningful program assessment.

Instructors are asked to choose suitable readings to complement the anchor texts. (Some suggestions for complementary texts are included here.) In addition, instructors should provide contextual frames for the readings, orienting students to time period, zeitgeist, and the broad outlines of the conversation each author is entering.

It is assumed that, when syllabi are designed, time will be allocated for feedback on writing-to-read assignments and paper drafts (e.g., group work, peer review, instructor responses).

Organization

Semester 1 engages students in enduring questions that emerge from different disciplinary emphases. In the sample below, the questions are as follows: (1) What is scientific thinking? (2) How do we balance freedom and responsibility? (3) How do narratives shape our thoughts and feelings?

Semester 2 connects enduring texts with current debates such as the following: Is material well-being a universal right? Is morality absolute or situational? Through source-based exercises connected to research questions that emerge from course content, students are introduced to basic inquiry methods and the broader aspects of information literacy.

Faculty Development

It is helpful for faculty to meet at least twice per semester to enable the benefits of teamwork, e.g., to discuss the anchor texts and how best to help students grapple with them, share and assess assignments, discuss students' progress, engage in grading workshops, and exchange advice on issues as they arise.

Good resources to help prepare faculty for teaching classes such as these include the following (for bibliographic details, see Works Cited in this volume):

- Anson, Chris (2017). "Writing to Read, Revisited." Advocates and illustrates the development of engaging low-stakes writing assignments to encourage better critical reading.

- Baehr, Jason (2013). "Educating for Intellectual Virtues: An Introductory Guide for College and University Instructors." Offers a framework to encourage students' reflection about their emerging selves in relation to ideas from their reading and writing; can serve as a bridge to first-year seminars that focus on student affective and emotional development. The "virtues" include traits such as curiosity, persistence, open-mindedness, intellectual humility, and intellectual courage.

- Carillo, Ellen C. (2016). "Engaging Sources through Reading-Writing Connections across the Disciplines." Maps out an assignment sequence for encouraging reading-writing connections leading to "critical conversations" using several sources.

- Horning, Alice S. (2011). "Where to Put the Manicules: A Theory of Expert Reading." Defines meta-reading and illustrates purposeful strategies to foster students' understanding of extended informational prose texts in any discipline.

Semester 1: Sample Reading and Writing Assignments

Introduction
Introduce students to Baehr's "intellectual virtues."

1. Consider having students assess their own traits, using the chart on p. 68.

2. Discuss William Cronon, "Only Connect: The Goals of a Liberal Education"

Writing to Read

1. What commonalities do you see between Cronon's definition of a liberal education and Baehr's "intellectual virtues"?
2. If a summer book has been assigned, pose the following question: How does the author or an individual described (if nonfiction) or the narrator, protagonist, or another character (if fiction) demonstrate or fail to demonstrate one or more of the intellectual virtues described by Cronon or Baehr?

Introduction to Reading Rhetorically (Meta-reading)
Use a short in-class reading, such as a well-written editorial, to practice identification of "they say" elements and their relation to "I say" elements (Graff and Birkenstein, op. cit.).

Sequence 1 Question: What is scientific thinking? How does it compare with earlier ways of explaining the material world?

Sequence 1 Anchor Texts

- Genesis 1–3
- Charles Darwin, "The Descent of Man" (abridged Chapter 1)

Sequence 1 Sample Writing-to-Read Assignments

1. Analyze the texts using rhetorical reading principles from Horning: metalinguistic, metatextual, metacontextual; or apply Carillo's annotation exercise. (See suggested resources for faculty development, above.)
2. Compare details of the creation account in Genesis Chapter 2 with those in Chapter 3, especially the relationship between the Creator and his creatures. Then compare the intellectual and emotional effects of the two narratives.
3. Create a list of questions that the narratives of Genesis 1–3 address, compare questions and answers inherent in a creation story from a different culture, and speculate on reasons for the similarities and differences.

Sequence 1 Sample Complementary Texts

- E. O. Wilson, "Intelligent Evolution"
- Brian Doyle, "Joyas Voladoras"
- Annie Dillard, "Living like Weasels"

- Ernst Mayr, "Darwin's Influence on Modern Thought"
- Stephen Jay Gould, "The Chain of Reason vs. the Chain of Thumbs"
- E. O. Wilson, "What Is Science?"

Sequence 1 Sample Complementary Writing-to-Read Assignments

1. Annotate one of the argumentative or expository essays (Wilson or Mayr) and then write a "they say/I say" or a "says/does" analysis. (For the latter, see John Bean, *Engaging Ideas,* pp. 171–72.)

2. Tease out *implicit* "they say/I say" elements from the essays by Doyle and Dillard. Try to express the overall theme of each essay in a sentence or two.

3. Unlike conventional expository or argumentative essays (e.g., Wilson's), the more literary essays by Doyle and Dillard evolve in unexpected ways and surprise readers with an unanticipated theme or message. Chart this development, noting the relationship of each part to the whole. Then compare this strategy, and its effects on you as a reader, with the argumentative strategies used by Darwin or Wilson.

4. Both Gould and Wilson aim to dispel misconceptions about science among the general public. Decide which essay makes a more effective appeal to readers and, using a rhetorical analysis, explain why.

5. Build a graphic organizer (Bean, *Engaging Ideas,* pp. 179–80) and/or use group work to highlight connections among readings so far.

Sample Topics for Sequence 1 Paper

1. Using at least two of the texts studied so far, write an essay that answers the following questions: What can we learn from considering both our *connection* with "lower" life forms and our *differences* from them? Why is it important to understand both?

   Answering the first question will require you to demonstrate good reading comprehension, since you will have to include brief summaries of the main ideas of the selected texts.

   Answering the second question will require you to consider the "So what?" aspect of your topic that your readers will naturally have in mind. That is, what choices do we make or face—individually or as a society—that reflect our understanding of humanity in relation to other animals? Length should be about three pages. Be sure to use evidence from the texts to make your case.

2. In "Intelligent Evolution," E. O. Wilson writes the following: "The inexorable growth of [biology] continues to widen, not to close, the tectonic gap between science and faith-based religion. . . . Rapprochement [emerging agreement] may be neither possible nor desirable."

   In an essay of about three pages, briefly *explain Wilson's claims* here and then *respond with your own perspective,* including ideas from one of the other texts we have discussed. This means you are required to use two readings—the one by Wilson (whose ideas you will clearly represent as the "conversation-starter") and one additional text.

   In your response, you may agree entirely with Wilson, agree in part ("Yes, but . . ."), or disagree. In each case, you will need to explain both his point of view and your own and, in explaining your own position, use at least one of the other texts specified above.

3. Using at least two of the texts studied in this thematic group, explain and illustrate the qualities that distinguish scientific inquiry from other approaches to understanding the material (physical) world. In your essay, explain how your selected authors acknowledge and attempt to dispel what they consider common misconceptions about science. Include your thinking on the importance of basic scientific understanding for nonscientists.

Sequence 2 Question: How has the tension between individual freedom and responsibility to authority shaped ideas and human behavior?

Sequence 2 Anchor Text

- Thomas Jefferson, the Declaration of Independence

Sequence 2 Sample Writing-to-Read Assignments

1. Look up five to ten words that are unfamiliar to you. Some of these will have multiple connotations. Considering Jefferson's historical contexts, and considering the use of the words in the context of the document as a whole, try to determine the meanings for each that Jefferson likely intended. Explain your thinking.

2. Analyze the (syllogistic) structure of Jefferson's argument, and consider its intended effects on target audiences.

3. Read the "rough draft" of the declaration and speculate on possible reasons for the revisions.

Sequence 2 Sample Complementary Texts

- Stanley Milgram, "Some Conditions of Obedience and Disobedience to Authority" and Stanley Milgram, "The Perils of Obedience"
- Susan Glaspell, "A Jury of Her Peers"
- Martin Luther King Jr., "Letter from Birmingham Jail"

Sequence 2 Sample Complementary Writing-to-Read Assignments

1. Compare the content and rhetoric of the two versions of Milgram's report, including reasons for and effects of the differences.
2. Work in groups to do a "they say/I say" analysis or a "says/does" analysis of selected sections of King's "Letter," relating your conclusions to the document's overall themes and purposes.
3. Consider the ways in which "A Jury of Her Peers," a piece of fiction, makes an implied argument. Tease out implied "they say/I say" elements, keeping in mind *genre* differences (short story versus essay).

Sample Topics for Sequence 2 Paper

1. According to Stanley Milgram's study of the conditions in which people choose to disobey authority, "Many subjects [could] not find the verbal formula that would enable them to reject the role assigned to them by the experimenter [an authority figure]. Perhaps our culture does not provide adequate models for disobedience" (67).

   Write an essay in which you apply Milgram's findings to the situation of either Jefferson or King. Explain: How did Jefferson or King, in his document, offer the "verbal formula" appropriate for his time that would embolden people to disobey long-standing and extremely powerful authority figures and structures? How did Jefferson or King help people rethink the "conditions" that might affect their choices? [Note: See Chapter 4 in this volume for a discussion of this assignment in the context of a composition class taught by the author.]

2. Use Milgram's various "conditions" to analyze the choices made by Mrs. Peters and Mrs. Hale in "A Jury of Her Peers" and to explain your interpretation of the story as a whole. Indicate in your analysis the role of larger social and cultural conditions

that shape the women's decisions. Support your analysis with evidence from both texts.

Sequence 2 Sample Alternative Complementary Texts (Media/Communication/Digital Data Emphasis)

- Nicholas Carr, "Is Google Making Us Stupid?"
- Kate Crawford, Kate Miltner, and Mary L. Gray, "Critiquing Big Data: Politics, Ethics, Epistemology"
- Neil Postman, *Amusing Ourselves to Death: Public Discourse in the Age of Show Business,* Chapters 6 ("The Age of Show Business") and 7 ("Now . . .This").
- Noam Cohen, "Facebook Doesn't Like What It Sees When It Looks in the Mirror"
- Henry Kissinger, "How the Enlightenment Ends"

Sample Alternative Topic for Sequence 2 Paper

Synthesizing ideas from two or three of the texts above, write a letter to Thomas Jefferson explaining how modern technologies have affected one or more of the "self-evident truths" that are the basis of a democracy or our "inalienable rights" as citizens of a democratic country. Offer your own thinking on the seriousness of the effects you describe and your level of optimism about potential remedies or safeguards.

Sequence 3 Question: How do narratives shape our thoughts and feelings?

Sequence 3 Anchor Text

- James Baldwin, "Sonny's Blues"

Show video clip of Baldwin interview (*Florida Forum,* 1963)

- Introduce *narrative point of view;* review distinction between *essay* and *story*.
- Distinguish *theme* from *thesis*. Introduce *verbal, situational,* and *dramatic irony*.

Sequence 3 Sample Writing-to-Read Assignments

1. Consider the 1963 interview with Baldwin. How do the interviewers' questions and responses create dramatic irony when considered today?

2. Consider the following questions with regard to "Sonny's Blues":

   - What is the effect of Baldwin's choice of narrator?
   - Why are events of the story related out of chronological order? Identify story details that enable readers to build a theme.
   - How does irony play a role in this story? Relate the ironic elements to the overall theme.
   - How do apparently disparate pieces of the story, by the end, merge into a coherent experience for readers?

Sequence 3 Possible Complementary Texts

- James Baldwin, "Stranger in the Village"
- Jane Brox, "Influenza 1918"
- Rachel Carson, *Silent Spring,* Chapters 1 ("A Fable for Tomorrow") and 2 ("The Obligation to Endure")
- Nadine Gordimer, "Once upon a Time" (fiction)
- Trevor Noah, "Chameleon"
- John Noble Wilford, "Discovering Columbus"

Sequence 3 Sample Complementary Writing-to-Read Assignments

1. Illustrate the difference between *thesis* and *theme* by comparing the qualities and effects of Baldwin's essay "Stranger in the Village" with those of his short story "Sonny's Blues" or with those of Gordimer's story "Once upon a Time."
2. In what ways is Carson's first chapter a "fable"? Do a "they say/I say "or a "says/does" analysis of Chapter 2. After considering the relationship between Chapter 1 and Chapter 2, explain why Carson decided to begin with a genre not typically associated with science writing.
3. What is a memoir? Speculate on the audience response Noah hoped to evoke in "Chameleon."
4. On its surface, Wilford's essay is simply an overview of changing views of Christopher Columbus. However, a careful analysis reveals that Wilford is writing about an idea bigger than the story of Columbus's reputation. Identify where his thesis (overall point) is stated or implied. Then do a "says/does" analysis to show how the parts of the essay contribute to the development of this general claim.

5. In her author's note, Brox lists the various sources she used for her nonfiction essay. Speculate on which sources might have supplied which details. Connect Brox's selection of detail and other aspects of her writing style with what you conclude is her purpose in writing this essay.

6. Selecting three of the readings from this group, create a chart showing how the genre of each is evident in selected characteristics. Consider how these differences affect you as a reader; consider both your strategies for reading and the insights you derive.

Sample Topics for Sequence 3 Paper

1. Explain in detail the strategies used by one or more of the writers in this section to convey a particular point of view on the topic at hand. What other perspectives, which some readers are likely to hold, are thereby modified, changed, complicated, or repudiated? What was the effect of these strategies on you as you read and thought about the text(s)?

2. If you created the chart described in Question 6 above, use it to write an essay explaining and illustrating the importance of genre in creating an impact on readers.

Semester 1 Final Paper

Write a final essay using selected texts and your prior writing to explain what you have learned about yourself from the work of the semester, focusing on one or more of the traits in Baehr's schema (open-mindedness, intellectual courage, intellectual humility, persistence, etc.). Be prepared to share drafts in class, get feedback, and submit during finals week.

Semester 2: Sample Reading and Writing Assignments

Debate 1 Question: Is Material Well-Being a Universal Right?

Debate 1 Anchor Text

- Herbert J. Gans, "The Uses of Poverty: The Poor Pay All"

Debate 1 Sample Writing-to-Read Assignment

Write a rhetorical précis (see Bean, *Reading Rhetorically*) or a "says/does" analysis of this essay that illustrates how poverty is "useful" to a society. Then write a one-paragraph response, explaining your reaction to Gans's argument.

Debate 1 Sample Complementary Texts

- Barbara Ehrenreich, "Nickel-and-Dimed: On (Not) Getting By in America"
- Barbara Ehrenreich, "Class Matters"
- Milton Friedman, "The Social Responsibility of Business Is to Increase Profits"
- John Mackey, "Rethinking the Social Responsibility of Business"

Debate 1 Sample Complementary Writing-to-Read Assignments

1. Write a short essay that makes an interesting connection between the perspectives of Gans and Ehrenreich.
2. Keeping in mind that Mackey's argument is an explicit response to Friedman's (thirty-five years after Friedman's essay was published), do the following:
   - Explain concisely the basic point on which they disagree.
   - Seek to discern any areas of common ground between Mackey and Friedman. If you can find any, then consider what basic difference in philosophy or assumptions might account for the divergence in their main arguments.
   - Speculate: How might Friedman, were he alive today, write a rebuttal to Mackey, using some aspects of Mackey's own argument?

Debate 1 Additional Sample Complementary Texts

- Robert Reich, "How Capitalism Is Killing Democracy"
- Karen L. Higgins, "Economic Growth and Sustainability: Are They Mutually Exclusive?"

Debate 1 Additional Sample Writing-to-Read Assignments

1. Analysis of Higgins
   - Briefly state the "paradox" that is the subject of Higgins's paper.
   - Locate and paraphrase language in Higgins's paper that states her *thesis* (main argument).

- Identify the *kinds of evidence* she uses to support her thesis.
- Observe the *kinds of data* chosen for graphic or quantitative representation, and comment on how visual and verbal data are used together.

2. Synthesis

   Reich is not responding directly to either Friedman or Mackey, but his argument addresses some of the same issues in ways that enable readers to put the three essays into a "conversation" with one another. In order to deeply imagine such a conversation, do the following, possibly using a graphic organizer for the first two tasks:

   - Identify the issues that all three essays address.
   - Infer from the evidence of Reich's essay the areas where he seems to agree with Friedman (and even to use Friedman's premises) and where he seems to agree with Mackey.
   - Use textual evidence to defend the claim that Reich's proposed remedies grow more logically from Friedman's assumptions than from Mackey's—or vice versa.

Sample Topic for Debate 1 Paper

Read Jeffrey Pfeffer, "Building Sustainable Organizations: The Human Factor." Then write an essay that uses Pfeffer along with Ehrenreich, Mackey, Reich, *or* Higgins to broaden the definition of *sustainability*.

Use the following questions to guide your synthesis:

- How have the writers explained the role of the "the human factor" in organizational management and its effect on the common good?
- Why, in their view, is altruism not a zero-sum dynamic?
- How might Herbert Gans respond to their arguments?
- Drawing on ideas from these essays, conclude your paper by suggesting a *policy decision* that you think would have a positive effect on both individuals and the larger communities or environments they belong to.

Debate 2 Question: Is Morality Absolute or Situational?

Debate 2 Anchor Texts

- Plato, "The Allegory of the Cave"

- Niccolò Machiavelli, "The Morals of the Prince"

Debate 2 Sample Complementary Texts

- Kwame Anthony Appiah, "The Case against Character"
- Steven Pinker, "The Moral Instinct"

Debate 2 Sample Writing-to-Read Assignments

1. Write a "they say/I say" analysis of Appiah's essay.
2. Build a graphic organizer and/or use group work to highlight similarities and differences among readings so far (synthesis skills).

Research Skills/Information Literacy

[Note: This link to the Indiana University–Purdue University Indianapolis Writing Center Resources can be used as a resource for skills related to research-based writing: liberalarts.iupui.edu/uwc/pages/resources-folder/index.php.

The instructions for composing an annotated bibliography include an example that can help students prepare the following assignment:]

Submit an annotated bibliography of three sources that address the policy idea—or a related one—considered in your Debate 1 paper.

If you are interested in psychology and ethics, you might emphasize the ethical aspects of essays from the prior text group (on material well-being for all) and also consider the following: How might any of the ethical theories we are discussing contribute to a specific political decision, action, or policy?

Suggestions for Short Stories Related to Ethical Choices

- Rebecca Goldstein, "The Legacy of Raizel Kaidish"
- Amy Tan, "The Red Candle"
- Chimamanda Ngozi Adichi, "Apollo"

Sample Topics for Debate 2 Paper

1. Using ideas from one of the nonfictional texts in this group (e.g., Plato's idealism, Machiavelli's pragmatic approach, Appiah's situational ethics, or Pinker's moral spheres) analyze and evaluate a moral choice made by a character in one of the short stories.

   Alternatively, you may assume the persona of Appiah or Pinker and use "your" scholarly expertise to do the analysis and evaluation. Before writing, define your audience—e.g., the character herself, a general audience of readers who may have read the story, students in an introductory class on ethics, etc.

2. For an essay on Machiavelli's "The Morals of the Prince" and on Plato's "Allegory of the Cave," imagine the following situation:

   Some students in your former high school are studying the European Renaissance in World History. You have been asked by your high school to return as a guest speaker in the World History class in order to share what you know about Machiavelli's philosophy. Because you would not feel comfortable speaking only from notes, you have decided to write a paper that you will read to the high school students.

Your paper will explain Machiavelli's ideas in language the students will easily understand, even though they have not read anything Machiavelli wrote. Because these students have already studied Plato's "Allegory of the Cave," you refer to Plato for purposes of comparison or contrast. In order to make sure they understand how Machiavelli's ideas are relevant to more recent times, you decide to include in your paper two examples drawn from your knowledge of history, and/or current events. One example will illustrate political behavior that you consider "Machiavellian"; the other will illustrate leadership that you consider "Platonic." You end by offering your own assessment of the relative value of both perspectives.

[Note: See Chapter 4 in this volume for a discussion of this assignment in the context of a composition class taught by the author.]

Preparation for Research-Based Paper

- Review your annotated bibliography and work on your mini-literature review; use examples at liberalarts.iupui.edu/uwc/files/documents/Lit_Review_Synthesis.pdf.
- Working with peers and using a rubric or guidelines supplied by your instructor, review a draft of your research-based paper, including in-text citations and works-cited pages.
- Write an abstract that will serve as the basis for your four-minute oral presentation, including the following:
  1. A statement of your research question
  2. A summary of your findings in response to the research question
  3. Something of particular interest that you learned
  4. A statement about why your subject matters to the world in general and/or is significant to you

Semester 2 Final Paper: A Reflection and Application

Write an essay using selected texts and your prior writing to reflect on what you have learned about yourself from the work of the semester, focusing on one or more of the traits in Baehr's schema (open-mindedness, intellectual courage, intellectual humility, persistence, etc.). Be prepared to share drafts in class, get feedback, and submit during finals week.

Selected Bibliography for Sample Assignments

Adichie, Chimamanda Ngozi. "Apollo." *The New Yorker*, vol. 90, no. 8, 13 Apr. 2015. https://www.newyorker.com/magazine/2015/04/13/apollo.

Appiah, Kwame Anthony. "The Case against Character." *A World of Ideas,* edited by Lee A. Jacobus, 10th ed., Bedford/St. Martin's, 2017, pp. 801–16.

Arp, Thomas R., and Greg Johnson, editors. *Perrine's Story and Structure: An Introduction to Fiction,* 13th ed. Wadsworth/Cengage Learning, 2012.

Baldwin, James. Interview by Tom Miller et al., *Florida Forum,* WCKT News, 28 June 1963, www.youtube.com/watch?v=FpRziHGxeEU.

———. "Sonny's Blues." *Going to Meet the Man,* by Baldwin, Dial Press, 1965, pp. 103–41.

———. "Stranger in the Village." *Notes of a Native Son,* by Baldwin, Beacon Press, 1984, pp. 159–75.

Brox, Jane. "Influenza 1918." *One Hundred Great Essays,* edited by Robert DiYanni, 5th ed., Pearson, 2013, pp. 79–87.

Carr, Nicholas. "Is Google Making Us Stupid?" *The Atlantic,* July–Aug. 2008, pp. 56–63.

Carson, Rachel. *Silent Spring. Internet Archive,* archive.org/stream/fp_Silent_Spring-Rachel_Carson-1962/Silent_Spring-Rachel_Carson-1962_djvu.txt.

Cohen, Noam. "Facebook Doesn't Like What It Sees When It Looks in the Mirror." *The New York Times,* 16 Jan. 2018, vol. 167, no. 57845, p. A19.

Crawford, Kate, et al. "Critiquing Big Data: Politics, Ethics, Epistemology." *International Journal of Communication,* vol. 8, 2014, pp. 1663–72, ijoc.org/index.php/ijoc/article/viewFile/2167/1164.

Dillard, Annie. "Living like Weasels." *One Hundred Great Essays*, edited by Robert DiYanni, 5th ed., Pearson, 2013, pp. 118–22.

Doyle, Brian. "Joyas Voladoras." Peterson et al., shorter 13th ed., pp. 291–93.

Ehrenreich, Barbara. "Class Matters." *Anglican Theological Review*, vol. 98, no. 1, Winter 2016, pp. 15–21.

———. "Nickel-and-Dimed: On (Not) Getting By in America." *Harper's Magazine*, vol. 298, no. 1784, Jan. 1999, pp. 37–52.

Friedman, Milton. "The Social Responsibility of Business Is to Increase Profits." *The New York Times Magazine*, 13 Sept. 13, 1970, sec. SM, p. 12.

Gans, Herbert J. "The Uses of Poverty: The Poor Pay All." *Social Policy*, July–Aug. 1971, pp. 20–24. Rpt. in *Down to Earth Sociology: Introductory Readings*, edited by James M. Henslin, 12th ed., Free Press, 2003, pp. 340–46.

Glaspell, Susan. "A Jury of Her Peers." Arp and Johnson, pp. 574–93.

Goldstein, Rebecca. "The Legacy of Raizel Kaidish." *Strange Attractors*, by Goldstein, Viking, 1993, pp. 229–40.

Gordimer, Nadine. "Once Upon a Time." *Salmagundi*, no. 81, 1989, pp. 67–73. Rpt. in Arp and Johnson, pp. 189–94.

Gould, Stephen Jay. "The Chain of Reason vs. the Chain of Thumbs." *Natural History*, vol. 98, no. 7, July 1989, pp. 1–8. Rpt. in *Bully for Brontosaurus*, W. W. Norton, 1989, pp. 182–97.

Higgins, Karen L. "Economic Growth and Sustainability: Are They Mutually Exclusive?" *Elsevier Connect*, 16 May 2013, www.elsevier.com/connect/economic-growth-and-sustainability-are-they-mutually-exclusive.

King, Martin Luther, Jr. "Letter from Birmingham Jail." Peterson et al., shorter 13th edition, pp. 502–15.

Kissinger, Henry A. "How the Enlightenment Ends." *The Atlantic*, vol. 321, no. 5, June 2018, pp. 11–14.

Machiavelli, Niccolò. "The Morals of the Prince." Trans. Robert M. Adams. Peterson et al., 13th ed., shorter version, pp. 485–91.

Mackey, John. "Rethinking the Social Responsibility of Business." *Reason*, vol. 37, no. 5, Oct. 2005, pp. 28–37.

Mayr, Ernst. "Darwin's Influence on Modern Thought." 2000. *Scientific American*, 24 Nov. 2009, www.scientificamerican.com/article/darwins-influence-on-modern-thought/.

Milgram, Stanley. "The Perils of Obedience." *Harper's Magazine*, vol. 247, no. 1483, Dec. 1973, pp. 62–66, 75–77.

———. "Some Conditions of Obedience and Disobedience to Authority." *Human Relations*, vol. 18, no. 1, Feb. 1965, pp. 57–76.

Noah, Trevor. "Chameleon." *Born a Crime: Stories from a South African Childhood*, by Noah, Spiegel & Grau, 2016, pp. 49–62.

Peterson, Linda H., et al., editors. *The Norton Reader: An Anthology of Nonfiction*. Shorter 13th ed., W. W. Norton, 2012.

Pfeffer, Jeffrey. "Building Sustainable Organizations: The Human Factor." *Academy of Management Perspectives*, vol. 24, no. 1, Feb. 2010, pp. 34–45.

Pinker, Steven. "The Moral Instinct." *The New York Times Magazine*, vol. 157, no. 54188, 13 Jan. 2008, pp. 32–58. Rpt. in Peterson et al., shorter 13th ed., pp. 321–38.

Plato. "The Allegory of the Cave." *A World of Ideas: Essential Readings for College Writers*, edited by Lee A. Jacobus, Bedford/St. Martin's, 2017, pp. 580–90.

Postman, Neil. *Amusing Ourselves to Death: Public Discourse in the Age of Show Business*. Twentieth anniversary ed., Penguin, 2005.

Reich, Robert B. "How Capitalism Is Killing Democracy." *Foreign Policy*, no. 162, 12 Oct. 2009, pp. 38–42.

Tan, Amy. "The Red Candle." *The Joy Luck Club*, by Tan, 1989, Penguin, 2019, pp. 42–63.

Wilford, John Noble. "Discovering Columbus." *The New York Times Magazine*, 11 Aug. 1991, sec. 6, p. 25.

Wilson, Edward O. "Intelligent Evolution." *From So Simple a Beginning: Darwin's Four Great Books*, edited by Wilson, W. W. Norton, 2006. Rev. and rpt. in Peterson et al., shorter 13th ed., pp. 547–57.

———. "What Is Science?" *Letters to a Young Scientist*, W. W. Norton, 2013, pp. 55–68. Rpt. in *A World of Ideas: Essential Readings for College Writers*, edited by Lee A. Jacobus, 10th ed., Bedford/St. Martin's, 2017, pp. 631–40.

Works Cited

Adams, G. Travis. "The Line That Should Not Be Drawn: Writing Centers as Reading Centered." *Pedagogy,* vol. 16, no. 1, 2016, pp. 73–90, doi:10.1215/15314200-3158637.

Anderson, Chris. "Teaching Students What Not to Say: Iser, Didion, and the Rhetoric of Gaps." *Journal of Advanced Composition,* vol. 17, no. 1–2, 1987, pp. 10–22.

Angelo, Thomas A., and K. Patricia Cross. *Classroom Assessment Techniques: A Handbook for College Teachers.* John Wiley & Sons, 1993.

Anson, Chris M. "The Intelligent Design of Writing Programs: Reliance on Belief or a Future of Evidence." *Writing Program Administration,* vol. 32, no. 1, 2008, pp. 11–36.

———. "The Pop Warner Chronicles: A Case Study in Contextual Adaptation and the Transfer of Writing Ability." *College Composition and Communication,* vol. 67, no. 4, 2016, pp. 518–49.

———. "We Never Wanted to Be Cops: Plagiarism, Institutional Paranoia, and Shared Responsibility." *Pluralizing Plagiarism: Identities, Contexts, Pedagogies,* edited by Rebecca Moore Howard and Amy E. Robillard, Boynton/Cook-Heinemann Publishers, 2008, pp. 140–57.

———. "Writing to Read, Revisited." *What Is College Reading?,* edited by Alice S. Horning et al., Across the Disciplines Books, WAC Clearinghouse and UP of Colorado, 2017, pp. 21–39, wac.colostate.edu/docs/books/collegereading/anson.pdf.

Argyris, Chris, and Donald A. Schön. *Theory in Practice: Increasing Professional Effectiveness.* Jossey-Bass, 1974.

Armstrong, Sonya L., and Mary Newman. "Teaching Textual Conversations: Intertextuality in the College Reading Classroom." *Journal of College Reading and Learning,* vol. 41, no. 2, Jan. 2011, pp. 6–21.

Arp, Thomas R., and Greg Johnson, editors. *Perrine's Story and Structure: An Introduction to Fiction.* 13th ed., Wadsworth/Cengage Learning, 2012.

Arum, Richard, and Josipa Roksa. *Academically Adrift: Limited Learning on College Campuses.* U of Chicago P, 2011.

Arum, Richard, Josipa Roksa, and Amanda Cook. *Improving Quality in Higher Education: Learning Outcomes and Assessments for the 21st Century.* John Wiley & Sons, 2016.

Attewell, Paul, et al. "New Evidence on College Remediation." *The Journal of Higher Education,* vol. 77, no. 5, 2006, pp. 886–924.

Baehr, Jason. "Educating for Intellectual Virtues: An Introductory Guide for College and University Instructors." 2015, jasonbaehr.files.wordpress.com/2013/12/e4iv_baehr.pdf.

Bain, Ken. *What the Best College Teachers Do.* Harvard UP, 2004.

Bartholomae, David, and Anthony Petrosky. *Facts, Counterfacts, and Artifacts: Theory and Method for a Reading and Writing Course.* Boynton/Cook Publishers, 1986.

Bartholomae, David, et al. *Ways of Reading: An Anthology for Writers.* 11th ed., Bedford/St. Martin's, 2017.

Bazerman, Charles. "Physicists Reading Physics: Schema-Laden Purposes and Purpose-Laden Schema." *Written Communication,* vol. 2, no. 1, 1985, pp. 3–23.

Bean, John C. *Engaging Ideas: The Professor's Guide to Integrating Writing, Critical Thinking, and Active Learning in the Classroom.* 2nd ed. Jossey-Bass, 2011.

Bean, John C., et al. *Reading Rhetorically.* 4th ed., Pearson, 2014.

Blau, Sheridan. "How the Teaching of Literature in College Writing Classes Might Rescue Reading as It Never Has Before." Sullivan et al., pp. 265–90.

Booth, Wayne C. "Boring from Within: The Art of the Freshman Essay." Peterson et al., shorter 10th ed., pp. 247–57.

———. "The Ethics of Teaching Literature." *College English,* vol. 61, no. 1, 1998, pp. 41–55.

Bosley, Lisa. "'I Don't Teach Reading': Critical Reading Instruction in Composition Courses." *Literacy Research and Instruction,* vol. 47, no. 4, 2008, pp. 285–308.

Bransford, John D., et al. *How People Learn: Brain, Mind, Experience, and School.* National Academy Press, 1999.

Bråten, Ivar, and Helge I. Strømsø. "Effects of Personal Epistemology on the Understanding of Multiple Texts." *Reading Psychology,* vol. 27, no. 5, Nov. 2006, pp. 457–84.

Brent, Doug. *Reading as Rhetorical Invention: Knowledge, Persuasion, and the Teaching of Research-Based Writing.* National Council of Teachers of English, 1992.

BRIDGE Participant Examples. Rider University, www.rider.edu/offices-services/bridge-faculty-development-program/participant-examples.

Brooks, Cleanth. "The New Criticism: A Brief for the Defense." *The American Scholar,* no. 13, 1944, pp. 285–95.

———. *A Shaping Joy: Studies in the Writer's Craft.* Methuen, 1971.

———. *The Well Wrought Urn: Studies in the Structure of Poetry.* Harcourt, Brace & World, 1947.

Brooks, David. "Goodness and Power." *The New York Times,* 28 Apr. 2015, sec. A, p. 27.

Brown, Stacy M. "Common Core vs. State Standards: What's the Difference?" *ESSA,* 2 Sept. 2017, nnpa.org/essa/common-core-vs-state-standards-whats-the-difference/.

Bunn, Michael. "Reimagining Workshop: Recognizing and Expanding the Role of Reading." *Pedagogy,* vol. 16, no. 1, 2016, pp. 53–71.

Carillo, Ellen C. "Creating Mindful Readers in First-Year Composition Courses: A Strategy to Facilitate Transfer." *Pedagogy: Critical Approaches to Teaching Literature, Language, Composition, and Culture,* vol. 16, no. 1, 2016, pp. 9–22.

———. "Engaging Sources through Reading-Writing Connections across the Disciplines." *Across the Disciplines,* vol. 13, no. 1, 2016, wac.colostate.edu/atd/articles/carillo2016.cfm.

———. "Reimagining the Role of the Reader in the Common Core State Standards." *English Journal,* vol. 105, no. 3, 2016, pp. 29–35.

———. *Securing a Place for Reading in Composition: The Importance of Teaching for Transfer.* UP of Colorado, 2015.

Chura, Patrick. "Prolepsis and Anachronism: Emmett Till and the Historicity of *To Kill a Mockingbird.*" *The Southern Literary Journal,* vol. 32, no. 2, 2000, pp. 1–26, www.jstor.org/stable/20078264.

Churchwell, Sarah. "*Go Set a Watchman* by Harper Lee Review—'Moral Ambition Sabotaged.'" *The Guardian,* 17 July 2015, www.theguardian.com/books/2015/jul/17/go-set-a-watchman-harper-lee-review-novel.

Clark, Irene L., and Andrea Hernandez. "Genre Awareness, Academic Argument, and Transferability." *WAC Journal,* vol. 22, Nov. 2011, pp. 65–78.

Coleman, David. "Bringing the Common Core to Life." NYSED, 28 Apr. 2011, usny.nysed.gov/rttt/docs/bringingthecommoncoretolife/fulltranscript.pdf.

Coleman, David, and Susan Pimentel. *Revised Publishers' Criteria for the Common Core State Standards in English Language Arts and Literacy, Grades 3–12.* National Association of State Boards of Education, 2012, www.corestandards.org/wp-content/uploads/Publishers_Criteria_for_Literacy_for_Grades_3-12.pdf.

Colomb, Gregory G. *Disciplinary "Secrets" and the Apprentice Writer: The Lessons for Critical Thinking.* Institute for Critical Thinking Resource Publication, series 1, no. 6, 1988, eric.ed.gov/?id=ED352331.

Committing to Inclusive Equity and Excellence. 2015. *Association of American Colleges and Universities,* www.aacu.org/sites/default/files/CommittingtoEquityInclusiveExcellence.pdf.

"Common Core Unit: A Close Reading of the Gettysburg Address." *U. S. Department of Education,* www2.ed.gov/programs/racetothetop/communities/day-1-gettysburg-address.pdf.

Connors, Sean P., and Rish, Ryan M. "Puzzle Solving and Modding: Two Metaphors for Examining the Politics of Close Reading." *Reader: Essays in Reader-Oriented Theory, Criticism, and Pedagogy,* no. 67, 2014, pp. 94–118.

Crane, R. S. *The Languages of Criticism and the Structure of Poetry.* U of Toronto P, 1953.

Cronon, William. "'Only Connect . . .' The Goals of a Liberal Education." *American Scholar,* vol. 67, no. 4, 1998, pp. 73–80.

Cunningham, Anne E., and Keith E. Stanovich. "Early Reading Acquisition and Its Relation to Reading Experience and Ability 10

Years Later." *Developmental Psychology,* vol. 33, no. 6, 1997, pp. 934–45.

———. "Reading Can Make You Smarter." *Principal,* vol. 83, no. 2, Nov.–Dec. 2003, pp. 34–39.

Dare, Tim. "Lawyers, Ethics, and *To Kill a Mockingbird.*" *Philosophy and Literature,* vol. 25, no. 1, 2001, pp. 127–41.

Devitt, Amy J. *Writing Genres.* Southern Illinois UP, 2004.

Dirk, Kerry. "The 'Research Paper' Prompt: A Dialogic Opportunity for Transfer." *Composition Forum,* vol. 25, Spring 2012, files.eric.ed.gov/fulltext/EJ985773.pdf.

Dobrin, David. *Writing and Technique.* National Council of Teachers of English, 1989.

Elbow, Peter. "The Doubting Game and the Believing Game: An Analysis of the Intellectual Enterprise." *Writing without Teachers,* 1973, 2nd ed., Oxford UP, 1998, pp. 147–91.

Eliot, George. "The Antigone and Its Moral." *Essays of George Eliot,* edited by Thomas Pinney, Columbia UP, Routledge & K. Paul, 1963, pp. 261–65.

Elish-Piper, Laurie, et al. "Scaffolding High School Students' Reading of Complex Texts Using Linked Text Sets." *Journal of Adolescent and Adult Literacy,* vol. 57, no. 7, Apr. 2014, pp. 565–74.

Endacott, Jason L., et al. "Robots Teaching Other Little Robots: Neoliberalism, CCSS, and Teacher Professionalism." *Review of Education, Pedagogy and Cultural Studies,* vol. 37, no. 5, Jan. 2015, pp. 414–37.

Endacott, Jason L., and Christian Z. Goering. "Speaking Truth to Power: Reclaiming the Conversation on Education." *English Journal,* vol. 103, no. 5, 2014, pp. 89–92.

Fahnestock, Jeanne, and Marie Secor. "The Stases in Scientific and Literary Argument." *Written Communication,* vol. 5, no. 4, Oct. 1988, pp. 427–43.

Ferguson, Daniel E. "Martin Luther King Jr. and the Common Core: A Critical Reading of 'Close Reading.'" *Rethinking Schools,* vol. 28, no. 2, Winter 2013–14, pp. 18–21.

Fish, Stanley. *Doing What Comes Naturally: Change, Rhetoric, and the Practice of Theory in Literary and Legal Studies.* Duke UP, 1989.

Fister, Barbara. "Teaching the Rhetorical Dimensions of Research." *Research Strategies,* vol. 11, no. 4, 1993, pp. 211–19, homepages.gac.edu/~fister/rs.html.

Flockhart, D. T. Tyler, et al. "Unravelling the Annual Cycle in a Migratory Animal: Breeding-Season Habitat Loss Drives Population Declines of Monarch Butterflies." *Journal of Animal Ecology,* vol. 84, no. 1, Jan. 2015, pp. 155–65.

Flower, Linda. "Taking Thought: The Role of Conscious Processing in the Making of Meaning." *Thinking, Reasoning, and Writing,* edited by Elaine Maimon et al., Longman, 1989, pp. 185–212.

Foa, Roberto Stefan, and Jascha Mounk. "The Danger of Deconsolidation: The Democratic Disconnect." *Journal of Democracy,* vol. 27, no. 3, July 2016, pp. 5–17, www.journalofdemocracy.org/wp-content/uploads/2016/07/FoaMounk-27-3.pdf.

Freedman, Aviva. "Show and Tell? The Role of Explicit Teaching in the Learning of New Genres." *Research in the Teaching of English,* vol. 27, no. 3, 1993, pp. 222–51.

Frost, Robert. "Design." *The Poems of Robert Frost,* edited by Edward Connery Lathem, Holt, Rinehart, and Winston, 1969.

Gay, Roxane. "Lots of People Love 'To Kill a Mockingbird.' Roxane Gay Isn't One of Them." Review of *Why 'To Kill A Mockingbird' Matters: What Harper Lee's Book and the Iconic American Film Mean to Us Today* by Tom Santopietro, *The New York Times Sunday Book Review,* 18 June 2018, www.nytimes.com/2018/06/18/books/review/tom-santopietro-why-to-kill-a-mockingbird-matters.html.

Gibbons, Louel C. To Kill a Mockingbird *in the Classroom: Walking in Someone Else's Shoes.* NCTE High School Literature Series, National Council of Teachers of English, 2009.

Gilbert, Chris. "A Call for Subterfuge: Shielding the ELA Classroom from the Restrictive Sway of the Common Core." *English Journal,* vol. 104, no. 2, 2014, pp. 27–33.

Gopnik, Adam. *Angels and Ages: A Short Book about Darwin, Lincoln, and Modern Life.* Alfred A. Knopf, 1999.

Graff, Gerald. *Clueless in Academe: How Schooling Obscures the Life of the Mind.* Yale UP, 2003.

Graff, Gerald, and Cathy Birkenstein. *They Say/I Say: The Moves That Matter in Academic Writing.* 3rd ed., W. W. Norton, 2016.

Green, Melanie C., and Timothy C. Brock. "In the Mind's Eye: Transportation-Imagery Model of Narrative Persuasion." *Narrative Impact: Social and Cognitive Foundations,* edited by Green et al., Lawrence Erlbaum Associates, 2002, pp. 315–41.

Griswold, W. Gary. "Postsecondary Reading: What Writing Center Tutors Need to Know." *Journal of College Reading and Learning,* vol. 37, no. 1, Jan. 2006, pp. 61–72.

Guterson, David. "Enclosed. Encyclopedic. Endured: The Mall of America." *Harper's Magazine,* vol. 287, no. 1719, Aug. 1993. Rpt. in Peterson et al., shorter 13th ed., pp. 102–14.

Haas, Christina. "Learning to Read Biology: One Student's Rhetorical Development in College." *Written Communication,* vol. 11, no. 1, Jan. 1994, p. 43–84.

Haas, Christina, and Linda Flower. "Rhetorical Reading Strategies and the Construction of Meaning." *College Composition and Communication,* vol. 39, no. 2, May 1988, pp. 167–83.

Harkin, Patricia, and James L. Sosnoski, "Whatever Happened to Reader-Response Criticism?" Helmers, pp. 101–21.

Harris, Muriel. "Writing Centers Are Also Reading Centers: How Could They Not Be?" Sullivan et al., pp. 227–43.

Hart Research Associates. *Fulfilling the American Dream: Liberal Education and the Future of Work: Selected Findings from Online Surveys of Business Executives and Hiring Managers.* Association of American Colleges and Universities, July 2018, www.aacu.org/sites/default/files/files/LEAP/2018EmployerResearchReport.pdf.

———. "It Takes More than a Major: Employer Priorities for College Learning and Student Success." *Liberal Education,* vol. 99, no. 2, Spring 2013, www.aacu.org/publications-research/periodicals/it-takes-more-major-employer-priorities-college-learning-and.

Hassel, Holly, and Joanne Giordano. "The Blurry Borders of College Writing: Remediation and the Assessment of Student Readiness." *College English,* vol. 78, no. 1, Sept. 2015, pp. 56–80.

Haswell, Richard H., et al. "Context and Rhetorical Reading Strategies: Haas and Flower (1988) Revisited." *Written Communication,* vol. 16, no. 1, Jan. 1999, pp. 3–27.

Heims, Neil. "Critical Contexts: 'Were You Ever a Turtle?': *To Kill a Mockingbird*—Casting the Self as the Other." *Critical Insights:* To Kill a Mockingbird, 2010, pp. 50–66.

Helmers, Marguerite, editor. *Intertexts: Reading Pedagogy in College Writing Classrooms,* Lawrence Erlbaum Associates, 2003.

Hirsch, E. D. "'You Can Always Look It Up' . . . Or Can You?" *American Educator,* Spring 2000, pp. 1–5.

Hogan, Tiffany P., et al. "On the Importance of Listening Comprehension." *International Journal of Speech-Language Pathology,* vol. 16, no. 3, 2014, pp. 199–207, www.ncbi.nlm.nih.gov/pmc/articles/PMC4681499/#R2.

Horning, Alice S. "Elephants, Pornography and Safe Sex: Understanding and Addressing Students' Reading Problems across the Curriculum." *Across the Disciplines,* vol. 10, no. 4, Nov. 2013, wac.colostate.edu/docs/atd/reading/intro.pdf.

———. "Reading Across the Curriculum as the Key to Student Success." *Across the Disciplines,* vol. 4, May 2007, wac.colostate.edu/atd/articles/horning2007.cfm.

———. *Reading, Writing, and Digitizing: Understanding Literacy in the Electronic Age.* Cambridge Scholars Publishing, 2012.

———. "Where to Put the Manicules: A Theory of Expert Reading." *Across the Disciplines,* vol. 8, no. 2, Oct. 2011, wac.colostate.edu/docs/atd/articles/horning2011.pdf.

Horning, Alice S., and Deborah-Lee Gollnitz. "What Is College Reading? A High School-College Dialogue." *Reader: Essays in Reader-Oriented Theory, Criticism, and Pedagogy,* vol. 67, Fall 2014, pp. 43–72, 149–50.

Howard, Rebecca Moore, Tanya K. Rodrigue, and Tricia C. Serviss. "Writing from Sources, Writing from Sentences." *Writing and Pedagogy,* vol. 2, no. 2, Fall 2010, pp. 177–92.

Hughes, Langston. "Salvation." *The Big Sea: An Autobiography,* by Hughes, Hill and Wang, 1963. Rpt. in Peterson et al., shorter 13th ed., pp. 620–21.

Iser, Wolfgang. *How to Do Theory.* Blackwell, 2006.

———. *The Implied Reader: Patterns of Communication in Prose Fiction from Bunyan to Beckett.* Johns Hopkins UP, 1974.

Jacobus, Lee A., editor. *A World of Ideas: Essential Readings for College Writers.* 10th ed., Bedford/St. Martin's, 2017.

Jamieson, Sandra. "Reading and Engaging Sources: What Students' Use of Sources Reveals About Advanced Reading Skills." *Across the Disciplines,* vol. 10, no. 4, Nov. 2013, wac.colostate.edu/docs/atd/reading/jamieson.pdf.

Jamieson, Sandra, and Rebecca Moore Howard. "Sentence-Mining: Uncovering the Amount of Reading and Reading Comprehension in College Writers' Researched Writing." *The New Digital Scholar: Exploring and Enriching the Research and Writing Practices of NextGen Students,* edited by Randall McClure and James P. Purdy, American Society for Information Science and Technology, 2013, pp. 111–33.

———. "Unraveling the Citation Trail." Interview by Alison Head for Project Information Literacy, 2011, www.projectinfolit.org/sandra-jamieson-and-rebecca-moore-howard-smart-talk.html.

Jolliffe, David A. "The Common Core Standards and Preparation for Reading and Writing in College." *Reconnecting Reading and Writing,* edited by Alice S. Horning and Elizabeth W. Kraemer, Parlor Press/WAC Clearinghouse, 2013, pp. 134–53.

———. "Learning to Read as Continuing Education." *College Composition and Communication,* vol. 58, no. 3, 2007, p. 470–94.

———. "'Learning to Read as Continuing Education' Revisited." Sullivan et al., pp. 3–22.

Jolliffe, David A., and Christian Z. Goering. "Guest Editors' Introduction: A Call for Revolution in High School to College Reading Instruction." *Reader: Essays in Reader-Oriented Theory, Criticism, and Pedagogy,* vol. 67, no. 1, 2014, pp. 3–11.

Jolliffe, David A., and Allison Harl. "Studying the 'Reading Transition' from High School to College: What Are Our Students Reading and Why?" *College English,* vol. 70, no. 6, 2008, pp. 599–617, www.jstor.org/stable/25472296.

Kalbfleisch, Elizabeth. "*Imitatio* Reconsidered: Notes toward a Reading Pedagogy for the Writing Classroom." *Pedagogy: Critical Approaches to Teaching Literature, Language, Composition, and Culture,* vol. 16, no. 1, Jan. 2016, pp. 39–51.

Kaufer, David S. "Cultural Literacy: A Critique of Hirsch and an Alternative Theory." *ADE Bulletin,* no. 94, Winter 1989, pp. 23–28.

Kegan, Robert. *In Over Our Heads: The Mental Demands of Modern Life.* Harvard UP, 1994.

Kidd, David Comer, and Emanuele Castano. "Reading Literary Fiction Improves Theory of Mind." *Science,* vol. 342, no. 6156, 18 Oct. 2013, pp. 377–80, doi:10.1126/science.1239918.

Kintsch, Walter. "An Overview of Top-Down and Bottom-Up Effects in Comprehension: The CI Perspective." *Discourse Processes: A Multidisciplinary Journal,* vol. 39, no. 2, May 2005, pp. 125–28.

———. "The Role of Knowledge in Discourse Comprehension: A Construction-Integration Model." *Psychological Review,* vol. 95, no. 2, 1988, pp. 163–82, doi:10.1037/0033-295X.95.2.163.

Kintsch, Walter, and Teun A. van Dijk. "Toward a Model of Text Comprehension and Production." *Psychological Review,* vol. 85, no. 5, 1978, pp. 363–94.

Klein, Alyson. "Two Words That Barely Appear in State ESSA Plans: 'Common Core.'" *Education Week,* 27 June 2017, blogs.edweek.org/edweek/campaign-k-12/2017/06/common_core_ESSA_plans_barely_appear.html.

Langer, Judith A. "Teaching Disciplinary Thinking in Academic Coursework." *Creating Powerful Thinking in Teaching and Students: Diverse Perspectives,* edited by John N. Mangieri and Cathy Collins Block, Harcourt Brace College, 1994, pp. 81–109.

Lanham, Richard A. *Style: An Anti-Textbook.* 2nd ed., revised, Paul Dry Books, 2007.

Leamnson, Robert. *Thinking about Teaching and Learning: Developing Habits of Learning with First Year College and University Students.* Stylus, 1999.

Lee, Harper. *Go Set a Watchman.* HarperCollins, 2015.

———. *To Kill a Mockingbird.* Warner Books, 1960.

Lewis, Anthony. *Freedom for the Thought We Hate: A Biography of the First Amendment.* Basic Books, 2007.

Liu, Eric. "What Every American Should Know: Defining Common Cultural Literacy for an Increasingly Diverse Nation." *The Atlantic,* 3 July 2015.

Lockhart, Tara, and Mary Soliday. "The Critical Place of Reading in Writing Transfer (and Beyond): A Report of Student Experiences." *Pedagogy,* vol. 16, no. 1, Jan. 2016. pp. 23–37.

"Lumina Foundation's Equity Imperative." *Lumina Foundation,* 2017, www.luminafoundation.org/files/resources/equity-impera tive-2017-01-25.pdf.

MacDonald, Susan Peck. "Problem Definition in Academic Writing." *College English,* vol. 49, no. 3, 1987, pp. 315–31.

———. *Professional Academic Writing in the Humanities and Social Sciences.* Southern Illinois UP, 2010.

Machiavelli, Niccolò. "The Morals of the Prince." Trans. Robert M. Adams. Peterson et al., 13th ed., shorter version, pp. 485–91.

"Making Excellence Inclusive." *Association of American Colleges and Universities,* www.aacu.org/making-excellence-inclusive.

Mallette, Jennifer, et al. "The Longest Conversation about Reading You've Never Heard." *Reader: Essays in Reader-Oriented Theory, Criticism, and Pedagogy,* vol. 67, Fall 2014, pp. 12–36, 149, 151.

Manarin, Karen, et al. *Critical Reading in Higher Education: Academic Goals and Social Engagement.* Indiana UP, 2015.

Mar, Raymond A., and Keith Oatley. "The Function of Fiction Is the Abstraction and Simulation of Social Experience." *Perspectives on Psychological Science: A Journal of the Association for Psychological Science,* vol. 3, no. 3, May 2008, pp. 173–92.

Martorell, Paco, and Isaac McFarlin Jr. "Help or Hindrance? The Effects of College Remediation on Academic and Labor Market Outcomes." *The Review of Economics and Statistics,* vol. 93, no. 2, 2011, p. 436–54.

Maxwell, Martha. "The Dismal State of Required Developmental Reading Programs: Roots, Causes and Solutions." MM Associates, 1997, files.eric.ed.gov/fulltext/ED415501.pdf.

McNamara, Danielle S., et al. "Are Good Texts Always Better? Interactions of Text Coherence, Background Knowledge, and Levels of Understanding in Learning from Text." *Cognition and Instruction,* vol. 14, no. 1, 1996, pp. 1–43.

Michaels, Walter Benn. "Against Formalism: The Autonomous Text in Legal and Literary Interpretation." *Poetics Today,* vol. 1, nos. 1–2, 1979, pp. 23–34.

Milgram, Stanley. "The Perils of Obedience." *Harper's Magazine,* Dec. 1973, pp. 62–66, 75–77.

———. "Some Conditions of Obedience and Disobedience to Authority." *Human Relations,* vol. 18, no. 1, Feb. 1965, pp. 57–76.

Moje, Elizabeth Birr. "Foregrounding the Disciplines in Secondary Literacy Teaching and Learning: A Call for Change." *Journal of Adolescent and Adult Literacy,* vol. 52, no. 2, Oct. 2008, pp. 96–107.

Monseau, Susanna C. "Multi-Layered Assignments for Teaching the Complexity of Law to Business Students." *International Journal of Case Method Research and Application,* vol. 17, no. 4, 2006, pp. 531–40, pdfs.semanticscholar.org/f18c/df5af84abf076982ba589a455b9e2e5c7280.pdf?_ga=2.26390264.432989508.1564666039-621860743.1564666039.

Murphy, Mary McDonagh, director. *Harper Lee: American Masters.* PBS, 10 July 2015, pbs.org/wnet/americanmasters/harper-lee-hey-boo-about-the-documentary/1972/.

Murray, Jennifer. "More than One Way to (Mis)Read a Mockingbird." *Southern Literary Journal,* vol. 43, no. 1, Fall 2010, pp. 75–91.

Nabokov, Vladimir. "Good Readers and Good Writers." *Lectures on Literature,* Nabokov, edited by Fredson Bowers, Estate of Vladimir Nabokov, 1980.Rpt. in Peterson et al., shorter 13th ed., pp. 571–76.

National Endowment for the Humanities. "Lesson 3: The Gettysburg Address (1863)—Defining the American Union." *EDSITEment!* edsitement.neh.gov/lesson-plans/lesson-3-gettysburg-address-1863-defining-american-union#sect-activities.

National History Education Clearinghouse. Teach History https://teachinghistory.org/best-practices/teaching-with-textbooks/19438#:~:text=Opening%20Up%20the%20Textbook%20is,inform%20a%20larger%20historical%20narrative.

Nelson, Craig E. "On the Persistence of Unicorns: The Tradeoff between Content and Critical Thinking Revisited." *The Social Worlds of Higher Education: Handbook for Teaching in a New Century,* edited by Bernice A. Pescosolida and Ronald Aminzade, Pine Forge Press, 1999, pp. 168–84.

———. "Teaching Evolution (and All of Biology) More Effectively: Strategies for Engagement, Critical Reasoning, and Confronting Misconceptions." *Integrative and Comparative Biology,* vol. 48, no. 2, 2008, pp. 213–25.

Nelson, Jennie. "The Research Paper: A 'Rhetoric of Doing' or a 'Rhetoric of the Finished Word'?" *Composition Studies/Fresh-*

man English News, vol. 22, no. 2, Fall 1994, pp. 65–75, eric .ed.gov/?id=EJ497430.

Nussbaum, Martha C. *Cultivating Humanity: A Classical Defense of Reform in Liberal Education.* Harvard UP, 1997.

Oatley, Keith. "Fiction: Simulation of Social Worlds." *Trends in Cognitive Sciences,* vol. 20, no. 8, Aug. 2016, pp. 618–28.

Olson, David R. "From Utterance to Text: The Bias of Language in Speech and Writing." *Perspectives on Literacy,* edited by Eugene R. Kintgen et al., Southern Illinois UP, 1988, pp. 175–89.

Orwell, George. "Shooting an Elephant." 1936. Rpt. in Peterson et al., shorter 13th ed., pp. 472–77.

Perry, William G. "Examsmanship and the Liberal Arts: An Epistemological Inquiry." 1963. *In the College Years: Selected Publications of the BSC,* Bureau of Study Counsel, Harvard University, 2012, pp. 1–13, bsc.harvard.edu/files/bsc/files/bsc_pub_-_examsmanship_and_the_liberal_arts.pdf.

———. *Forms of Intellectual and Ethical Development in the College Years: A Scheme.* Holt, Rinehart and Winston, 1970.

Peskin, Joan, and Janet Wilde Astington. "The Effects of Adding Metacognitive Language to Story Texts." *Cognitive Development,* vol. 19, no. 2, Jan. 2004, pp. 253–73.

Peterson, Linda H., et al., editors. *The Norton Reader: An Anthology of Nonfiction.* Shorter 10th ed., W. W. Norton, 2000.

———. *The Norton Reader: An Anthology of Nonfiction.* Shorter 13th ed., W. W. Norton, 2012.

Pinker, Steven. "The Moral Instinct." *The New York Times Magazine,* vol. 157, no. 54188, Jan. 13, 2008.

Plato. "The Allegory of the Cave." *A World of Ideas: Essential Readings for College Writers,* edited by Lee A. Jacobus, Bedford/St. Martin's, 2017, pp. 580–90.

Rabinowitz, Peter J. "Against Close Reading." *Pedagogy Is Politics: Literary Theory and Critical Teaching,* edited by Maria Regina Kecht, U of Illinois P, 1992, pp. 230–43.

———. *Before Reading: Narrative Conventions and the Politics of Interpretation.* Cornell UP, 1987.

Rabinowitz, Peter J., and Corinne Bancroft. "Euclid at the Core: Recentering Literary Education." *Style,* vol. 48, no. 1, Spring 2014, pp. 1–34.

Rabinowitz, Peter J., and Michael W. Smith. *Authorizing Readers: Resistance and Respect in the Teaching of Literature.* Teachers College Press, 1998.

Raines, Howell. "Harper Lee and Her Father, the Real Atticus Finch." Review of *Atticus Finch: The Biography,* by Joseph Crespino, *The New York Times Sunday Book Review,* 18 June 2018, pp. 1+.

Reading between the Lines: What the ACT Reveals about College Readiness in Reading. ACT, 2006, achievethecore.org/content/upload/act_reading_between_the_lines_research_ela.pdf.

Relles, Stefani R., and William G. Tierney. "The Challenge of Writing Remediation: Can Composition Research Inform Higher Education Policy?" *Teachers College Record,* vol. 115, no. 3, Mar. 2013, pp. 1–45.

Rhodes, Lynne A. "When Is Writing Also Reading?" *Across the Disciplines,* vol. 10, no. 4, 2013, wac.colostate.edu/atd/reading/rhodes.cfm.

Richards, Ivor A. *Practical Criticism: A Study of Literary Judgment.* Harcourt, Brace, & World, 1929.

Rivera, Edward. "First Communion." Peterson et al., shorter 10th ed., pp. 618–31.

Robbins, Mari Lu. *A Guide for Using* To Kill a Mockingbird *in the Classroom.* Teacher Created Resources, 2011, rpt. 2016.

Rose, Mike. "The Language of Exclusion: Writing Instruction at the University." *College English,* vol. 47, no. 4, 1985, pp. 341–59, www.jstor.org/stable/376957.

Rosenblatt, Louise M. *Literature as Exploration.* 1938. 2nd ed., Noble & Noble Publishers, 1968.

———. *The Reader, the Text, the Poem: The Transactional Theory of the Literary Work.* Southern Illinois UP, 1994.

———. "The Transactional Theory: Against Dualisms." *College English,* vol. 55 no. 4, Apr. 1993, pp. 377–86.

Rosenfeld, Mordecai. "Genesis, Chapter 22—A Respectful Dissent." Peterson et al., shorter 13th ed., pp. 631–33.

Russell, David R. *Writing in the Academic Disciplines, 1870–1990: A Curricular History.* Southern Illinois UP, 1991.

Rutenberg, Jim. "Fair Play in a Fact-Challenged Political Landscape." *The New York Times,* 3 July 2016, sec. B, p. 1.

Salvatori, Mariolina Rizzi. "Reading Matters for Writing." Helmers, pp. 195–217.

Salvatori, Mariolina Rizzi, and Patricia Donahue. "Guest Editors' Introduction: Guest Editing as a Form of Disciplinary Probing." *Pedagogy: Critical Approaches to Teaching Literature, Language, Composition, and Culture,* vol. 16, no.1, 2016, pp. 1–8, doi:10.1215/15314200-3158557.

———. "What Is College English? Stories about Reading: Appearance, Disappearance, Morphing, and Revival." *College English,* vol. 75, no. 2, Feb. 2012, pp. 199–217.

Schecter, Barnet. *The Battle for New York: The City at the Heart of the American Revolution.* Walker, 2002.

Scholes, Robert. *Textual Power: Literary Theory and the Teaching of English.* Yale UP, 1985.

———. "The Transition to College Reading." *Pedagogy: Critical Approaches to Teaching Literature, Language, Composition, and Culture,* vol. 2, no. 2, Spring 2002, pp. 165–72.

Schön, Donald A. *Educating the Reflective Practitioner: Toward a New Design for Teaching and Learning in the Professions.* Jossey-Bass, 1987.

———. *The Reflective Practitioner: How Professionals Think in Action.* Basic Books, 1983.

Seitz, James E. "How Literature Learns to Write: The Possibilities and Pleasures of Role-Play." *Critical Theory and the Teaching of Literature: Politics, Curriculum, Pedagogy,* edited by James F. Slevin, National Council of Teachers of English, 1996, pp. 328–40.

Shanahan, Cynthia, et al. "Analysis of Expert Readers in Three Disciplines: History, Mathematics, and Chemistry." *Journal of Literacy Research,* vol. 43, no. 4, 2011, pp. 393–429.

Shanahan, Timothy. "The Common Core Ate My Baby and Other Urban Legends." *Educational Leadership,* vol. 70, no. 4, Dec. 2012–Jan. 2013, pp. 10–16.

———. "How Bad Are the Common Core Lessons on the Gettysburg Address?" *Commentary*, Thomas B. Fordham Institute, 20 Dec. 2013, edexcellence.net/commentary/education-gadfly-daily/common-core-watch/how-bad-are-the-common-core-lessons-on-the.

———. "Letting the Text Take Center Stage: How the Common Core State Standards Will Transform English Language Arts Instruction." *American Educator*, Fall 2013, pp. 4–11, 43.

Shanahan, Timothy, and Cynthia Shanahan. "Teaching Disciplinary Literacy to Adolescents: Rethinking Content-Area Literacy." *Harvard Educational Review*, vol. 78, no. 1, Spring 2008, pp. 40–59.

———. "What Is Disciplinary Literacy and Why Does It Matter?" *Topics in Language Disorders*, vol. 32, no.1, Jan.–Mar. 2012, pp. 7–18.

Shulman, Lee S. "Teaching as Community Property: Putting an End to Pedagogical Solitude." *Change*, vol. 25, Nov. 1993, pp. 6–7.

Singer, Alan. "Reading without Understanding: Common Core versus Abraham Lincoln." *Huffington Post*, 22 Nov. 2013, www.huffingtonpost.com/alan-singer/reading-without-understan_b_4323239.html.

Slevin, James F., and Art Young, editors. *Critical Theory and the Teaching of Literature: Politics, Curriculum, Pedagogy*. National Council of Teachers of English, 1996.

Smith, Michael W., and Peter J. Rabinowitz. "Playing a Double Game: Authorial Reading and the Ethics of Interpretation." *Journal of Language and Literacy Education*, vol. 1, no. 1, Sept. 2005, pp. 9–19.

Smith, Michael W., and Jeffrey D. Wilhelm. *Fresh Takes on Teaching Literary Elements: How to Teach What Really Matters about Character, Setting, Point of View, and Theme*. National Council of Teachers of English, 2010.

Sommers, Nancy. "Revision Strategies of Student Writers and Experienced Adult Writers." *College Composition and Communication*, vol. 31, no. 4, Dec. 1980, pp. 378–88, athena.rider.edu:2111/stable/pdf/356588.pdf.

Spiegelberg, Bryan D. "A Focused Assignment Encouraging Deep Reading in Undergraduate Biochemistry." *Biochemistry and Molecular Biology Education*, vol. 42, no. 1, Nov. 2013, pp. 1–5, doi:10.1002/bmb.20744.

Stanford History Education Group. https://sheg.stanford.edu/.

Stanovich, Keith E. "Matthew Effects in Reading: Some Consequences of Individual Differences in the Acquisition of Literacy." *Reading Research Quarterly,* 1986, vol. 21, no. 4, pp. 360–407.

Stanovich, Keith E., and Anne E. Cunningham. "Studying the Consequences of Literacy within a Literate Society: The Cognitive Correlates of Print Exposure." *Memory & Cognition,* 1992, vol. 20, no. 1, pp. 51–68.

———. "Where Does Knowledge Come From? Specific Associations between Print Exposure and Information." *Journal of Educational Psychology,* vol. 85, no. 2, June 1993, pp. 211–29.

Stevenson, Bryan. *Just Mercy: A Story of Justice and Redemption.* Spiegel & Grau, 2014.

Sullivan, Patrick. "'Deep Reading' as a Threshold Concept in Composition Studies." Sullivan et al., pp. 143–71.

Sullivan, Patrick, et al. *Deep Reading: Teaching Reading in the Writing Classroom.* National Council of Teachers of English, 2017.

Tan, Amy. *The Joy Luck Club.* Putnam, 1989.

Tinkle, Theresa, et al. "Teaching Close Reading Skills in a Large Lecture Course." *Pedagogy: Critical Approaches to Teaching Literature, Language, Composition, and Culture,* vol. 13, no. 3, 2013, pp. 505–35.

"*To Kill a Mockingbird:* Main Ideas." *SparkNotes,* www.sparknotes.com/lit/mocking/themes/.

van den Broek, Paul, et al. "Integrating Memory-Based and Constructionist Processes in Accounts of Reading Comprehension." *Discourse Processes: A Multidisciplinary Journal,* vol. 39, no. 2, 2005, pp. 299–316.

Walker, Alice. "Beauty: When the Other Dancer Is the Self." Peterson et al., shorter 13th ed., pp. 38–44.

Walvoord, Barbara E., and Lucille P. McCarthy. *Thinking and Writing in College: A Naturalistic Study of Students in Four Disciplines.* National Council of Teachers of English, 1990.

Wardle, Elizabeth. "'Mutt Genres' and the Goal of FYC: Can We Help Students Write the Genres of the University?" *College Composition and Communication,* vol. 60, no. 4, June 2009, pp. 765–89.

Warren, James E. "Rhetorical Reading and the Development of Disciplinary Literacy across the High School Curriculum." *Across the Disciplines,* vol. 10, no. 1, June 2013, wac.colostate.edu/atd/articles/warren2013.cfm.

———. "Rhetorical Reading as a Gateway to Disciplinary Literacy." *Journal of Adolescent and Adult Literacy,* vol. 56, no. 5, Feb. 2012, pp. 391–99.

Watt, Ian. *The Rise of the Novel: Studies in Defoe, Richardson, and Fielding.* 1957. U of California P, 1965.

Wexler, Natalie. "The Radical Case for Teaching Kids Stuff." *The Atlantic,* Aug. 2019, pp. 20–23.

Williams, Joseph M., and Gregory G. Colomb. "The Case for Explicit Teaching: Why What You Don't Know Won't Help You." *Research in the Teaching of English,* vol. 27, no. 3, Jan. 1993, pp. 252–64.

Willingham, Daniel T. "Critical Thinking: Why Is It So Hard to Teach?" *American Educator,* vol. 109, no. 4, Summer 2007, pp. 8–19.

———. *The Reading Mind: A Cognitive Approach to Understanding How the Mind Reads.* Jossey-Bass, 2017.

Wills, Gary. *Lincoln at Gettysburg: The Words That Remade America.* Simon and Schuster, 1992.

Wilner, Arlene. "Asking for It: The Role of Assignment Design in Critical Literacy." *Reader: Essays in Reader-Oriented Theory, Criticism, and Pedagogy,* vol. 52, 2005, pp. 56–91.

———. "Confronting Resistance: Sonny's Blues—and Mine." *Pedagogy,* vol. 2, no. 2, 2002, pp. 173–96.

———. "Fostering Critical Literacy: The Art of Assignment Design." *New Directions for Teaching and Learning,* no. 103, edited by Ned Laff, Jossey-Bass, 2005, pp. 23–38.

———. "Multidisciplinary Faculty Learning Communities for SoTL: Rethinking 'Rigor.'" *Learning Communities Journal,* vol. 6, 2014, pp. 5–30.

Wimsatt, W. K. *The Verbal Icon: Studies in the Meaning of Poetry.* U of Kentucky P, 1954.

Wimsatt, W. K., and M. C. Beardsley. "The Intentional Fallacy." *The Sewanee Review,* vol. 54, no. 3, 1946, pp. 468–88, www.jstor.org/stable/27537676.

Wineburg, Samuel S. "On the Reading of Historical Texts: Notes on the Breach between School and the Academy." *American Educational Research Journal,* vol. 28, no. 3, September 1, 1991, pp. 495–519.

"WPA Outcomes Statement for First-Year Composition (3.0), Approved July 17, 2014." *Council of Writing Program Administrators,* wpacouncil.org/aws/CWPA/pt/sd/news_article/243055/_PARENT/layout_details/false.

Yancey, Kathleen Blake, et al. "Device. Display. Read: The Design of Reading and Writing and the Difference Display Makes." Sullivan et al., pp. 33–56.

Young, Justin A., and Charlie R. Potter. "The Problem of Academic Discourse: Assessing the Role of Academic Literacies in Reading across the K–16 Curriculum." *Across the Disciplines,* vol. 10, no. 4, Dec. 2013.

Zull, James E. *The Art of Changing the Brain.* Stylus, 2002.

Zunshine, Lisa. "Theory of Mind as a Pedagogical Tool." *Interdisciplinary Literary Studies,* vol. 16, no. 1, 2014, pp. 89–109.

———. "What Reading Fiction Has to Do with Doing Well Academically." *Style,* vol. 48, no. 1, Spring 2014, pp. 87–93.

Zwaan, Rolf A. "Effect of Genre Expectations on Text Comprehension." *Journal of Experimental Psychology: Learning, Memory, and Cognition,* vol. 20, no. 4, July 1994, pp. 920–33.

Index

Author

Arlene Fish Wilner, professor of English at Rider University in Lawrenceville, New Jersey, holds a PhD in English literature from Columbia University and was trained in the study of higher education pedagogy as a Fellow of the Carnegie Academy for the Scholarship of Teaching and Learning (CASTL). Inspired by the CASTL experience, she designed and directed BRIDGE (2001–15), a collaborative campuswide faculty development program that facilitated classroom-inquiry projects and supported participants in publishing their research. Her studies in literary theory and interpretation, composition pedagogy, and faculty development have appeared in venues such as *Eighteenth-Century Fiction, Children's Literature, Modern Language Studies,* the *Journal of Narrative Theory,* the *CEA Critic, College Literature, Reader, Composition Forum, Pedagogy, Learning Communities Journal, Criticism,* and *New Directions in Teaching and Learning.* Throughout her career, Wilner has been an advocate for more purposeful attention in higher education to the interdependence of reading and writing, with a focus on assignment design.

This book was typeset in Sabon by Barbara Frazier.
Typefaces used on the cover include Eveleth and Proxima Nova.
The book was printed on 50-lb. White Offset paper
by Seaway Printing Company, Inc.

www.ingramcontent.com/pod-product-compliance
Lightning Source LLC
LaVergne TN
LVHW050619100826
845148LV00011B/1651

* 9 7 8 0 8 1 4 1 4 1 2 2 9 *